BIOINFORMATICS

Basics, Algorithms and Applications

Ruchi Singh
Formerly Lecturer, Department of Bioinformatics,
SRM University (Deemed University),
Ramapuram, Tamil Nadu

Richa Sharma
Assistant Professor and Head,
Department of Information Science and Engineering,
The Oxford College of Engineering,
Bangalore, Karnataka

Universities Press

UNIVERSITIES PRESS (INDIA) PRIVATE LIMITED

Registered Office
3-6-747/1/A & 3-6-754/1, Himayatnagar, Hyderabad 500 029 (A.P.), India
info@universitiespress.com; www.universitiespress.com

Distributed by
Orient Blackswan Private Limited

Registered Office
3-6-752 Himayatnagar, Hyderabad 500 029 (A.P.), India

Other Offices
Bangalore / Bhopal / Bhubaneshwar / Chandigarh / Chennai
Ernakulam / Guwahati / Hyderabad / Jaipur / Kolkata
Lucknow / Mumbai / New Delhi / Noida / Patna

ISBN 978 81 7371 713 0

Typeset in Life BT 10.5/13.5 *by*
OSDATA, Hyderabad

Printed at
Graphica Printers
Hyderabad 500 013

Published by
Universities Press (India) Private Limited
3-6-747/1/A & 3-6-754/1, Himayatnagar,
Hyderabad 500 029 (A.P.), India

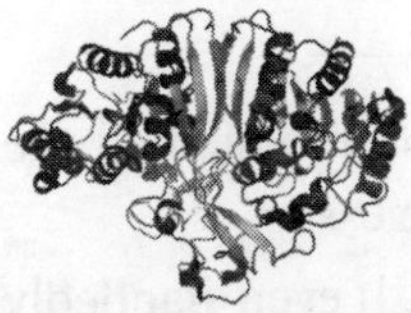

Foreword

Bioinformatics, a multidisciplinary subject, is increasingly evolving into a discipline of its own, and books like the present one, written by biologists/ bioinformaticians with the assistance of a computer scientist, help accelerate this process. In India, Bioinformatics is now taught and practiced at various levels, in both undergraduate and postgraduate teaching and research institutions. The credit for this rapid spread must be shared between dedicated teachers and researchers, such as the authors of this book, and the Government agencies, in particular the Department of Biotechnology (DBT), Government of India.

In the late 1980s, almost as soon as the first DNA and protein sequences were reported in literature and were recorded in computer databases, the DBT set up information centres to make this information available to all interested biologists. Initially regarded as a curiosity by classical biologists, the data, and the computational techniques required to collate, access, process and interpret them, soon became indispensible to the advance of biology. Along with this realisation of the tremendous utility of the data, biologists also understood the importance of devising and using better, faster and more reliable computational tools. This task required collaboration between biologists and computer scientists; later, physicists, chemists and mathematicians also joined the team. Consequently, there was a great demand for cross-disciplinary books, authored either by experts who straddled more than one discipline or by teams of collaborating authors with expertise in different disciplines. Many such books have since appeared, and cater to the large audience of not only senior researchers and scientists, but also novice students. This latter section of the audience, which still comes largely from an educational system that builds tight, impermeable boundaries between the disciplines, requires especial treatment. Students who have studied biology in its various avatars (i.e., botany, zoology, biochemistry, microbiology, etc.), will require a gentle introduction to mathematics and computer science, while those with a background in physics, chemistry and mathematics will need detailed explanations of the biological principles, on the basis of which all the data is interpreted, and without which all the analyses—no matter how sophisticated the tools—are useless.

In this context, the book at hand is particularly welcome. It even-handedly deals with subjects that are part of a conventional bioinformatics course, such as databases, database access and analyses tools, as well as many of the principles of computer science that underlie the algorithms which are built into those tools. Extensive explanations of the core algorithms of sequence analyses and phylogeny construction are also given. Altogether, this emphasis on introducing the concepts of algorithms, and fundamental explanations for many of the more important ones in bioinformatics, will ideally suit the vast majority of the students coming into bioinformatics courses with an undergraduate degree in one of the biological sciences. I congratulate the authors on a job well done.

I have been associated with the principal force behind this book, Ms Ruchi Singh, for many years now, and see in it all the meticulous attention to detail and the needs of the student community that I have experienced in all my interactions with her. I wish her and the co-author, Ms Richa Sharma, every success with not only the present book, but also all their future endeavours in the service of the bioinformatics student community.

N Gautham
CAS in Crystallography and Biophysics,
University of Madras, Chennai

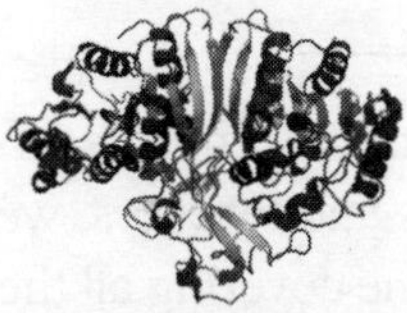

Preface

Biologists analyse biological data to find answers to the origin, function and structure of living organisms. Sequencing projects that generate enormous numbers of nucleotide sequences have been initiated for advanced research into the genetic structure of life. For the interpretation of this massive data gathered by the biologists, computational tools are required. Computers have provided the necessary accuracy, speed and precision for handling vast quantities of biological data. The introduction of computers to biology has changed the face of biology, leading to a new and important subject area called 'bioinformatics'. Bioinformatics is a set of computational methods used for capturing diverse sources of biological information and preparing models for analysing them to aid basic and advanced research. Only in the last decade has it been recognised and studied as a separate discipline. It is a multidisciplinary subject that requires knowledge of several subjects, such as molecular biology, biochemistry, computer science and others. Since bioinformatics is such a young and rapidly evolving field, it is essential to get a general understanding of the principles and technologies involved, before studying the applications and latest developments. This book attempts to provide a simple and concise explanation of the basic principles, tools and applications of bioinformatics. Algorithms, which are fundamental to solving a problem, have been used throughout the book to illustrate how the various tools are applied to obtain meaningful solutions.

Keeping in mind that students of bioinformatics are from diverse backgrounds, equipped with only a modest knowledge of biology, the book begins with a brief overview of the terms used frequently in bioinformatics. The book is divided into five sections—bioinformatics and algorithms, databases and matrices, how sequences can be aligned and compared, algorithms or computational approaches to analyse data gathered from various sources and applications of bioinformatics, including a brief introduction to genomics and proteomics.

The book has been planned and structured as a textbook for the foundation course. We hope it will be of help to readers in understanding the principles and computational approaches of bioinformatics. In order to make the book more useful for a wider section of students and teachers, we have deliberately kept it simple and concise, at the same time covering all the important aspects. Care has been taken to explain algorithms so that even a beginner can understand them without difficulty.

We wish to thank our students who have inspired us by their eagerness to learn more about this fascinating and expanding subject. We are grateful to Dr N Gautham, Professor and Head, Department of Crystallography and Biophysics, University of Madras, who has kindly provided the foreword for the book.

We are thankful to Universities Press, for publishing this book, especially Ms Javanthi Singaram and Ms Madhavi Sethupathi, for their continued encouragement, guidance and careful editing which have given shape to the book.

We thank our family members for their blessings and constant support, which have been an enduring source of encouragement for us.

Ruchi Singh
Richa Sharma

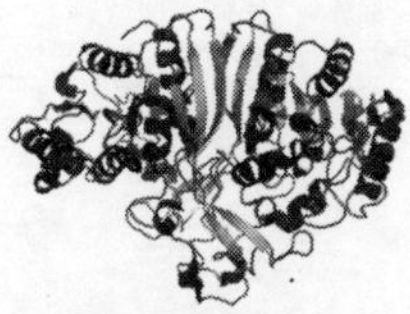

Contents

Dedicated
to
Abu

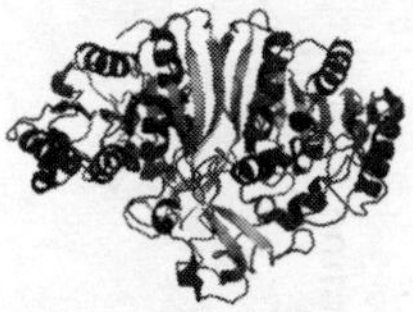

Getting Started

To study bioinformatics, a basic knowledge of biomolecules is essential. A number of terms such as sequencing, sequence alignment, phylogenetics, metabolomics and many others, also relating to the structure and function of biomolecules, are used in defining and establishing the purpose of bioinformatics. Hence it was felt that it would be helpful to the reader to begin with definitions of the seemingly complex terms that are encountered throughout the book.

A **biomolecule** is a chemical compound found in living organisms. It consists primarily of carbon and hydrogen, along with nitrogen, oxygen, phosphorus and sulphur. Proteins, nucleic acids, lipids and sugars are examples of biomolecules.

Nucleic acids are macromolecules composed of nucleotides. They are the structural units of RNA and DNA. A nucleotide consists of a five-carbon sugar (either ribose or 2'-deoxyribose), one to three phosphate groups and a nitrogenous base, which is either a purine or a pyrimidine, linked together (Fig. 1). Purines are heterocyclic aromatic organic compounds and have a pyrimidine ring fused to an imidazole ring. Pyrimidines are also heterocyclic aromatic organic compounds and are similar to pyridine. They contain two nitrogen atoms at positions 1 and 3 of the benzene ring. Purines and pyrimidines have the ability to form a hydrogen bond between them. Adenine (A) and guanine (G) are purines, and thymine (T) and cytosine (C) are pyrimidines. The nucleic acids have two main parts: a backbone composed of alternating sugar and phosphate molecules bonded together in a long chain, and the sugar groups in the backbone attached to the nitrogenous base. This is represented below:

```
NUCLEOTIDE BASE                     NUCLEOTIDE BASE
       |                                   |
     SUGAR ——————  PHOSPHATE  —————— SUGAR
```

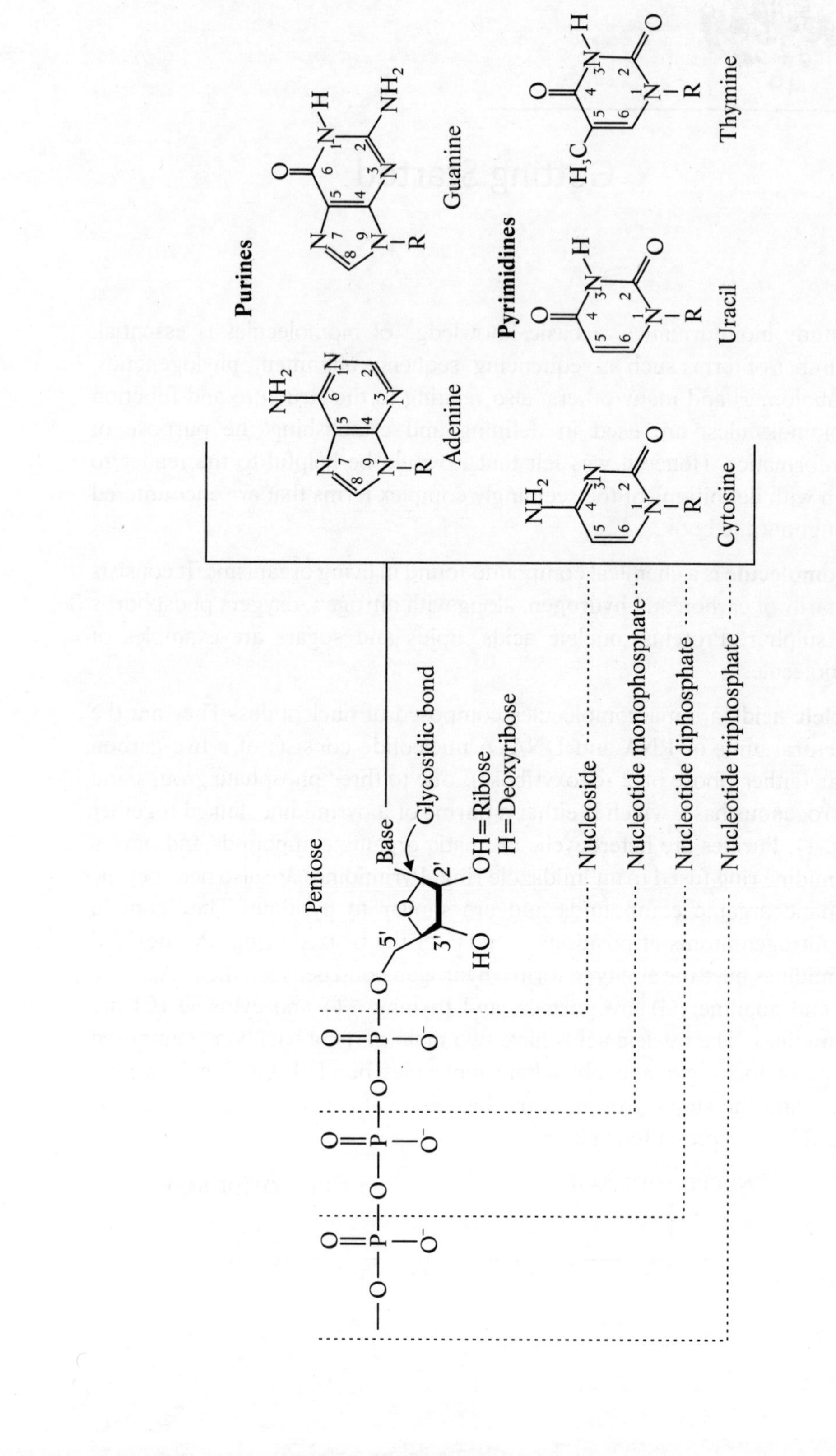

FIGURE 1 *Structure of a nucleotide*

Ribonucleic acid (RNA) is a long linear polymer of nucleotides consisting of a nitrogenous base, a ribose sugar (instead of deoxyribose as in DNA) and a phosphate. It is found in the nucleus, cytosol and in intercellular fluid. RNA plays a vital role in protein synthesis and other cell activities. There are three types of RNA: mRNA (messenger RNA) that contains information, tRNA (transfer RNA) that reads the code and carries the amino acid to be incorporated into the developing protein and rRNA (ribosomal RNA) that serves as the site and carries the enzymes necessary for protein synthesis. Other RNAs include snRNA (small nuclear RNA), snoRNA (small nucleolar RNA), miRNA (mitochondrial RNA), dsRNA (double-stranded RNA), piRNA (Piwi-interacting RNA), siRNA (small interfering RNA), tmRNA (transfer-messenger RNA) and others.

Deoxyribonucleic acid (DNA) is a nucleic acid consisting of a nitrogenous base, a deoxyribose sugar and a phosphate. It has a double-helical structure. The two deoxyribose residues are attached by a phosphodiester bond, while the nucleotides are attached by a hydrogen bond (Fig. 2). The DNA segments that carry this genetic information are called ***genes***. DNA is usually referred to as chromosomal DNA, mitochondrial DNA and chloroplast DNA. Chromosomal DNA is found in the nucleus while chloroplast and mitochondrial DNA are found in the chloroplast and mitochandria, respectively. Four forms of DNA structures are known. A-, B- and C-DNA are composed of a right-handed helix, while Z-DNA contains a left-handed helix and is found in vitro under high salt.

The gene is the basic unit of inheritance. It is a portion of an organism's DNA. Each organism has a set of genes providing the complete hereditary information. The ***genome*** is the complete set of genes in an organism.

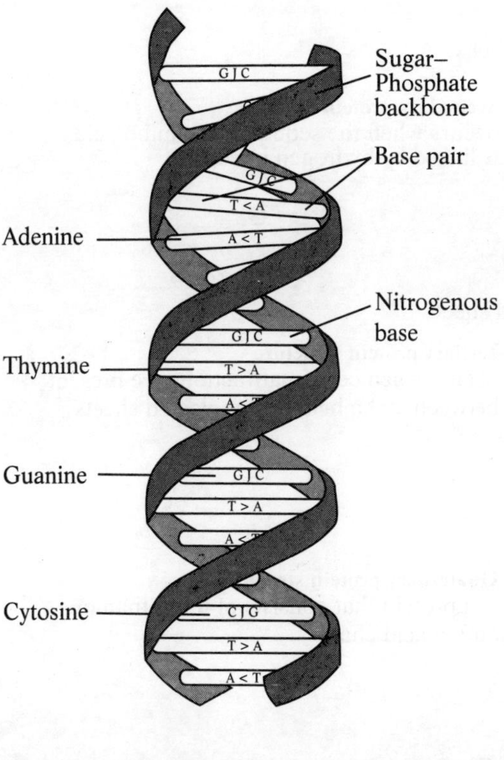

FIGURE 2 *DNA structure showing the position of nucleotide bases*

Proteins are polymers built from amino acids (molecules containing an amine and a carboxyl functional group), and are the most important building blocks. The amino acid sequence gives the primary structure of a protein. There are twenty essential amino acids (Table 1). The secondary structure refers to the folding of the chain of amino acids of proteins. It provides information about local inter-residue interactions by the formation of hydrogen bonds. The most common secondary structures are α-helices and β-sheets. The tertiary structure of the protein is the three-dimensional structure formed by the folding of the secondary structure (α-helices and β-sheets) upon themselves. Sometimes many folded protein molecules combine to make a multi-subunit complex (like haemoglobin), usually bound by hydrogen bonds. This complex structure is called the quaternary structure of the protein (Fig. 3).

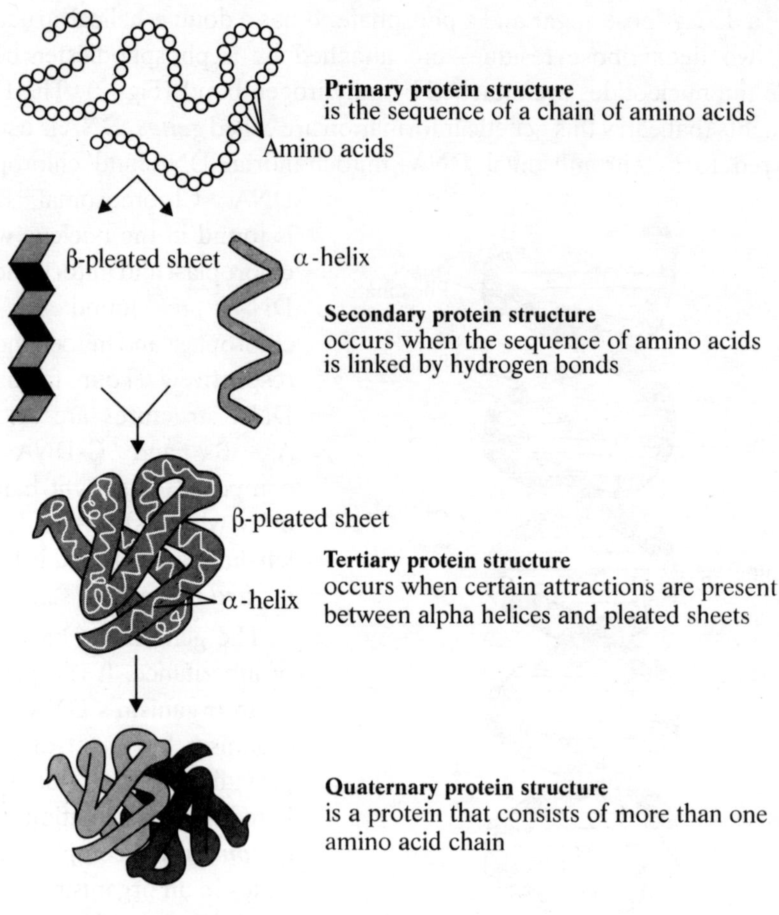

FIGURE 3 *Protein structure*

(http://commons.wikimedia.org/wiki/File:Protein-structure.png)

A **protein domain** or **protein conserved region** is the functional part of the protein sequence. It has certain functions and exists independently of the rest of the protein chain. These domains form a compact three-dimensional structure which is mostly stable on its own. The information stored in DNA has to be translated to produce proteins in the cells.

TABLE 1 *Twenty essential amino acids*

Amino acid	3-Letter code	1-Letter code
Alanine	Ala	A
Arginine	Arg	R
Asparagine	Asn	N
Aspartic acid	Asp	D
Cysteine	Cys	C
Glutamic acid	Glu	E
Glutamine	Gln	Q
Glycine	Gly	G
Histidine	His	H
Isoleucine	Ile	I
Leucine	Leu	L
Lysine	Lys	K
Methionine	Met	M
Phenylalanine	Phe	F
Proline	Pro	P
Serine	Ser	S
Threonine	Thr	T
Tryptophan	Trp	W
Tyrosine	Tyr	Y
Valine	Val	V

A **codon** is a sequence of three nucleotides, or a ***nucleotide triplet***. Each codon represents a particular amino acid. As there are four nucleotides in DNA, there are sixty-four (4^3) possible triplets. Most of the organisms use twenty amino acids. Each of these twenty amino acids has more then one codon to represent it. For example, glutamine (gln) can be coded by CAA and CAG, and arginine (arg) by CGU, CGC, CGA, CGG, AGA and AGG (Fig. 4). It is not necessary for all organisms to use all the codons equally.

Human beings use 22% of AGA and 23% of AGG and the rest in a very low percentage. *Drosophila* uses 49% of CGC and the rest in a very low percentage. This is termed ***codon bias***, where a particular organism is more biased towards a specific codon for an amino acid and is used sometimes to compare two organisms.

The term **sequence** refers to the ordered list of characters. A nucleotide sequence is a succession of nucleotide characters (A, T, G, C) representing the primary structure of a DNA molecule or DNA strain. A protein sequence or amino acid sequence gives the order of the amino acid residues connected by peptide bonds in a protein. In sequence analysis, a sequence is analysed to find various kinds of information pertaining to it. Due to the critical need to obtain more genomic sequences to learn about life, several sequencing projects for genomes of various organisms are underway.

Second position

First position	U		C		A		G		Third position
U	UUU	Phe	UCU	Ser	UAU	Tyr	UGU	Cys	U
	UUC		UCC		UAC		UGC		C
	UUA	Leu	UCA		UAA	*Stop*	UGA	*Stop*	A
	UUG		UCG		UAG	*Stop*	UGG	Trp	G
C	CUU	Leu	CCU	Pro	CAU	His	CGU	Arg	U
	CUC		CCC		CAC		CGC		C
	CUA		CCA		CAA	Gln	CGA		A
	CUG		CCG		CAG		CGG		G
A	AUU	Ile	ACU	Thr	AAU	Asn	AGU	Ser	U
	AUC		ACC		AAC		AGC		C
	AUA		ACA		AAA	Lys	AGA	Arg	A
	AUG	Met	ACG		AAG		AGG		G
G	GUU	Val	GCU	Ala	GAU	Asp	GGU	Gly	U
	GUC		GCC		GAC		GGC		C
	GUA		GCA		GAA	Glu	GGA		A
	GUG		GCG		GAG		GGG		G

FIGURE 4 *A codon table showing 64 codons and the amino acids coded*

Sequence alignment is a way of arranging the primary sequences of DNA, RNA or protein to find the regions of similarity. These sequences are written across a page in different rows by keeping one character above the other. Gaps are inserted between the residues so that identical or similar characters are aligned in successive columns. The alignment is said to be better when there are more similar characters in the two rows. ***Pairwise sequence***

alignment is the comparison of two sequences for a common pattern. It can be of two kinds: local alignment, when a portion of the sequence is aligned providing conserved domains, that is, a portion of the sequence is present in both the sequences; and global alignment, when the full sequence is aligned. ***Multiple sequence alignment*** is a sequence alignment of three or more biological sequences. The sequences with good alignment (fewer mutations) can be interpreted as having either the same ancestry or being evolutionarily related.

Sequence 1: A C C C G T T G A	Sequence 1: A C C A G T A
Sequence 2: A C C _ G T T G A	Sequence 2: A C _ A G T A
	Sequence 3: A C C A _ T A
Pairwise sequence alignment	**Multiple sequence alignment**

Analyses of gene sequences and other data suggest that the 5 to 100 million species of organisms living on Earth are genetically related. The genealogical relationships of living things can be represented by a vast Tree of Life, the evolutionary tree or ***phylogenetic tree***. The evolutionary tree is a record of the history of the heredity of organisms as they changed through time. This is also referred to as the phylogeny of organisms. The branches of the phylogenetic tree represent the genological links between the different organisms. All organisms—from the smallest microbe to the largest plant and vertebrate—are found on this tree.

Phylogenetics is the field of biology dealing with the characterisation of relationships among various organisms on Earth and their evolutionary history. Multiple sequence alignment provides the base for phylogenetic analysis.

Transcriptomics is the study of genes and pathways involved in biological processes. It is also defined as the study of the ***transcriptome***—the complete set of RNA transcripts produced by the genome at any one time.

In an organism, metabolites are formed during metabolic or cellular processes. They are usually small molecules. A ***metabolome*** is the complete set of small-molecule metabolites found in an organism. **Metabolomics** studies the small-molecule metabolite profile or "unique chemical fingerprints of all the cellular processes" and provides an understanding of metabolic pathways.

Pharmacogenomics or **pharmacogenetics** is a combination of pharmacology and genomics. It studies how an individual's genetic inheritance influences the body's response to drugs. Though used to a limited extent, this study has opened the way for tailor-made drugs for each individual and has a promising future.

A **biological database** is a kind of library that collects and stores data from various biological sources (sequence, structure, function, location and other related information) in digital form in a particular format. ***Data designing*** is the conceptual, logical and physical structure of any database.

Data mining is the process of sorting and analysing large volumes of data and selecting the relevant information. There are various data mining software available for analysing data. Technically, finding relationships or patterns among dozens of fields in large relational databases is considered as data mining.

Annotation is the overall information emphasised or the explanation of a specific region in a genomic sequence. In biological evaluation, for example, a genomic sequence may reach a finite endpoint, but the annotations will continue to evolve indefinitely as biological knowledge increases. It bridges the gap between the sequence and the biology of the organism. The aim of high-quality annotation is to identify the key features of the genome, that is, the genes and their products. Many new tools and resources for annotation are being developed, and scientists are relying on them to access different kinds of biological information.

Simulation is an imitation of a real or imaginary situation. In bioinformatics, simulation software is used to simulate the biological environment.

Section I

INTRODUCTION

Chapter 1: Introduction to Bioinformatics
Chapter 2: Introduction to Algorithms

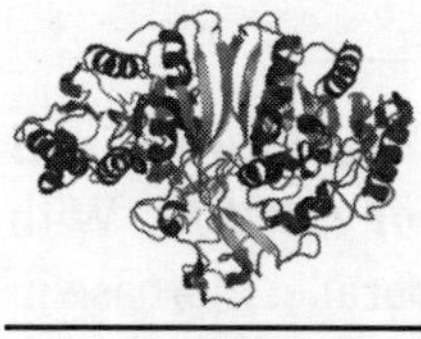

CHAPTER 1

Introduction to Bioinformatics

LEARNING OUTCOME

- Define bioinformatics
- Define related terms
- State the goals of bioinformatics
- Define sequencing
- Describe database management systems
- Describe biological databases
- List the applications of bioinformatics

The introduction of computers in the field of biology has completely changed the way we work in this field. Now an enormous amount of information is just a click away. This chapter introduces the basic concept of bioinformatics and its applications in biological and computer research. ***Bioinformatics*** can be broadly defined as a group of methods used to capture diverse sources of biological information and to prepare models to analyse that information and other advanced research. It offers opportunities for developing innovative data analysis methods.

In recent years there has been an explosive growth in biological data due to increased biological research. A large number of sequencing projects have been initiated to gain further knowledge of life and life processes, and they have produced enormous amounts of nucleotide sequences. The nucleotide databases are growing exponentially in size. ***As of May 2008, there were 85,759,586,764 bases in 82,853,685 sequence records in the traditional GenBank divisions and 108,635,736,141 bases in 27,439,206 sequence records in the whole genome shotgun (WGS) in***

GenBank, a nucleotide sequence database developed and maintained by the National Center for Biotechnology Information (NCBI). With the rapid increase in sequence data, there has also been a parallel increase in the related analytical data. To manage this splurge in data, a new scientific discipline, bioinformatics or computational biology, has emerged.

Bioinformatics was first introduced in the late 1980s to manage the flood of biological data. It was initially called ***biocomputing*** and its application was limited to standalone computers and the intranet. The practical applications started appearing in the early 1990s after the internet was opened up to commercial interests.

Bioinformatics is a rapidly growing multidisciplinary science and uses techniques and concepts from biology, computer science, informatics, statistics, mathematics, chemistry and biochemistry. Imagine that all the biological data in the form of research papers have been stacked in a room. How can this stack be searched physically to find a specific piece of information? It would be like searching for a needle in a haystack. Bioinformatics combines the computing power of a computer with the wealth of information available in biology to help us search and retrieve data and thereby solve problems as well.

DEFINITION OF BIOINFORMATICS

Defining bioinformatics is not an easy task. While writing this book, a Google search for "definitions of bioinformatics" returned 2,550,000 results. There is no universally approved definition of bioinformatics. Generally biologists define bioinformatics as, "the use of *computers* to *store, retrieve, analyse* or *predict* the *composition* or *structure* of biomolecules". Bioinformatics is the application of computational techniques and information technology to the organisation and management of biological data. 'Classical' bioinformatics deals primarily with *sequence analysis.*

Some other definitions of bioinformatics and computational biology from the internet are given below:

- The science of informatics as applied to biological research. Informatics is the management and analysis of data using advanced computing techniques. Bioinformatics is particularly important as an adjunct to genomics research, because of the large amount of complex data this research generates. (http://www.biology.gatech.edu/graduate-programs/bioinformatics/new/whatis.php)
- Bioinformatics derives knowledge from the computer analysis of biological data. These can consist of information stored in the genetic code, but also experimental results from various sources,

patient statistics and scientific literature. Research in bioinformatics includes method development for storage, retrieval and analysis of data. Bioinformatics is a rapidly developing branch of biology and is highly interdisciplinary, using techniques and concepts from informatics, statistics, mathematics, chemistry, biochemistry, physics and linguistics. It has many practical applications in different areas of biology and medicine. (http://www.pasteur.fr/recherche/unites/Binfs/definition/bioinformatics_definition.html)

BIOINFORMATICS FOR BIOLOGISTS

Among the sciences, biology has played a key role in this century. However, for the interpretation of the enormous amount of data gathered by biologists we require computational tools. Thus bioinformatics is closely linked to computer science and the internet. Computers have changed the face of biology. They provide the accuracy, speed and precision needed to cope with huge amounts of biological data.

Biologists use biological data to answer different queries. They deal with biological sequences and other related data for their research. These sequences are stored in computer files that can be accessed via the World Wide Web. The data are universally available in databases like GenBank (for DNA sequences) and SwissProt (for protein sequences). This topic is explained in detail in *Section II, Chapter 3*.

Database management systems (DBMSs) have been developed to manage the large volumes of biological data currently available. MySQL and Oracle, which are relational database management systems (RDBMS), are software programs that can be used for this purpose.

BIOINFORMATICS FOR COMPUTER SCIENTISTS

Computer science or informatics is concerned with the organisation, maintenance and manipulation of data in the digital form. An important task of this discipline is the development of various analytical software tools. These tools are programmed to accept input in a certain format, and then by means of calculations or manipulations, produce certain or required output.

Bioinformatics is a quick and easy means to get results. Starting from accumulating and organising scientific information, it progresses to comparing sequences, generating protein structures, transcriptomics, metabolomics and pharmacogenomics (explained in brief in *Section V*).

For the sustained growth and development of bioinformatics, it is necessary that all the concerned disciplines work together.

Current approaches in biocomputation are very helpful in identifying patterns, domains and functions of proteins and genes, but they are still not perfect. Therefore it is necessary to use biological reasoning and common sense while evaluating the results obtained from a biocomputing program. Various algorithms used in bioinformatics are explained in this book. Bioinformatics software tool development requires knowledge of various computer languages like BioJava, BioPerl, C++, Python and others.

WORLD WIDE WEB AND BIOINFORMATICS

The World Wide Web is the major source for the data which is to be manipulated to obtain an insight into yet unexplored areas of living science. The working of all bioinformatics tools and databases is deeply entwined with the web; programming languages and specific commands are used to develop tools and databases. Communication between computers, via the Internet, has to follow certain 'protocols'.

The Internet differs from other computer networks in the particular set of rules or 'protocols' they use to communicate. This protocol is called Transmission Control Protocol/Internet Protocol (TCP/IP). TCP protocols guarantee the delivery of the information in the same order as it was sent, and the IP protocol (like135.134.88.19) provides the rules for the path that is used to transfer the information. HyperText Markup Language (HTML), Hypertext Transfer Protocol (HTTP) and Universal Resource Locator (URL) aid communication between computers. Other than web servers, email servers, telnet servers and FTP servers also help in communication between computers.

GOALS OF BIOINFORMATICS

- Development of a database containing all biological information.
- Progress of content with continual research and effectiveness of databases with updated information.
- Development of better tools for data designing, annotation and mining.
- Creation and development of software to improve tools for analysing sequences for their function and similarity with other sequences.
- Design and development of software tools for protein structure prediction function, annotation and docking analysis.
- Design and development of drugs by using simulation software.

SEQUENCING

Sequencing gives the exact order of a biopolymer, for example, the nucleotide bases (adenine, guanine, cytosine and thymine) as a linear sequence. Determination of the primary sequence of an unbranched amino acid is called sequencing. Determination of the exact order of the chemical building blocks was not an easy job. The Maxam–Gilbert DNA sequencing method based on the chemical modification of DNA and subsequent cleavage at specific bases, Sanger's chain termination method for sequencing DNA and the automated DNA sequencing method provided enormous volumes of biological data for further interpretation. Figuring out the order of DNA nucleotides, or bases, in a genome is called ***genome sequencing***. Clone contig and shotgun sequencing is used for genome sequencing where first the genome is cut into smaller pieces and then sequenced, as it is difficult to sequence the full genome as such. The sequences of these pieces are then joined to give the sequence of the complete genome. Various programs like the Phred and Phrap assemblers that join the small fragments of genome sequence and generate the full genome have been developed to facilitate and accelerate sequencing.

SEQUENCE ANALYSIS

Pairwise protein sequence alignments can be very useful in determining the conserved portions of a protein. For example, an active site is likely to be highly conserved while other portions of the protein are less likely to be conserved. This is a valuable way to establish relationships between sequences from different proteins. One important application is phylogenetic analysis, where the degree of sequence homology between proteins can be used to determine the relationship between species.

The goal of sequence alignment is to allow a researcher to determine whether two sequences show enough similarity to infer that they are homologous to one another. With this application, we will be able to perform pairwise comparisons of a single sequence with sequences in a database using programs such as BLAST (41), WU-BLAST and FASTA (43).

STRUCTURE ANALYSIS

Several programs that give scientists the ability to look at the three-dimensional shape of proteins and nucleotides have been developed. By examining a protein in three dimensions, we get a better understanding of its functions, as well as a visual understanding that cannot always be conveyed through still photographs or descriptions. Using nuclear magnetic resonance (NMR) and x-ray crystallography, protein structures are visualised three-dimensionally using software such as Cn3D, Chimera, SPDBV and Rasmol. These programs are freely available and can be downloaded from the internet. Commercial software such as Accelrys (Insight II and Discover), YASARA and the EXOME-Horizon™ package can also be used.

HUMAN GENOME PROJECT

The human genome project (HGP) was formally begun in October 1990 and was completed two years ahead of schedule, owing to the enormous progress in bioinformatics. HGP used the shotgun method to sequence the genome. Information about the draft sequence was ready in 2001 and the finished sequence was published in 2003. The information obtained from the HGP has become more useful owing to the explanation provided by bioinformatics.

HGP was initiated with the following goals:

- To identify the genes present in human DNA
- To determine the sequences that make up human DNA
- To store the information about the sequences in databases
- To improve the tools for data analysis
- To transfer the related technologies to the private sector
- To address the ethical, legal and social issues (ELSI) that may arise from the project

Visit the HGP official site: http://www.ornl.gov/sci/techresources/Human_Genome/home.shtml for more information.

SEQUENCE DATABASES AND DATABASE SEARCHES

A ***database*** is a store of persistent related data, organised in such a way that it is accessible and can be queried. Sequencing has given rise to enormous amounts of data to manage. A sequence database contains sequence data and other related information in a computer readable form.

Databases must have easy and simple methods for accessing and mining the stored data. It is very important to search a database in an efficient manner as larger the database, more the information. The methods used for small databases (such as dynamic programming) will not be effective with larger databases in terms of time and space efficiency. Other methods (such as heuristics like BLAST or FASTA) are used instead. Initially data was stored in a flat file format which enabled easy parsing. Now many file formats are used. These are discussed in *Chapter 3*. A database can be managed and queried by a computer program known as a database management system (DBMS).

DATABASE MANAGEMENT SYSTEM (DBMS)

A DBMS is a software package that controls the organisation, storage, management and retrieval of data in a database. It is a set of pre-written programs that are used to store, update and retrieve a database. DBMSs are categorised according to their data structures or types. A user can retrieve and update the information in a DBMS. It accepts requests for data from the application program and instructs the operating system to transfer the appropriate data. Database servers are specially designed computers that hold the actual databases and run only the DBMS and related software. The following are examples of database applications:

- computerised library systems
- automated teller machines
- flight reservation systems

Properties

A DBMS should have ACID properties. The ACID acronym stands for Atomicity, Consistency, Isolation and Durability.

Atomicity: Atomicity refers to the ability of the DBMS to guarantee that either all or none of the tasks of a transaction are performed. For example, the transfer of funds from one account to another can be completed or it can fail for a multitude of reasons; but atomicity guarantees that one account will not be debited if the other is not credited. Atomicity states that database modifications must follow an "all or nothing" rule.

Consistency: The consistency property ensures that the database remains in a consistent state before the start of the transaction and after the transaction is over (whether successful or not).

Isolation: Isolation refers to the requirement that other operations cannot access or see the data in an intermediate state during a transaction.

Durability: Durability refers to the guarantee that once the user has been notified of success, the transaction will persist and not be undone.

A DBMS provides independently stored, non-redundant, consistent, secure and accurate data. It protects the data from inconsistent changes made by different users accessing data concurrently and it also ensures that the data is restored to a consistent state if the system crashes.

Advantages

The advantages of a DBMS are:

- Data independence
- Efficient data access
- Data integrity and security
- Data administration
- Concurrent access and crash recovery
- Reduced application development time

Example 1.1

A student's personal and academic database in a college. It will be similar to the following personal databases of all students:

Table 1.1: Personal databases of all students

Register No.	Student's name	Date of birth	Father's name	Address
0001	BK Ram	05.11.86	BS Ramesh	32 K,Tagore Town, Bangalore
0002	Ishita Sinha	11.01.87	Yogesh Sinha	D 301,Golden Park Apartments, Chennai
0003	Vinoth	29.03.85	T Gurunathan	C11, Bhatiya Garden, Vellore

Table 1.2: Academic database of all students

Register No.	Student's name	Internal assessment marks (Max. Marks 50)			
		Maths	Physics	Chemistry	Biology
0001	BK Ram	10	44	25	36
0002	Ishita Sinha	44	49	37	48
0003	Vinoth	50	48	46	43

The attribute common to both tables is the Register No. This attribute is called the ***primary key***. It is a unique key for searching any data and is used to retrieve data from Tables 1.1 and 1.2. The DBMS can be effectively used to send feedback to the parents of students whose marks are less than 30% in any of the subjects. First we have to query Table 1.2 for all those with less than 30% in any subject. Only BK Ram has got less than 30% in Maths.

We can find his address from Table 1.1 and dispatch the report to his address.

Here the completed array is called a ***table***; a row in each table is called a ***tuple***; each column head (Name/ID/Grade) is called an ***attribute***; and the data in each attribute is called ***value***.

BIOLOGICAL DATABASE

As we have already mentioned, the biological database is one of the most important tools and is mandatory for any bioresearcher. The biological database is a collection of biological data in computer readable form which is accessible and can be queried. Biological databases usually contain genomics (data obtained from gene analysis) and proteomics (data obtained from protein analysis) data. Scientists use them to explain biological phenomena and to unfold the mystery of evolution. A detailed discussion of this is found in *Chapter 3*.

APPLICATIONS OF BIOINFORMATICS

The applications of bioinformatics are so vast that a separate book can be written on it. The most important application is the use of classical bioinformatics to find biological data quickly in a computer readable form, and using various bioinformatics tools to get information from that data. Bioinformatics applications specifically include designing and developing biological databanks, and tools for retrieving, querying, visualising and evaluating data. Designing tools is essential as they enable scientists to perform in silico experiments and test them in wet labs. Figure 1.1 illustrates the applications of bioinformatics.

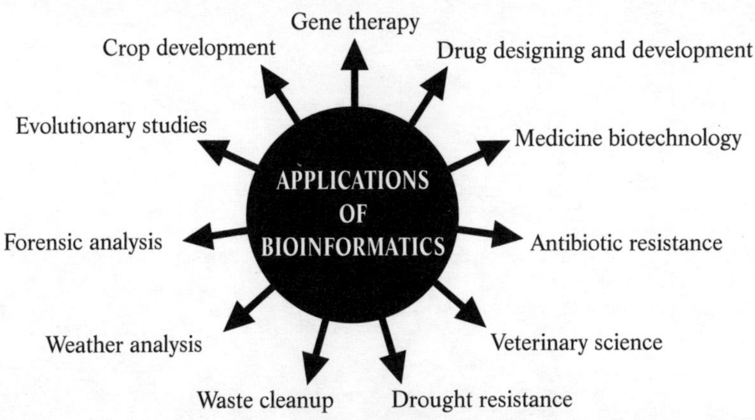

FIGURE 1.1 *The applications of bioinformatics*

EXERCISES

1. How has bioinformatics changed the face of biology?
2. "Bioinformatics is a multidisciplinary science". What are the various sciences dealing with bioinformatics?
3. How does the definition of bioinformatics by a molecular biologist and a computer scientist differ?
4. Give a brief outline of the history of bioinformatics.
5. What is a DBMS? Explain tuple and attribute with respect to DBMS.
6. List the applications of bioinformatics.
7. Explain in your own words what bioinformatics represents.
8. Before the advent of bioinformatics, how were biologists sorting and storing biological data?

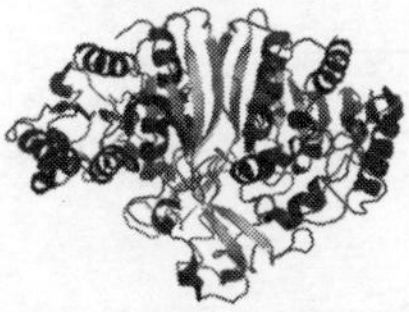

CHAPTER 2

Introduction to Algorithms

LEARNING OUTCOME

- Define an algorithm
- Define a pseudocode
- Define deterministic and non-deterministic algorithms
- Describe probabilistic and heuristic algorithms
- List the differences between algorithms and computer programs
- List the applications of algorithms
- Describe the best, average and worst case in algorithm analysis
- Define big 'O' notation

The word algorithm has a curious connection to the title of an algebra book, *On Calculation with Hindu Numerals,* written by the Persian mathematician Mohammed ibn-Musa al-Khwarizmi (AD 780–850). The title of the Latin translation was *Algoritmi de numero Indorum,* where 'algoritmi' was the translator's name for the author. The first algorithm for a computer was written by Ada Byron in 1842 for Charles Babbage's analytical engine. It is pronounced as al-go-rith-um; the algorithm for resolving bioinformatics tasks is called a ***bioinformatics algorithm***. It can be defined in terms of the actions to be executed and in the order in which these actions are to be executed. The study of algorithms, or ***algorithmics***, has been developed to solve a wide variety of problems.

Keyword: Words that have predefined meaning in a computer language are called keywords or reserved words. For example, the keywords in C language are int, float, const, if, else, while, etc.

Identifier: An identifier is a word consisting of a sequence of one or more letters or digits. For example: marks1, marks2.

Variable: It is an identifier that is used to store a value. The stored value in the variable may change during the execution of the program. For example, marks1, marks2, sum, A, B, etc.

Constant: It is a data item that will not change during the execution of the program. The keyword available in C language for a constant is const. For example, any integer or floating point number can be called a constant. Sometimes even an alphabet or a word can be declared as a constant in a program.

Integer: An integer is any whole number. For example, 1, 2, 3, 4......etc. The keyword available in C language for an integer is int.

For example, int A = 6; // initialise integer variable A with value 6

It will first allocate a memory location and name the location as A and store 6 at that location. This is called initialising A with the integer value 6, i.e., value 6 at location A.

6
A

Here A is a variable because by default in computer programming it is assumed that all data are variables.

So, if the next command in C language is

A = A+1

it means that the new value assigned to memory location A is 6 + 1=7.

7
A

If we modify the initial command as

const int A = 6 // initialise constant integer A with value 6

A is always a constant. If the next command in C language is A = A+1, it is invalid as the value of A will always remain the same throughout the execution of the program. Only X = A+1 is possible where X is the next position with A+1 as the value.

6	7
A	X

Floating point numbers: All real numbers are called floating point numbers. For example, 5.53, 0.12, 3.333, 2.0, etc. The keyword available in C language for a floating point number is float.

Swap: Swapping two variables means the exchange of data between the variables. For example, if we have two variables A and B, let the initial value of A be 1 and that of B be 2 (A = 1,B = 2). If we say: swap A and B, this implies that after swapping, the new value of A is 2 and B is 1, or A = 2, B = 1.

Assigning the value: Copying or storing data into a memory location is called assigning. For example, location A has the value 6 in the integer example above.

Definition of an algorithm

An algorithm is used to solve problems by breaking it up into several smaller tasks to be executed stepwise. An algorithm can be defined as "a set of steps, to solve a particular problem". Any procedure written in a finite number of steps in such a way that it is understood and that terminates to give at least one result is called an algorithm. This set of steps must be unambiguous, finite and must have an end. Algorithms are expressed in natural language, that is, how we speak, such that we can understand it. A computer program, on the other hand, is written in a programming language, which can be read and executed by a computer. An algorithm must be correct in all conditions specific to the problem, have a fixed number of definite steps and must terminate. We can also define an algorithm as, "a sequence of instructions executed in an order to solve a well-formulated problem." It is a technique or method that translates the given input into a certain type of output. An algorithm must be correct in all conditions; if it is incorrect for even one input instance, it will be considered incorrect.

The best algorithm is one that is simple and is written in the fewest possible steps. Writing best-case algorithms (in terms of the time taken to execute and the space or memory required for the process) is one of the principal challenges of programming. This is explained in brief at the end of this chapter. We use algorithms every day. Even the recipe for baking a cake, given in a stepwise manner, is an algorithm. Designing an algorithm to solve a specific problem and analysing a given algorithm are the two main tasks of a programmer. A computer program to process information is basically an algorithm that tells computers what specific steps to perform and in what sequence.

PSEUDOCODE

A pseudocode is a description of what a computer program should do, given in general language rather than in programming language. Its language can be easily understood by both programmers and non-programmers who are not familiar with a specific programming language. It resembles the source code of widely used programming languages such as C and Java. While writing a pseudocode, it is not necessary to be concerned about keywords, case (i.e., lower case and upper case) and details of punctuation.

DETERMINISTIC AND NON-DETERMINISTIC ALGORITHMS

A deterministic algorithm always produces the same correct output for a particular input. Deterministic algorithms are one of the most practical algorithms and can be run on real machines efficiently. In a deterministic algorithm, future states can be predicted based on a previous state. A fully automatic washing machine has five states—pre-wash, wash, rinse, spin and dry. Now, if at a given time the washing machine is in state 3, that is, rinse, it can be easily predicted that the next state will be spin. Any mathematical function is deterministic as it always produces the same output for a given input, that is, A + B is always equal to 10 if A = 6 and B = 4.

Non-deterministic algorithms have multiple choice points where different continuations are possible. Picking a choice for the execution of an algorithm generally produces a different output or final state. For example, in any undirected graph, if we want the path to go from one node to another, various paths are available. In the given graph there are two ways to go from node A to node D: ACD or ABD. So if we are writing an algorithm to find a path from A to D, both outputs are correct. In that case, the algorithm is non-deterministic.

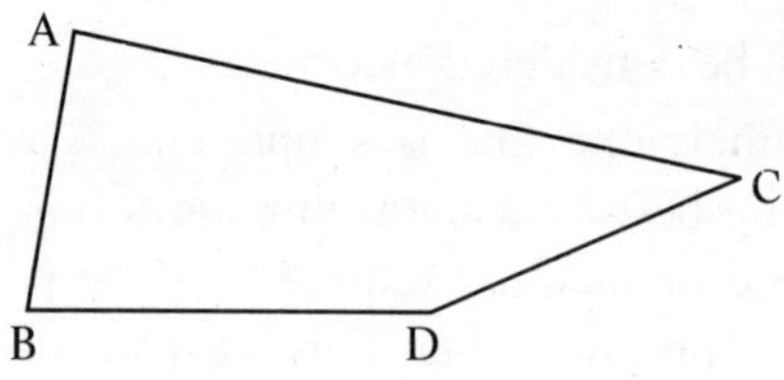

HEURISTIC ALGORITHMS

Heuristic algorithms search for an approximate solution. In the heuristic approach, the time or resources required to find a perfect solution is not practical; hence it gives an optimal solution. A heuristic algorithm is an algorithm that can produce an acceptable solution to a problem in many practical scenarios, but for which there is no formal proof of its correctness. Alternatively, it may be correct, but may not be proven to produce an optimal solution or to use reasonable resources. Heuristics are typically used when there is no known method to find an optimal solution, under the constraints of time, space, etc.

Example 2.1

What is the perfect solution to pinning odd-shaped circulars on a notice board?

Finding the perfect solution is difficult, as there is no known way which is significantly faster than trying every possible way of pinning them. What most people do is to pin the largest circular first, then fit the smaller circulars in the space left around it. This is not necessarily the perfect arrangement, but it will usually give one that is satisfactory. It is an example of a heuristic solution.

The travelling salesman problem is also an interesting example of a heuristic algorithm. A salesman has to visit all the cities and he has to choose the shortest path in such a way that each city is visited only once and all the cities allotted to him are visited.

Example 2.2

An algorithm to find if a given number is odd or even

Step 1: Receive a number.

Step 2: If it is divisible by 2, go to Step 3, else Step 4

Step 3: If the given number is even, go to Step 5.

Step 4: If the given number is odd, go to Step 5.

Step 5: Stop.

A flow chart to identify odd or even numbers

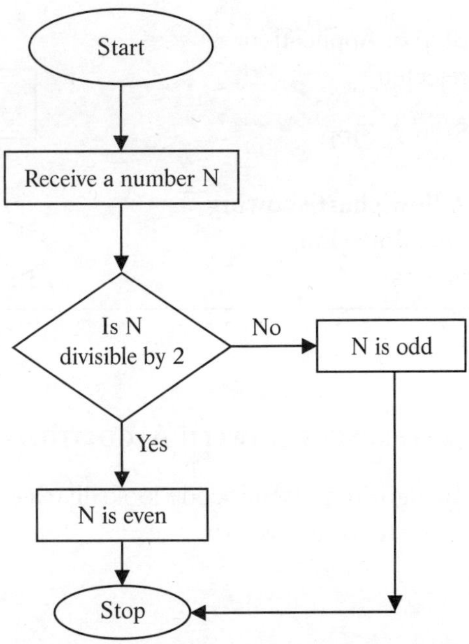

Example 2.3

The student admission process can also be written as an algorithm.

Step 1: Receive the application form.

Step 2: If percentage of marks is less than 75% reject the form. Go to Step 6, else Step 3.

Step 3: Seat allotted.

Step 4: If fees have been paid, go to Step 5, else Step 6.

Step 5: Admitted. Go to Step 7.

Step 6: Application rejected.

Step 7: Stop.

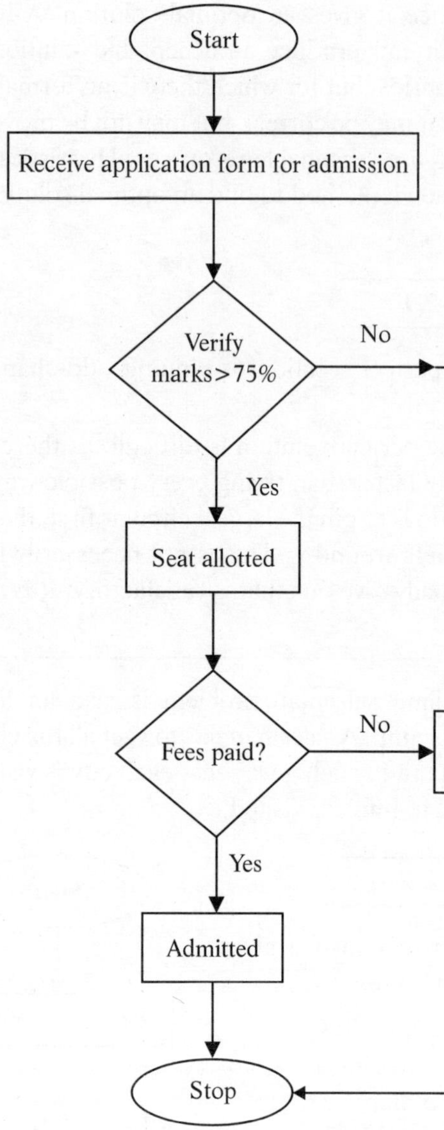

A flow chart showing the admission process

DIFFERENCES BETWEEN ALGORITHMS AND COMPUTER PROGRAMMING

An algorithm pseudocode looks like a computer program but differs from it in the following ways:

- An algorithm is written in algorithmic language (natural languages, pseudocode and flowcharts), while a computer program is written in a programming language such as C, C++, Perl or Java.
- An algorithm must terminate, while a computer program need not.

Applications: Some of the most common applications of algorithms in computers are:

- Searching for text
- Sorting files or lines of text in alphabetic order
- Compressing and decompressing data
- Detecting errors in the transmission of data
- Encrypting and decrypting data
- Compiling (that is, converting) source code, which is written in programming language, into machine language so that it can be understood by computer processors.

Analysis of algorithms: Best, average and worst case

The effectiveness of an algorithm is determined by analysing it. Analysis involves determining the amount of time and space taken to compute or run a certain algorithm. The central processing unit (CPU) of a computer performs algorithmic operations and stores the code and information about its execution in its memory.

The same algorithm may give different complexities for the same instance size, depending on the input provided by the user. An instance is the input for which the problem needs to be solved, that is, the input provided by the user. Depending on the complexity of an algorithm, it can be classified as best case, worst case or average case complexity.

BEST CASE COMPLEXITY

Among all problems of the same size (the number of bits needed to represent the instance in a computer), the one that encounters least complexity is called best case complexity for the given problem size. For example, for time complexity, the one that takes the minimum number of steps on a size 'n' instance is the best case. If we plot a graph with size of problem on the x-axis and number of steps taken on a size 'n' instance along the y-axis, the lowest curve represents the best-case algorithm.

WORST CASE COMPLEXITY

Among all the problems of the same size, the one that encounters maximum complexity is called the worst case complexity for the given problem size. For example, if you are concerned with time complexity, the one that takes the maximum number of steps (and hence time) on a size 'n' instance is the worst case. In a graph, the highest curve represents the worst-case algorithm.

AVERAGE CASE COMPLEXITY

This function is defined by the average number of steps taken on any instance of size n. The curve passing through the middle in the graph represents the average case algorithm.

An algorithm with the least complexity or low complexity is suitable for problem solving and yields the best results in the least time.

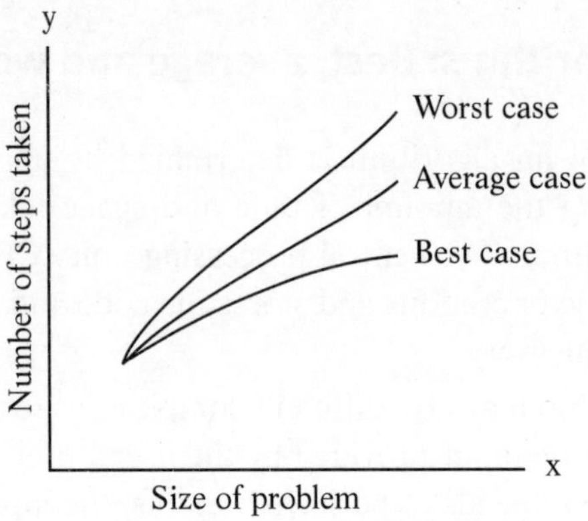

A graph showing the complexity of an algorithm

BIG 'O' NOTATION

To explain the running time of an algorithm, computer scientists use the big 'O' notation. First introduced by a German intellect, Paul Bachman, in 1892 in his book *Analytisch Zahlentheoric*, it is used to explain the asymptotic behaviour of functions. The big 'O' stands for 'order of'. Originally, the symbol for the Greek capital letter omicron was used, but now a capital 'O' is used; zero is never used.

The processing time to get the desired output after giving a certain input is called the running time:

Input ⟶ Executable file ⟶ Output

The efficiency of an algorithm is a measure of the time taken to run the algorithm by a user—not the compilation time taken by a programmer. An efficient algorithm will take less time to give the output through an executable file, or we can say that it is a theoretical measure of the execution of an algorithm.

Computing time in big 'O'	Implication
O (1)	Computing time is constant
O (n)	Computing time is linear
O (n^2)	Computing time is quadratic
O (n^3)	Computing time is cubic
O (2^n)	Computing time is exponential
O (log n)	Computing time is logarithmic

ITERATIVE ALGORITHM

In the iterative method, unlike direct methods, a problem is solved by successive approximation, where an initial guess is made first to solve the problem. When we have a large number of variables and it is difficult to use the direct methods, we use the iterative method. Selection sort is a good example of this method.

Selection sort

Assume that a teacher has collected the answer books after a test. She now wants to arrange it in ascending order of roll number. If she uses selection sort, she will first find roll number 1 from the bunch of books and swap it with the top one. Next she will find roll number 2 and swap it with the second answer book from the top. She will repeat the same procedure till the entire bunch is sorted. Here, every time she searches for a particular roll number, she has to go through the entire lot of books. Hence it takes a long time to sort the books.

The procedure given above follows the steps of an iterative algorithm. Since there are a large number of books, it is difficult to use the direct method.

Selection sort is an iterative method. The following steps are followed:

1. Get a list of various data.
2. Locate the smallest data.
3. Swap the smallest data with the first position.
4. Find the next smallest and swap it with the second position.
5. Repeat the process till the last number is sorted.

Example 2.4

Sort the given data in ascending order

14	2	7	24

↓ Swap 2 with 14

2	14	7	24

↓ Swap 7 with 14

2	7	14	24

Given above is the sorted list. 14 is smaller than 24 so no more swapping is necessary.

Algorithm

SELECTION_ SORT (s, n) /*n is the total number of elements, s is the set of elements (s_i, s_{i+1}, s_{i+2}....s_n), i is a variable used in the algorithm to execute a loop of step 2 and step 3 'n' number of times, because we need to repeat the process of selecting the smallest element and swapping till the last element. Step 1 states that i has been assigned the initial value 1 and its value is incremented by 1 every time we repeat the loop*/

Step 1: Repeat steps 2 and 3 for $i \leftarrow 1$ to $n - 1$

Step 2: $s_j \leftarrow$ pick the smallest element among (s_i, s_{i+1}, ... s_n)

Step 3: Swap s_i and s_j

Step 4: Return s

RECURSIVE ALGORITHM

A recursive algorithm is one which uses smaller input values which are easy to solve. In mathematics, the term 'recursion' is used more generally to describe a process of repeating objects in a self-similar way.

Example 2.5

Calculation of the factorial of a number n.

As we know, factorial (n) = 1 × 2 × 3 ×...× n = Factorial (n – 1) × n

The pseudocode for calculating the factorial can be written in a very simple way.

```
Factorial (n)
{
If n=0 or 1 Return 1;
Return n*(Factorial (n–1);
}
```

For n = 5, the above pseudocode can be traced to understand recursion better. For the first time the function named Factorial will be called with argument value n = 5 as given below:

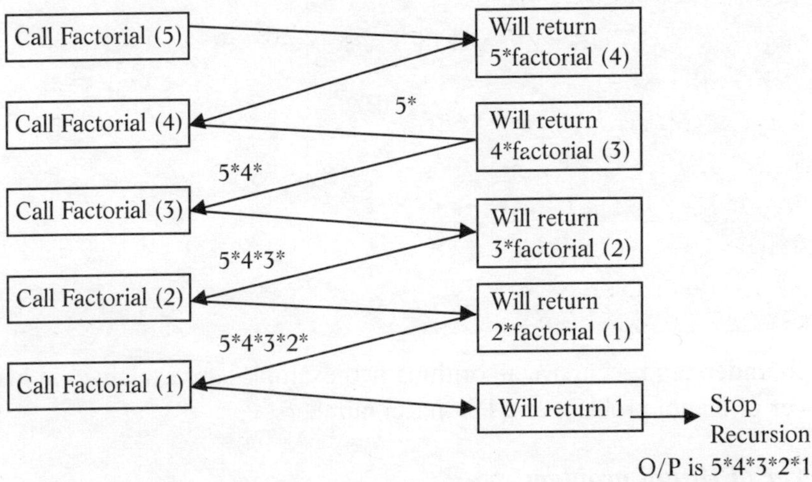

Algorithm

RECURSIVE_FACTORIAL(N)

Step 1: If N=0 or 1 Return 1; go to step 3

Step 2: Return N* RECURSIVE_FACTORIAL(N–1)

Step 3: Stop

Algorithm for recursive selection sort:

Start End

/*S is the array of elements to be sorted. 'Start' is a pointer pointing to the beginning of array and 'End' is pointing to the end of the array. Initially Start=0 and End=3 */

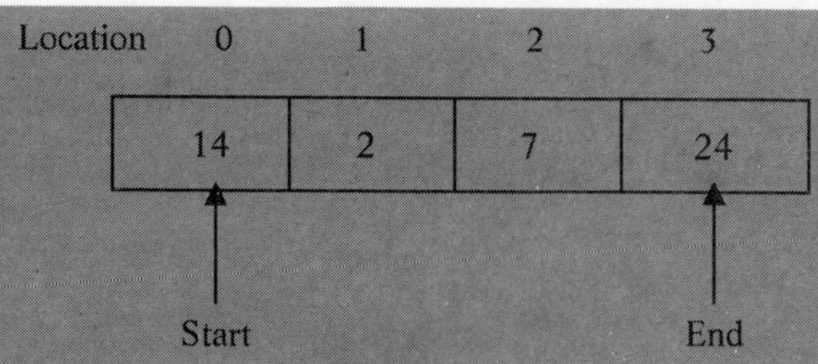

RECURSIVE_SELECTION_ SORT (S, Start, End)
Step 1: If Start < End goto steps 2,3 & 4; else go to step 5
Step 2: LOC← Location_of_min (A, Start, End) /* Is a function to find the location of the smallest element in the array S*/

Step 3: Swap A [Start] with A [LOC]
Step 4: A← RECURSIVE_SELECTION_SORT (A, Start+1, End)
Step 5 : Return A.
Location_of_min (A, Start, End)
Step 1: LOC ← Start
Step 2: For i ← Start + 1 to End
If Array [i] < Array [LOC], LOC ← i
Step 3: Return LOC

To understand recursive algorithms two examples are explained in brief: Tower of Hanoi problem and Fibonacci numbers.

Tower of Hanoi problem

The Tower of Hanoi (TOH) problem is a very interesting one which can be solved through recursion. It is a mathematical problem puzzle invented by the French mathematician Edward Lucas in 1803. In this puzzle, three pegs and a number of discs are used. Each player is supposed to stack the discs from the first peg to the third.

The rules of this game are:

1. Move the entire stack from the first peg to the third peg (each player can choose the number of discs).
2. Only one disc can be moved at a time.
3. A bigger disc cannot be placed on a smaller disc and the *task has to be completed in* a minimum number of moves.

Algorithm

This puzzle can be solved by a recursive algorithm in the following steps:

1) Total numbers of pegs are 3 and discs D.
2) Move top D–1 disk to the free peg.
3) Move the D disk to the other free peg.
4) Now move D–1 disk on top of D disk.
5) This algorithm has 2^n-1 moves.

For example, for 3 disks this puzzle can be solved in a minimum of seven moves:

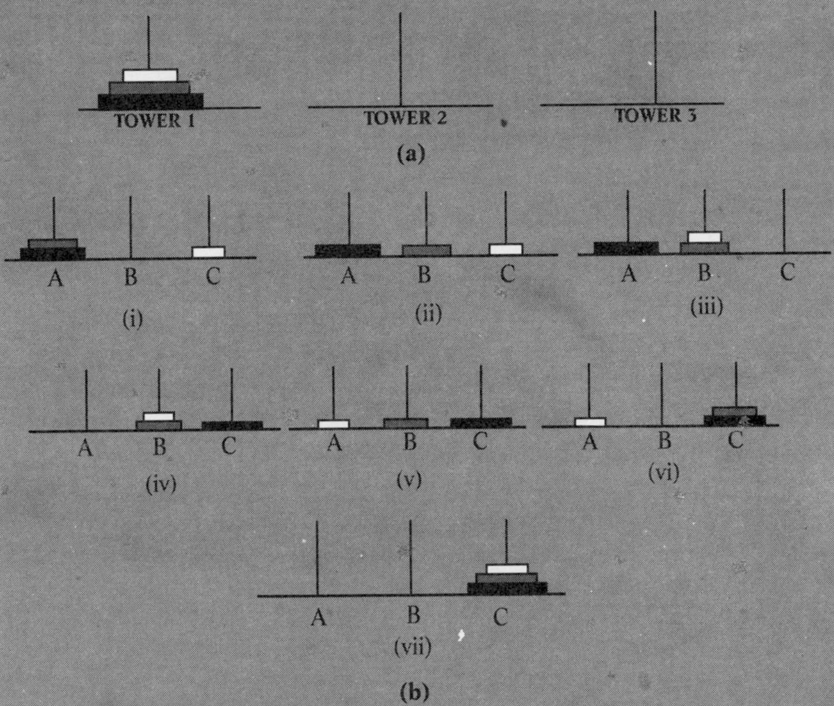

FIGURE 2.1(a) *Three pegs and three disks. (b) Seven moves running recursively to solve the puzzle*

Fibonacci numbers

The Fibonacci numbers are named after Leonardo of Pisa, known as Fibonacci. The Fibonacci sequence is based on the rabbit breeding problem. According to the Fibonacci rule, there is only one newborn rabbit per month. From the second month, the newborn pairs become fertile and each month every fertile pair produces a new pair. This process goes on year after year and as the rabbits do not die, we can count them all. Though it sounds unrealistic, this pattern appears in nature in the branching pattern of some flowers and arrangement of seeds in a sunflower. Fibonacci numbers are studied as part of number theory and are applied in mathematical object counting like sets, permutations and sequences. This is also applied in computer science. In a Fibbonacci number set, at time n the next number is equal to the two previous numbers, that is, F (n−1) and F (n−2), respectively.

In mathematical terms, the sequence F(n) of Fibonacci numbers is defined by the recurrence relation. So the nth Fibonacci number F(n) is equal to F (n−1) + F (n−2) (where $F_1 = F_2 = 1$)

A series of Fibonacci numbers can be generated by the following algorithm.

Algorithm

FIBONACCI (N)

Step 1: Initialize F_1 and F_2 with 1 that is $F_1 \leftarrow 1$ and $F_2 \leftarrow 1$

Step 2: Repeat step 3 for i ← 3 to N /* This step will repeat step 3 with various values for variable i .i.e., i = 3,4,5....N */

Step 3: $F_i \leftarrow F_{i-1} + F_{i-2}$ /* In the first iteration , i carry value 3; i.e. i=3. So

$F_3=F_2+F_1 = 1+1=2$. In second iteration i=4. So

$F_4=F_3+F_2 =2+1=3$ and so on.*/

Step 4: Return F (N)

Using the recursive algorithm the Fibonacci number can be returned as:

RECURSIVE FIBONACCI (N)

Step1: if N=1 or N=2 return 1

Step 2: else

Step 3: temp1 ← recursive _ Fibonacci (N-1)

Step 4: temp2 ← recursive _ Fibonacci (N-2)

Step 5: return (temp1+temp2) /* As temp1 carries F_{n-1} and temp2 carries F_{n-2}, temp1 + temp2 carries $F_{n-1} + F_{n-2} = F_n$ */

EXERCISES

1. How is computer programming different from algorithms? List the important characteristics of an algorithm.
2. Write an algorithm to travel from one city to another where you started by train but had to change routes due to a problem on the tracks.
3. What is big 'O' notation? Explain the linear and exponential running time algorithms.
4. With a suitable example, explain the best case and worst case algorithms. Which one is suitable or best suited for a problem solving algorithm and why?
5. "An algorithm must be correct in all conditions". Explain by giving examples for correct and incorrect algorithms.
6. Differentiate between iterative and recursive algorithms.
7. Explain the selection sort algorithm with an example. Differentiate iterative and recursive selection sort procedures.
8. Sort the given input using the selection sort algorithm: {7, 2. 9. 6, 1, 8, 5, 3}.
9. What are Fibonacci numbers? Explain an example using both iterative and recursive algorithms.
10. Explain the Tower of Hanoi puzzle. Write an algorithm for TOH.
11. Write a recursive algorithm to find the greatest common factor of two numbers.

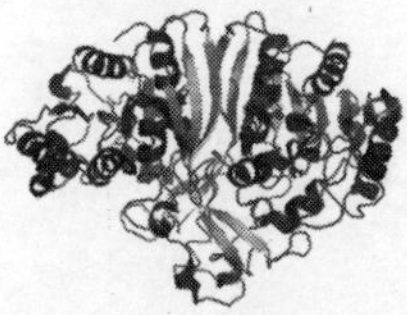

Section II

DATABASES AND MATRICES

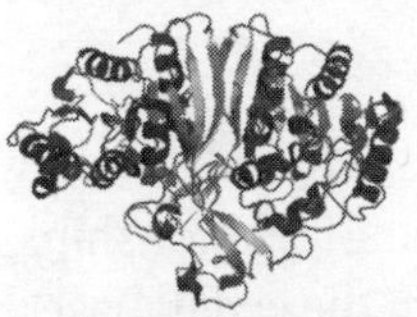

CHAPTER 3

Biological Databases

LEARNING OUTCOME

- List the primary protein sequence databases
- List the primary protein sequence patterns or motif databases
- Define secondary databases
- Describe a macromolecular 3D structure database
- Define gene expression databases
- Define metabolic pathway databases
- Explain genome databases
- Explain virological databases
- Describe world biodiversity databases
- Define model organism databases
- Describe other specialised databases
- List examples of database file structures

Biological data are complex, exception-ridden, vast and incomplete (missing data). Therefore, several databases must be created and interpreted to ensure unambiguous results. A collection of biological data arranged in computer readable form that enhances the speed of search and retrieval and is convenient to use is called a ***biological database***.

It is an important tool that researchers use to explain a host of biological phenomena—from the structure of biomolecules and their interaction to the whole metabolism of organisms—and also to understand the evolution of species. Biological databases are of immense importance and are created to manage distinct sets or types of information, from basic sequences to very high functional annotation.

A range of information like biological sequences, structures, binding sites, metabolic interactions, molecular action, functional relationships, protein families, motifs and homologs can be retrieved from these databases. ***The main purpose of a biological database is to store and manage biological data and information in computer readable form.***

Keywords: Databases must have methods for accessing and mining the stored data. The most important objective is 'keyword searching'. A keyword can be the name of the gene or protein, species, taxonomical term or reference title that is present in that database, or any other. More specific data can be retrieved by just entering the ID or the accession number—a unique identifier given to a biological polymer sequence (DNA, protein) when it is submitted to a sequence database.

Hyperlinks: There are many public databases in the field of life sciences. The data in each of them change regularly as researchers find and add new information. Hyperlinks are used to constantly update and retrieve information from one database to another. The Hyperlink Management System keeps checking when the information in one or more databases changes, and instantly retrieves and updates the database on which it is installed (Fig. 3.1).

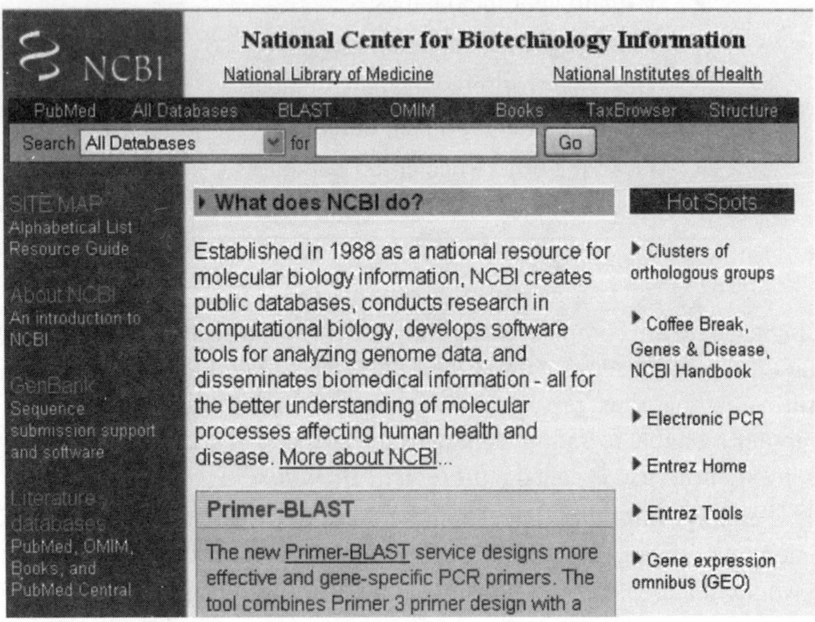

Figure 3.1: *An example from NCBI which has hyperlinks for PubMed, BLAST, OMIM, GenBank, Entrez Tools, etc.*

A good database must have updated information. It includes broad coverage and support staff, and has future prospects for development and changes and a good query interface. A database needs to collect, manage and organise data in such a way that it is easy to find standardised data representation and extract the required information (Fig. 3.2).

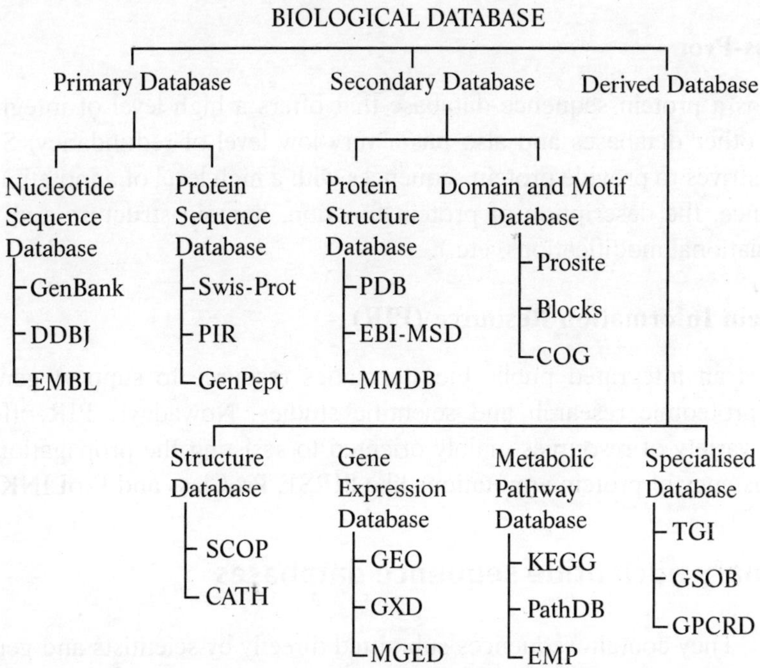

FIGURE 3.2 *Classification of biological databases*

Primary database

A primary database contains only sequence or structure information. Examples of these include GenBank and EMBL for genome sequences, Swiss-Prot and PIR for protein sequences and Protein Data Bank for protein structures.

GenBank

One of the fastest growing repositories of known nucleotide sequences, GenBank (Genetic Sequence Databank), has a flat file structure. It is an ASCII text file, readable by both humans and computers. Besides sequence data, GenBank files contain information such as accession numbers and gene names, phylogenetic classification and references to published literature.

EMBL

A comprehensive database of DNA and RNA sequences, EMBL Nucleotide Sequence Database is collected from scientific literature and is directly submitted by researchers. EMBL has been prepared in collaboration with GenBank (USA) and the DNA Database of Japan (DDBJ).

Swiss-Prot

This is a protein sequence database that offers a high level of integration with other databases and also has a very low level of redundancy. Swiss-Prot strives to provide protein sequences with a high level of annotation (for instance, the description of protein function, domain structure and post-translational modifications, etc.).

Protein Information Resource (PIR)

PIR is an integrated public bioinformatics resource to support genomic and proteomic research and scientific studies. Nowadays, PIR offers a wide variety of resources mainly oriented to assisting the propagation and consistency of protein annotations like PIRSF, ProClass and ProLINK.

Primary nucleotide sequence databases

- They contain sequences submitted directly by scientists and genome sequencing groups, and sequences taken from literature and patents.
- The ***three*** primary nucleotide sequence databases are EMBL (www.ebi.ac.uk/embl/), GenBank (www.ncbi.nlm.nih.gov/Genbank/) and DDBJ (www.ddbj.nig.ac.jp).
- Database entries are ***updated*** every day between these three primary nucleotide databases.
- These databases can be used without any ***legal restrictions***.
- To manage the huge influx of primary nucleotide data and minimise its search and download time, some subdivisions have been made. For example: UniGene (www.ncbi.nlm.nih.gov/UniGene/), Ensembl (www.ensembl.org), SGDgenome (www.stanford.edu/Saccharomyces/), EBI Genomes (www.ebi.ac.uk/genomes/), Genome Biology (www.ncbi.nlm.nih.gov/Genomes/), etc.

Primary protein sequence databases

- These databases contain documentation entries which describe protein domains, families and functional sites. They also contain associated patterns and profiles to identify protein domains and families.
- Swiss-Prot (http://www.expasy.org/sprot/), PIR (http://pir georgetown.edu) and TrEMBL translation of EMBL Nucleotide Sequence Database are the primary protein databases and are different from the nucleotide databases. These databases are curated, that is, they are created/maintained with a great deal of 'manual labour'.
- PIR has UniProt Universal Protein Resource that provides a single, centralised, authoritative resource for protein sequences and functional information.
- Swiss-Prot provides a high level of annotations and a minimum level of redundancy. It is highly integrated with other databases.
- TrEMBL, a ***computer-annotated supplement*** of Swiss-Prot, contains all the translations of EMBL nucleotide sequence entries that are not integrated in Swiss-Prot.
- GenPept (at NCBI) is a database of translated coding sequences from GenBank (and EMBL and DDBJ).

Secondary databases

The databases derived from the analysis or treatment of primary data are secondary databases. These databases contain data that is delivered by and licensed from other databases. These databases consolidate, summarise, standardise, classify, index and comment on primary databases. Secondary databases are very important for inferring protein function.

MOTIF DATABASES

Protein sequence motif is a set of conserved amino acid residues that are important for protein function and are located within a certain (short) distance from one another. These motifs usually provide clues to the functions of otherwise uncharacterised proteins.

- The PROSITE database (http://www.expasy.org/prosite/) consists of documentation entries describing protein domains, families and functional sites as well as associated patterns and profiles to identify them.

- PROSITE is complemented by ProRules (http://www.expasy.ch/prosite/prorule.html), which consists of manually created rules that increase the discriminatory power of PROSITE motifs.
- Blocks are multiple aligned ungapped segments (without gap) corresponding to the most highly conserved regions of proteins. These databases are made automatically by looking for the most highly conserved regions in groups of proteins represented in the PROSITE database.
- There are two Block databases: one derived automatically from sequence families classified in InterPro, and the other derived directly from motifs stored in PRINTS.
- Version 14.2 of the Block database consists of 29,767 blocks representing 6149 groups (March, 2006).
- PRINTS (http://www.bioinf.man.ac.uk/dbbrowser/PRINTS/) is a database for protein fingerprints. A fingerprint is a group of conserved motifs used to characterise a protein family.

DOMAIN DATABASES

A protein domain is an independently folded, structurally compact unit that forms a steady three-dimensional structure and shows a certain level of evolutionary conservation. Typically, a conserved domain contains one or more motifs.

- ProDom(http://prodom.prabi.fr/prodom/) is a protein domain database automatically generated from the Swiss-Prot and TrEMBL sequence databases.
- Pfam (http://www.sanger.ac.uk/Software/Pfam/) is a protein family database of alignments and hidden Markov.
- SMART (http://smart.embl-heidelberg.de/) is a highly reliable and sensitive tool for domain identification.
- COG (http://smart.embl-heidelberg.de/) is a database and a convenient tool for motif and domain search.

Macromolecular 3D structure databases

PDB (Protein Data Bank at http://www.rcsb.org/pdb/) ***is the main primary database for 3D structures*** of biological macromolecules determined by x-ray crystallography and NMR. It also accepts experimental data used to determine the structures (x-ray structure factors and NMR restraints) and homology models. PDB entries contain **atomic coordinates**, and some structural parameters connected with atoms (B-factors, occupancies) or computed from structures (secondary structure). As on 3 March 2009, there were 56217 structures in PDB.

- SCOP (Structural Classification of Proteins database at scop.mrc-lmb.cam.ac.uk/scop/) ***classifies protein 3D structures in a hierarchical scheme of structural classes***. All the protein structures in PDB are classified here, and the updated new structures are deposited in PDB. It is a ***typical secondary database***; with some added information through protein sequence and structure analysis. It is based on data in the primary database.
- The CATH database (Class, Architecure, Topology, Homologous superfamily at www.biochem.ucl.ac.uk/bsm/cath/) contains a hierarchical classification of protein domain structures.
- EBI-MSD is a Macromolecular Structure Database at EBI, UK, at http://www.ebi.ac.uk/msd/.
- NDB (Nucleic Acid Structure Database at Rutgers State University of New Jerseyat http://ndbserver.rutgers.edu/) is a repository of three-dimensional structural information about nucleic acids.
- MMDB (Molecular Modeling Database at NCBI(http://130.14.29.110/Structure/MMDB/mmdb.shtml), is a database of experimentally determined three-dimensional biomolecular structures.

Gene expression databases

- GEO or Gene Expression Omnibus at http://www.ncbi.nlm.nih.gov/geo/ is a curated, online resource and a gene expression/molecular abundance repository for gene expression data browsing, query and retrieval.
- GXD or Gene Expression Database is a community resource for gene expression information from the laboratory mouse at http://www.informatics.jax.org/mgihome/GXD/aboutGXD.shtml
- MGED or Microarray Gene Expression Data at http://www.mged.org/ contains microarray data, generated by functional genomics and proteomics experiments.
- ArrayExpress from European Bioinformatics Institute at http://www.ebi.ac.uk/arrayexpress/ is a repository for transcriptomics data.

Metabolic pathway databases

- KEGG PATHWAY Database (http://www.genome.ad.jp/kegg/metabolism.html) contains graphical pathway maps for all known metabolic pathways from various organisms.
- BRITE or Biomolecular Relations in Information, Transmission and Expression at http://www.genome.jp/kegg/brite.html is a collection of hierarchical classifications representing our knowledge on various aspects of biological systems.
- LIGAND (http://www.genome.jp/kegg/ligand.html) is a chemical database for enzyme reactions at the Institute for Chemical Research, Kyoto. It is a composite database currently consisting of the COMPOUND, DRUG, GLYCAN, REACTION, RPAIR and ENZYME databases.
- BRENDA at http://www.brenda.uni-koeln.de/ is an enzyme database that contains information on all aspects of enzymes and enzymatic reactions.
- The WIT2 (What is There?) is an integrated pathway/genome database; the metabolic reconstruction project produces metabolic reconstructions for sequenced or partially sequenced genomes. Presently it is disconnected and superseded by the two new systems PUMA2 (ttp://compbio.mcs.anl.gov/puma2/) and SEED, an annotation or analysis tool (http://theseed.uchicago.edu/FIG/index.cgi).
- EcoCyc (http://ecocyc.org), an *E. coli* database, stores information regarding the genome and biochemical machinery of *E. coli*.
- Boehringer Mannheim Biochemical pathways maintained at ExPASy (http://www.expasy. ch/cgi-bin/search-biochem-index) provides access to the digitised version of the Boehringer Mannheim 'Biochemical Pathways' wall chart.
- BioCyc (http://www.biocyc.org/) is a microbial species-specific integrated pathway/genome database. The BioCyc databases are divided into three tiers, based on their quality: intensively curated databases, computationally-derived databases subject to moderate curation and computationally-derived databases subject to no curation.
- MetaCyc (http://metacyc.org/) is a non-redundant, experimentally elucidated metabolic pathway database.

- EMP is the database of Enzymes and Metabolic Pathways at http://www.empproject.com/. It answers queries for pathways, metabolic outlines, software, nomenclature (enzymes), etc.
- UM-BBD (Microbial Biocatalysis/Biodegradation Database) is a database containing information on microbial biocatalytic reactions and biodegradation pathways for primarily xenobiotic, chemical compounds (http://umbbd.msi.umn.edu).
- PathDB, a functional research tool for biochemistry and functional genomics, is a project to capture distinct metabolic steps. It helps in building tools to construct metabolic networks de novo from a set of defined steps.
- GEPASI (http://dbk.ch.umist.ac.uk/softw/gepasi) is a software package for modelling biochemical systems. It simulates the kinetics of systems of biochemical reactions and provides a number of tools to fit models to data, optimise any function of the model and execute metabolic control analysis and linear stability analysis.

Genome databases

Genome databases give absolute information on the heritable properties of an organism. These databases help to identify genes and predict their functions. A few genome databases have links with specific organism databases.

- GOLD (Genomes Online Database at the University of Illinois, USA) contains a list of all the complete and ongoing genome projects worldwide.
- Genomes at NCBI (NCBI, USA).
- TIGR database (TDB), at the Institute for Genomic Research at Rockeville MD, USA.
- Microbial Genomes, the completed microbial genomes in GenBank.
- PEDANT at MIPS, Munich, Germany, helps you browse computationally analysed completed and unfinished genomes.
- Ensembl, a database of automatically annotated genomes at EBI, UK.

Virological databases

A virological database contains all the sequences and related information of viruses of animals, plants, bacteria, fungi and archea; for example, the

HIV protease database. A committee called The International Committee on Taxonomy of Viruses (ICTV) authorises and organises the taxonomic classification of viruses. ICTVdB contains taxonomic information for over thousands of virus species.

World biodiversity databases

Taxonomic databases are built to document all known species and make them available and accessible worldwide. These databases contain taxonomic hierarchies, species names, synonyms, descriptions, illustrations and references. For example: CCINFO, STRAIN and ALGAE.

Model organism databases

Escherichia coli

- *E. coli* Genome Center (Wisconsin University, USA)
- The *E. coli* index (University of Birmingham, UK)

S. cerevisiae (Baker's yeast)

- SGD (Yeast genome database at Stanford, USA)
- CYGD (MIPS Comprehensive Yeast Genome Database, Neuherberg, Germany)

Arabidopsis thaliana

- MATDB (MIPS *A. thaliana* database, Munich, Germany)
- TAIR (The *Arabidopsis* Information Resource)
- TIGR *Arabidopsis thaliana* Database (TIGR, Rockeville, MD, USA)

Oryza sativa (rice)

- RGP (Rice Genome Research Programme, Japan)
- Gramene (comparative mapping resource for grains)
- INE (integrated rice genome explorer: common database of the International Rice Genome Sequencing Project, Japan)

Caenorhabditis elegans

- WormBase (*C. elegans* database at Cold Spring Harbor Laboratories, USA)

Drosophila melanogaster (fruit fly)

- FlyBase (*Drosophila* genome database)
- BDGP (Berkeley *Drosphila* Genome Project)

Danio rerio (zebrafish)

- ZFIN (Zebrafish Information Network at the University of Oregon, USA)
- WashU-Zebrafish Genome Resources (Zebrafish EST database at Washington University, USA)

Mus musculus (mouse)

- MGI (Mouse Genome Informatics)

Homo sapiens

- GDB (The Human Genome Database, Toronto, Canada)
- HIB (HumanInfoBase of annotated UniGene clusters—putative human gene transcripts—at MIPS, Germany)
- Human genome resources at NCBI, USA
- Human genome browser at the University of California, Santa Cruz, USA
- HGP (Human Genome Project at the Sanger Institute, Cambridge, UK)
- Gene Links (portal to hyperlinks for each human gene at the Center for Genomics and Bioinformatics, Karolinska Institutet, Stockholm, Sweden)

Other specialised databases

- dbEST (Database of Expressed Sequence Tags) at http://www.ncbi.nlm.nih.gov/dbEST/
- TGI (TIGR Genome Indices, integrated analysis of public EST data) at TIGR, USA
- dbSNP (Database of Single Nucleotide Polymorphisms) at NCBI, USA
- GPCRD (G-protein–coupled receptor data) at http://www.gpcr.org/7tm/
- SNPper (SNP explorer by Children's Hospital Informatics Program) at Boston, USA
- dbSTS (Database of Sequence Tagged Sites) at NCBI, USA
- GSDB (The Genome Sequence Database) is a complete, relational database of annotated DNA sequences
- FlyBase (*Drosophila* database)
- MITOMAP (human mitochondrial genome database)

TABLE 3.1 *Some commonly used database formats*

S. No.	Format Name	Example	Explanation
1	FASTA	>seq (name & information) ACAGTTGCGATTAACGGC GCGATTAACCCTTTTACG	First line starting with a > symbol followed by the sequence identification (name/accession number, etc.); sequence starts from second line. The sequence is in one-letter symbol (DNA/amino acid).
2	NBRF	>seq (name) seq info ACAGTTGCGATTAACGGC	First line starting with a > symbol followed by the sequence identification. Second line has other information about the sequence, and the sequence starts from third line.
3	GCG	Seq (name) Length: 18 Check: 23.. 1 acgtgtgccc acggttgc	The first line contains the name, length, date, type of the sequence and the GCG checksum. The start of the sequence is marked by a line ending with two dot ("..") characters. GCG-RSF (rich sequence format) can contain several sequences in one file.
4	GenBank	LOCUS seq1 18 bp DEFINITION seq1, 18 bases, 245 checksum ORIGIN 1 ACAGTTGCGATTAACGGC //	One sequence in the GenBank format starts with a line containing the word LOCUS and a number of annotation lines. The start of the sequence is marked by a line containing "ORIGIN" and the end of the sequence is marked by two slashes ("//").
5	EMBL	ID accession no. standard; DNA Textual description of sequence SQ sequence 19 BP;3A;5C;6G;5T; TACGGTTGCGGGCTTACAC 19//	One sequence entry starts with an identifier line ("ID"), followed by further annotation lines. The start of the sequence is marked by a line starting with "SQ" and the end of the sequence is marked by two slashes ("//").
6	PIR	>code; sequence identification code Textual description of sequence MDITIHNPLI RRPLFSWLAP SDVPERSIPI AQRK*	It looks similar to the FASTA format but the sequence ends with a '*' and there is a second description line that is needed by the GCG importing programs.

- SWISS-2DPAGE (database of two-dimensional polyacrylamide gel electrophoresis)
- PRINTS, ENZYME, EcoCyc (metabolic databases)

Examples of database file structures

Sequence analysis and other bioinformatics programs require the sequences to be given in a standard ASCII file and in a specific format. These standard ASCII files contain certain characters that indicate various types of information. The ASCII format contains only sequences without any other related information. A database consists of a number of related files containing related records. These records consist of a number of linked fields and the final data consists of a number of characters.

Description of some database formats

GENBANK

This database has been developed and maintained at the National Center for Biotechnology Information (NCBI), Bethesda, MD, USA, as part of the International Nucleotide Sequence Database Collaboration (INSDC). GenBank is an open access sequence database. It coordinates with individual laboratories and other sequence databases like the European Molecular Biology Laboratory (EMBL) and the DNA Database of Japan (DDBJ). GenBank is a genetic sequence databank and is a rapidly increasing international repository of identified genetic sequences from a variety of organisms. It is an annotated collection of all the nucleotide sequences that are available to the public. Recently, the nucleotide database was divided into three databases at NCBI: CoreNucleotide database, Expressed Sequence Tag (EST) and Genome Survey Sequence (GSS). CoreNucleotide database has most of the nucleotide sequences used. It also encloses all nucleotide records that are not in the EST or GSS databases. Submission of sequences to GenBank can be done using BankIt (an internet-based submission tool), Sequin (NCBI's standalone submission software) and tbl2asn (a command line program used primarily for the submission of complete genomes and large batches of sequences).

Each entry in GenBank (all biological databases are associated with a specific format) contains identification, description and other information in the ASCII format (Table 3.1). A GenBank format has the following details in the order given below:

LOCUS	Information about the accession number, length and type (DNA/mRNA, etc.) of the sequence
DEFINITION	Single line description of the sequence and whether it is complete or incomplete
SOURCE	Source organism's name and type of cell
ORGANISM	Taxonomy of the organism
REFERENCE	Number of citations, names of authors and titles
FEATURE	About the gene and coding sequences
SOURCE	Organism, type and strain
ORIGIN	Sequence in batches of ten and each line has sixty residues. It should end with a double slash (//). Sequence includes numbers on each line for convenience.

```
LOCUS AF261270 1254 bp mRNA linear PLN 30-APR-2004
DEFINITION Oryza sativa beta-expansin (EXPB1) mRNA, complete
cds.
ACCESSION AF261270
VERSION AF261270.1 GI:8118420
SOURCE Oryza sativa (rice)
ORGANISM Oryza sativa
Eukaryota; Viridiplantae; Streptophyta; Embryophyta; Tracheophyta;
Spermatophyta; Magnoliophyta; Liliopsida; Poales; Poaceae; BEP
clade; Ehrhartoideae; Oryzeae; Oryza.
REFERENCE 1 (bases 1 to 1254)
AUTHORS Cosgrove,D.J., Bedinger,P. and Durachko,D.M.
TITLE Group I allergens of grass pollen as cell wall-loosening agents
JOURNAL Proc. Natl. Acad. Sci. U.S.A. 94 (12), 6559-6564 (1997)
PUBMED 9177257
REFERENCE 2 (bases 1 to 1254)
AUTHORS Cosgrove,D.J.
TITLE Characterization of beta-expansin in rice
JOURNAL Unpublished
source 1..1254
/organism="Oryza sativa"
/mol_type="mRNA"
/db_xref="taxon:4530"
gene 1..1254
```

```
/gene="EXPB1"
CDS 22..825
/gene="EXPB1"
/function="putative cell wall loosening activity"
/note="putative group-1 pollen allergen Ory s1; OsEXPB1"
/codon_start=1
/product="beta-expansin"
/protein_id="AAF72983.1"
/db_xref="GI:8118421"
/translation="MASSSLLLACVVVAAMVSAVSCGPPKVPPGPNITT
SYGDKWLEA

KATWYGAPKGAGPKDNGGACGYKDVDKAPFLGMNSCGNDP
IFKDGKGCGSCFEIKCSKKASNPNYLALLVKYVAGDGDVVEVEI
KEKGSEEWKALKESWGAPKPLKGPFSVRVTTEGGEKIIAEDAIP
DGWKADSVYKSNVQAK"

ORIGIN
1 caataacatt atattgcagc aatggcatcc tcctcccttc tactcgcctg tgttgtggtg
61 gcggctatgg tgtccgccgt ctcctgcggg ccacccaagg tgccaccggg
ccccaacatc
121 acgacaagct acggcgacaa gtggctggaa gccaaggcca cctggtatgg
tgcgcccaag
181 ggtgctggcc ccaaggacaa cggcggcgcc tgcgggtaca aggatgtcga
caaggctccc
------------------------------------------------------------------------
1201 gcgctattta tttaaaaaaa aaaaaaaaaa aaaaaaaaaa aaaaaaaaaa aaaa
```

FIGURE 3.3 *A curtailed output from GenBank for* Oryza sativa *beta-expansin (EXPB1)*

PROTEIN DATA BANK

PDB is a repository for 3D structural data obtained by x-ray crystallography or NMR spectroscopy of proteins and nucleic acids. Research Collaboratory for Structural Bioinformatics (RCSB) PDB provides a variety of tools and resources for studying the structures of biological macromolecules and their relationship with other sequences, its function and diseases caused if any. The PDB file format is a textual file format that describes the 3D structures of PDB molecules. The PDB format includes atom position information, sequence information and information about the researchers who defined the structure and citations. Every PDB file is broken into a number of lines and is terminated by an end-of-line indicator. Each line in the PDB entry file consists of 80 columns with an end-of-line indicator towards the end. The first six columns of every line contain a record name. The PDB file is a collection of record types with one or more lines in each record. Each record type is further divided into fields. All records in a PDB coordinate entry must appear in a defined order.

HEADER	First line of the entry contains the PDB ID code
TITLE	Contains records used to describe the experiment and the biological macromolecules present in the entry
REMARK	Encode experimental details under the title section
SOURCE	Source of the structure
AUTHOR	Author(s) name
SEQRES	Under primary structure section, contains observed residue sequence within the ATOM record
HET	The heterogen section contains identification of non-standard groups or residues (heterogens) and its complete description
ATOM	In coordinate section, it encodes atomic coordinate data as X, Y and Z coordinates
TER	Chain terminator

```
HEADER CYTOSKELETON 02-DEC-97 1A0K
TITLE PROFILIN I FROM ARABIDOPSIS THALIANA
COMPND MOL_ID: 1;
COMPND 2 MOLECULE: PROFILIN;
SOURCE MOL_ID: 1;
SOURCE 2 ORGANISM_SCIENTIFIC: ARABIDOPSIS THALIANA;
KEYWDS PROFILIN, CYTOSKELETON, ACTIN-BINDING
EXPDTA X-RAY DIFFRACTION
AUTHOR R.SHIGETA JUNIOR,D.HUDDLER,U.LINDBERG,C. E.SCHUTT
REVDAT 2 01-APR-03 1A0K 1 JRNL
```

```
REVDAT 1 18-MAR-98 1A0K 0
JRNL REFN ASTM STRUE6 UK ISSN 0969-2126
REMARK 1
REMARK 1 REFERENCE 1
REMARK 1 AUTH H.E.CHRISTENSEN,S.RAMACHANDRAN,C.
T.TAN,U.SURANA,
REMARK 1 TITL 2 BOVINE PROFILIN AT 2.0 A RESOLUTION
-------------------------------------------------------------------
DBREF 1A0K A 1 131 UNP Q42449 PROF1_ARATH 1 131
SEQRES 1 A 131 MET SER TRP GLN SER TYR VAL ASP ASP HIS
LEU MET CYS
SEQRES 2 A 131 ASP VAL GLU GLY ASN HIS LEU THR ALA ALA
ALA ILE LEU
-------------------------------------------------------------------
SEQRES 9 A 131 PHE TYR ASP GLU PRO MET THR GLY GLY
GLN CYS ASN LEU
SEQRES 10 A 131 VAL VAL GLU ARG LEU GLY ASP TYR LEU
ILE GLU SER GLU
SEQRES 11 A 131 LEU
FORMUL 2 HOH *26(H2 O)
HELIX 1 H1 TRP A 3 CYS A 13 1HAS A SINGLE I+5 TURN 11
HELIX 2 H2 PRO A 44 GLU A 55 1 12
HELIX 3 H4 GLY A 112 GLU A 128 1SEE REMARK 650 17
SHEET 1 A 6 MET A 73 ILE A 75 0
SHEET 2 A 6 VAL A 82 LYS A 87 -1 N LYS A 86 O MET A 73
CISPEP 1 GLU A 108 PRO A 109 0 -0.03
SITE 1 PLY 6 TRP A 3 TYR A 6 ILE A 25 TRP A 33
SITE 2 PLY 6 TYR A 125 LEU A 126
-------------------------------------------------------------------
SITE 3 AIN 14 THR A 111 GLY A 112 GLY A 113 ASN A 116
SITE 4 AIN 14 LEU A 117 ARG A 121
CRYST1 43.050 43.530 59.870 90.00 90.00 90.00 P 21 21 21 4
ORIGX1 1.000000 0.000000 0.000000 0.00000
ORIGX2 0.000000 1.000000 0.000000 0.00000
ORIGX3 0.000000 0.000000 1.000000 0.00000
SCALE1 0.023229 0.000000 0.000000 0.00000
```

```
SCALE2 0.000000 0.022973 0.000000 0.00000
SCALE3 0.000000 0.000000 0.016703 0.00000
ATOM 1 N SER A 2 0.880 13.177 –3.774 1.00 7.40 N
ATOM 2 CA SER A 2 1.878 14.106 –4.368 1.00 7.45 C
ATOM 3 C SER A 2 2.603 14.776 –3.228 1.00 7.32 C
ATOM 4 O SER A 2 2.295 14.497 –2.083 1.00 7.91 O
ATOM 5 CB SER A 2 1.130 15.162 –5.126 1.00 6.86 C
ATOM 12 CB TRP A 3 5.502 17.022 –2.903 1.00 5.05 C
-----------------------------------------------------------------------------------------
HETATM 1277 H1 HOH 26 -1.325 12.569 -0.426 1.00 0.00 H
HETATM 1278 H2 HOH 26 -1.683 11.122 -0.163 1.00 0.00 H
MASTER 258 0 0 3 8 0 11 6 1277 1 0 11
END
```

FIGURE 3.4 *A curtailed output from PDB for Profiling I from* Arabidopsis thaliana

PROSITE

PROSITE is a software program containing a database of protein domains, families and functional sites, related patterns and profiles to identify the protein domains and families. The entries are deposited in PROSITE in two distinct files. The first of these houses the pattern and lists all matches. The second one is a documentation file, which provides details of the characterised family, a description of the biological role of the chosen motifs and supporting bibliography. It is a free format text file.

Each entry contains an identification number (ID) and an accession number (AC).

ID line	Indicates the type of discriminator to expect in the file
DE line	Description of the family
PA lines	Description of the pattern itself
NR lines	Scientific details about the source and diagnostic performance of the pattern
CC line	Gives information on the taxonomy of the family, the maximum number of observed repeats of the pattern, functional site annotations, etc.

The sequence line next to the information lines has all the true matches to the pattern (denoted by T) and any visible matches (denoted by P) which are often in the form of fragments. The false positive and negative is denoted as P and N. The final line of the file (as DO) points to the associated family documentation file.

PROSITE PROFILE

The file structure is based on the PROSITE structure with some differences.

- ***ID line,*** where the word matrix indicates the type of discrimination to expect in a profile.
- ***Pattern (PA) lines*** are replaced by matrix (MA) lines which list the parameter specifications used to derive and describe the profile. They include details of the alphabet used, the length of the profile, cutoff scores, etc.
- ***I and M lines*** include position-specific profile scores for insert and match positions, respectively.

For example: RecR protein signature in a zinc finger motif:

C – x(2) – C – x(3,5) – [STACD] – x(4) – C – x – [LIVFQ] – C – x(4) – [RD] – [NQDS]

The above example can be explained as follows: RecR protein signature in a zinc finger motif sequence should first have amino acid C followed by any amino acid twice, next amino acid C again followed by any amino acid three to five times (either three, four or five times). Next, this should have amino acids STAC and D followed by any amino acid four times, and, in a similar way, the rest of the result can be explained.

EXERCISES

1. Give a brief outline of databases for the human genome.
2. Name a database for orthologous genes, gene expression data, essential genes and protein–protein interaction.
3. How are various interactions like protein–protein interaction or gene expression reactions represented in KEGG?
4. What are model organisms? How are these genome studies used in the human genome project?
5. Retrieve the nucleotide sequence for HelA2 (*Helianthus anus*) from GenBank. Translate it into protein sequence and observe. (Hint: http://www.expasy.ch/tools/dna.html)

6. Retrieve the protein sequence for Ory S1 from *Oryza sativa* from Swiss-Prot. Reverse translate it into nucleotide sequence and report. (Hint: http://www.bioinformatics.org/sms2/rev_trans.html)
7. What is PDB? What is the significance of PDB in bioinformatics?
8. Retrieve the complete structure of any multidomain protein from PDB.
9. Give the important characteristics of a PROSITE profile.
10. What is a sequence format? How do you write the following DNA sequence in the FASTA format? TGCAGACGTTCGTATCGTCAATCGTCG. (Hint: See sequence format table)

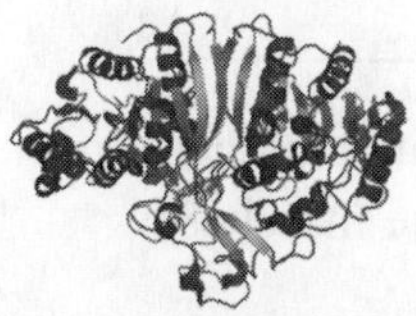

CHAPTER 4

Database Searching

LEARNING OUTCOME

- Explain primary database searching: FASTA, BLAST
- Explain secondary database searching: Motif, Patterns
- Define profile search
- Describe the hidden Markov model (HMM)
- Describe profile HMM

Managing the huge influx of biological data is a complex job, and maximum use of database searching is possible only when proper database search methods and interpretation of those results are known. Searching a database in an efficient manner is a matter of prime importance, as databases contain large amounts of information. So, methods that can run on small databases (exhaustive search or dynamic programming) may not be effective with larger databases in terms of time and space efficiency. We need other methods (heuristics like BLAST or FASTA) to perform such operations.

Database searching is the matching of query nucleotide or protein sequences with database sequences. To do this, we align the query sequence with database sequences to find similarity among them. Database searching is the application of knowledge achieved (information gathered) from previous biological experiments to the gene discovery problem.

Selectivity is the ability of a method to find the members of a protein family without any false positive matches. In other words, it is a measure of your ability to not include the false matches erroneously.

Selectivity = True negative/True positive + False positive

Sensitivity is the ability of a method to find the most similar sequences from the database or a measure of your ability to find all the true matches.

Sensitivity = True positive/True negative + False negative

Score (S) value, also called bit score, is derived from the raw alignment score 'S'. Here the statistical properties of the scoring system used have been taken into account to produce 'S'.

Expect (E) value is a parameter which depicts the expected number of hits that happen just by chance when searching a database of a particular size. Thus, a match is more 'significant' if the E value is lower (or closer to 0). The length of the query sequence is also taken into account for the E value, as shorter sequences have a higher probability of occurring in the database purely by chance.

K value is a statistical parameter that is used to calculate BLAST scores. This value is used to convert a raw score (S) to a bit score (S´).

Probability (P) value is the probability of obtaining a result by chance alone. The P- values closer to 0 are highly significant. Like the E value, it is a different way of representing the significance of the alignment.

Database searching is a balancing act between sensitivity and selectivity. The suitable method used for a certain query to perform a database search is one that has both high selectivity and sensitivity.

Scoring matrices, gap, gap extension penalties and type of gaps (*see Chapter* 5) as well as filtering low complexity regions affect database searches. As it is difficult to find optimal alignments dynamically from large databases, heuristic approaches are used to make the search faster, though they do not guarantee that the best alignment will be found.

Primary database searching

A ***primary sequence*** is one that has been experimentally determined, and a ***primary database*** is one that stores experimentally derived data. It is difficult to perform a database search using dynamic programming as it is a computationally intensive program and is therefore too slow. So, heuristic methods are used for database search. These programs are local similarity search programs that provide short matches. These short matches, called local alignment (a segment of sequence showing similarity, *see Chapter* 6), are more informative than global alignment (complete sequence showing similarity, *see Chapter* 6). Local alignments can return highly conserved regions of the sequence even in two sequences that do not produce any reasonable alignment when aligned globally. Dynamic algorithm programs can return local alignments and are guaranteed to find the best alignment, but are very insensitive due to their mathematical rigour. So BLAST and FASTA are used to carry out database searches. These heuristic database search programs are the major primary database search methods and are very fast though less sensitive.

Database searching algorithms search for similarity, not homology. So, once similarity is determined, it can be concluded that it is a result of homology or it has come from 'another source', such as regions of low sequence complexity, biases in nucleotide or amino acid usage or shared motifs that have been acquired.

FASTA (FAST ALIGNMENT)

FASTA was developed by Pearson and Lipman in 1905, and was so named because it was faster than other methods used for sequence alignment at that time. However, BLAST is now much faster than FASTA for database search. FASTA uses the Pearson and Lipman algorithm for similarity search between a query sequence and a database sequence. Given a query sequence, FASTA searches for local alignment with the sequences in the database.

Important characteristics of FASTA

- A heuristic approximation to the algorithm is performed.
- It is a rapid alignment program for protein and DNA sequence pairs.
- It searches for matching patterns called k tuples/words.
- No individual residue search is performed, saving time.
- Uses the hash method to find regions of similarity.
- The needs input sequence must be in the FASTA format for alignment.

Algorithm

It is basically a two-step algorithm. First, a word search for a specific word size is made and then alignment of the highly similar sequence fraction is done (found at diagonals), restricted to window size. This algorithm can be explained in the following steps:

1. The query sequence is placed on one axis (say the X axis) and the database sequence on another axis (Y axis) of the two-dimensional

table, as given below. This two-dimensional graph is called a hash plot or dot plot.

	G	C	G	T	G	G	A	T	A	C	G
A							*		*		
C		*								*	
G	*		*		*						*
T				*				*			
G	*		*		*	*					*
T				*				*			
A							*		*		
C		*								*	
G	*		*		*	*					*

FIGURE 4.1: *Query sequence on the X-axis and database sequence on the Y-axis.*

2. A specific word size, which is known as k tuple, is taken for finding identities shared between two sequences. Word size one takes one character from the query sequence and one from the database sequence for similarity search (Fig. 4.1). Word size one shows many hits (as *) resulting in noise (i.e. clustering of dots) in dot plot; similarly word size four will take four characters together for the search (Fig. 4.2).

	G	C	G	T	G	G	A	T	A	C	G
A											
C											
G			*								
T											
G											
T											
A									*		
C											
G											

Figure 4.2: *Query sequence on the X-axis and database sequence on the Y-axis. Word size four shows two hits, i.e. both the sequences have only two positions with four consecutive identical characters.*

3. The query sequence is divided into its constituent overlapping words of word length k or k tuples.

   Sequence: A C G T G T A C G

   A C G T

   C G T G

   G T G T

   Word list for FASTA with word size equal to 4.

4. The database sequence is also divided into its constituent overlapping words. A larger k tuple enables rapid alignment but becomes less sensitive.

   Sequence: G C G T G G A T A C G

   G C G T

   C G T G

   G T G G

   Word list for FASTA with word size equal to 4.

5. Both these lists (words from sequence and database sequence) are compared to find the identical words.

6. Significantly matching pairs of words are indicated by drawing a dot in a position representing the middle of the matched words. Once all possible words of the horizontal sequence have been compared to all possible words of the vertical sequence, a number of dots are plotted. Roughly diagonal runs of dots indicate roughly similar regions in the two sequences being compared.

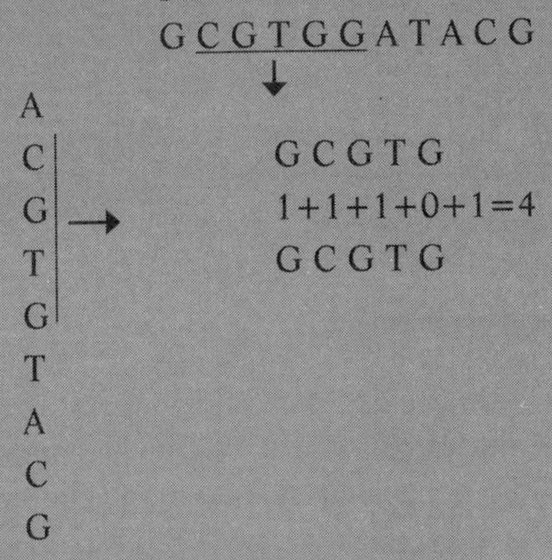

Figure 4.3 *Positioning of a dot in a dot plot based on word size 4 and cut-off score 3.*

7. Using a scoring scheme (+1 for a matched pair of bases, 0 for a mismatched pair, say), a similarity score is computed for each pair of compared words. Significant similarity is defined by the selection of a cut-off score (say 3, indicating 3 or more matched bases between words of size 4 to be significant).
8. Like the dot matrix, a hash plot is constructed for identical runs of residues on the table (Fig. 4.4 a).
9. An initial score based on identical residues is computed in the dot plot and the top scoring local diagonals are selected. The identical runs of residues that are found together are supposed to have a higher score than small runs of residues: more dots together means more number of similar characters (Fig. 4.4 b).
10. If the initial score is high enough, a second score is computed to find out which two identical segments can be joined to a consistent alignment using only gaps of the allowed number (Fig. 4.4 c).
11. The maximum number of gaps allowed is set by the window size parameter.
12. If the score is high enough, the algorithm is performed within the dot plot region. This finally gives rise to a final optimal score (Fig. 4.4 d).
13. Highly similar segments are found as closely spaced diagonals in the table.

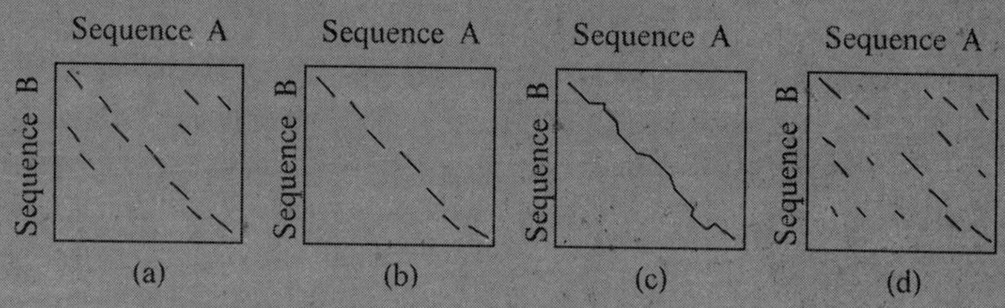

Figure 4.4 *FASTA algorithm*

BLAST (BASIC LOCAL ALIGNMENT SEARCH TOOL)

A local similarity search program, BLAST compares nucleotide or protein sequences to sequence databases and calculates the statistical significance of the matches (Fig. 4.5). The functional and evolutionary relationships between sequences are construed and members of gene families identified by the BLAST search program.

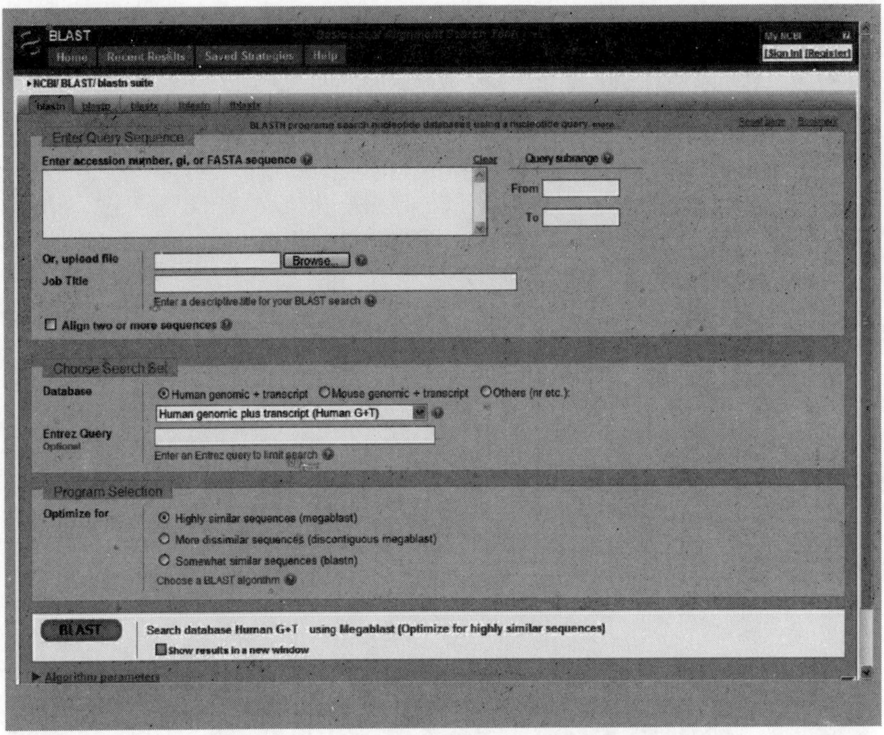

FIGURE 4.5 *Screenshot showing NCBI's BLAST web interface*

Important characteristics of BLAST

- It is faster than FASTA and more sensitive.
- It uses a word-based heuristic algorithm.
- It does not allow gaps in the alignment. Though, at present, some BLAST programs (like WU 1+1 BLAST, Gapped blast) allow less than the maximum number of gaps.
- It is more selective and less sensitive.
- It is more sensitive for protein sequences as it uses a word size of three, though FASTA uses a word size of two.
- FASTA is more sensitive than BLAST for nucleic acid sequences, as it uses a word size of 7 and BLAST uses a word size of 11.

Algorithm

This algorithm has the following steps.

1. For the query sequence, a list of a particular word size is made as explained in the FASTA algorithm (usually word size 2 or 3 for protein sequences and 11 for nucleic acid sequences are used by NSBI BLAST)

   ```
   Sequence:  F S A G W
              F S
                S A
                  A G
                    G W
   ```

   Word list for BLAST with word size equal to 2

2. Now this word list is expanded. The first word list contains only identical characters. The expanded list contains not only identical characters but physiologically similar characters as well, as explained below. This increases the sensitivity of the method, i.e., even a sequence with some non-identical characters with physiological similarity gets a hit.

Word List	**Expanded list**
FS	FS, FA, FN, FG, FP, FD, FT, YS
SA	No words
AG	AG
GW	GW, AW, NW, RW, EW, KW, SW, TW

   Expanded list; using PAM 120 matrix with word-containing score of at least eight.

3. A threshold score is selected. A hit is found when a word is aligned with the initial list of words and gets a score of more than the minimum threshold.

4. BLAST searches for the exact matches with any word of the expanded list in both directions until the score increases or remains the same (as explained earlier, match positive and mismatch negative value, so higher negative matches reduce the overall score). This is called as high scoring pair.

5. A cut-off score "S" is used now to limit this extension till a desired score is obtained. It keeps only the extended matches that have a score at least "S", the cut-off score.

For example: a sequence AFSAGWTT is searched for two characters in the database sequence and gets an exact hit at SA which gives a match value (say +1). Now search will be done on both the sides to see if it is only a two-letter identity or more similar characters are present in the alignment. This search is expanded in both the directions till it encounters a threshold or cut-off value (say 5).

Sequence 1: A F S A G W T T

←S A⟶

5. This way we can align many segments of the sequence. The two segments with very few characters unaligned in between can be aligned by using the dynamic programming algorithm. This gives rise to gapped alignment (as in WU-BlAST). the types of BLAST are discussed in *Chapter 6*. *For example,* two segments that have a hit in the database are F S A A W and T S R S with a two-space gap. Dynamic programming algorithm can be used to fill this gap (say with D G based on the characters found in database). The resultant sequence segment will be FSAAWDGTSRS. A long segment of sequence similarity is more meaningful than a short segment of sequence similarity.
6. Optionally the sequence is first filtered to remove the low complexity regions, as they hinder the production of meaningful alignment.

PSI-BLAST OR POSITION SPECIFIC ITERATIVE-BLAST

In this program, the query sequence is first queried against a protein database using the BLASTp program. This program searches for a certain pattern or conserved region by working interactively. In the first round, PSI-BLAST works like a normal BLAST program producing hits. Significant hits are collected and an MSA (multiple sequence alignment) table is constructed between the query sequence and significant conserved matches.

This MSA provides a profile. The database is once again queried using this profile and local matches are investigated and statistically significant matches are taken. The steps are repeated again (from step two) until no significant change occurs in the final alignment. Some types of low complexity sequences may not be detected by the filtering option in BLAST. This program provides better results to identify distant relatives (Fig. 4.6).

Sequences producing significant alignments:	Score (Bits)	E Value	
NEW ☑ ref|NP_942075.1|phosphoenolpyruvate carboxykinase 1 [Rattus ...	1303	0.0	U G
NEW ☑ ref|NP_035174.1| phosphoenolpyruvate carboxykinase 1, cytosol...	1278	0.0	U G
NEW ☑ dbj|BAC26903.1| unnamed protein product [Mus musculus]	1277	0.0	U G
NEW ☑ gb|AAH37629.1| Phosphoenolpyruvate carboxykinase 1, cytosolic [M	1276	0.0	U G
NEW ☑ ref|XP_5147452| PREDICTED: cytosolic phosphoenolpyruvate car...	1204	0.0	G
NEW ☑ sp|Q5R5J1|PPCKC_PONPY Phosphoenolpyruvate carboxykinase, cyto...	1201	0.0	
NEW ☑ gb|AAX41025.1|phosphoenolpyruvate carboxykinase 1 [synthetic co	1201	0.0	
NEW ☑ gb|AAV50001.1| phosphoenolpyruvate carboxykinase 1 (soluble) ...	1201	0.0	G
NEW ☑ ref|NP_002582.2|cytosolic phosphoenolpyruvate carboxykinase ...	1200	0.0	U G
NEW ☑ sp|P35558|PPCKC_HUMAN Phosphoenolpyruvate carboxykinase, cyto..	1200	0.0	G

FIGURE 4.6 *A curtailed A PSI-BLAST result showing hits for phosphoenolpyruvate carboxykinase 1 from* R. norvegicus. *Each hit shows from left to right the database reference sequence (sequence can be retrieved by clicking the link), name of protein and the species name, bits score and E value.*

NCBI BLAST

This has three options for 'Batch' BLAST searches:

1. Web Mega BLAST (for aligning nucleotide sequences that differ slightly as a result of sequencing or other similar 'errors').
2. Standalone BLAST (command line programs which run BLAST searches against local downloaded copies of the NCBI BLAST databases).
3. BLAST Network Client (submit a sequences in FASTA format over an internet connection to the NCBI BLAST databases).

Secondary database searching

Primary database searching does not always provide a satisfactory answer to the questions of sequence analysis. The presence of highly repetitive and low complexity sequences can result in irrelevant matches and may even complicate the interpretation. Secondary databases provide information about the relationship of a given sequence with other sequences within multiple alignment and some more information (family, domain and motif) as well, depending on the method used. These databases contain the results of primary sequence analysis. Some important secondary database searches are motif or pattern search and Profile search. PROSITE is a database and a tool consisting of documentation entries describing protein domains, families and functional sites as well as associated patterns and profiles to identify them.

Major approaches to search secondary databases

MOTIF SEARCH

Motifs are specific geometric arrangements of protein secondary structure elements (alpha, beta and loops). Some motifs are associated with a particular function and some are part of other structural and functional arrangements. Simple motifs are combined to form complex motifs. These are biologically conserved regions from protein sequences.

The different types of simple motifs (Fig. 4.7) are:

The Greek key motif: In this motif, four adjacent antiparallel β sheets are arranged in a Greek style ornamental pattern (Fig. 4.7a).

Hairpin β motif: This motif is built from two adjacent β strands, connected by a loop, and occurs repeatedly in protein structure (Fig. 4.7b).

β α β motif: This is a commonly used method to connect two β sheets. It comprises an α sheet connected with a loop to a β helix and again a loop connecting the next β sheet.

Helix loop helix motif: This motif is specific to a DNA binding region and comprises two helixes connected with a loop (Fig. 4.7c).

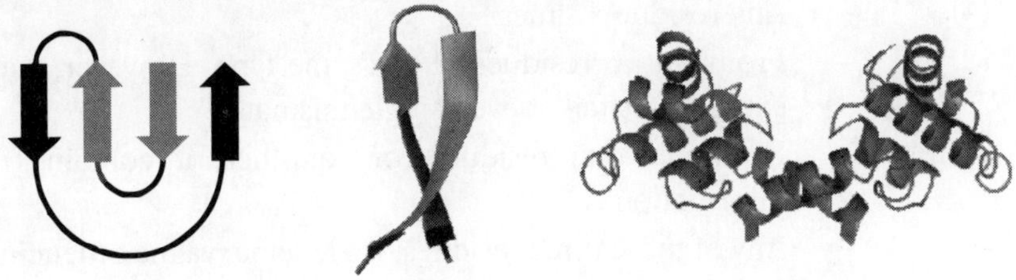

(a) (b) (c)

Figure 4.7 *(a) Greek key motif, (b) Hairpin beta motif, (c) Helix loop helix motif*

PATTERN SEARCH

The pattern from a conserved residue of a multiple sequence alignment, if used in the right way, can give an enormous amount of information about a protein sequence. Various pattern search methods include regular expressions, rules and block search.

Regular expression

This approach is based on pattern recognition, and a single conserved motif found in the multiple sequence alignment gives details about a family. Regular expression gives information about a sequence based only on the conserved region or consensus (Fig. 4.8). To obtain more authentic information, regular expression uses only identical matches and does not allow similarity. The regular expression can be used to check whether other sequences fit in that pattern or not. To obtain better interpretation from a regular expression, a highly conserved motif is required. It is important to mention here that if a query does not match the expression, it does not conform. It is likely that the query is not a member of that family. It may be the case that the query sequence deviates from the given pattern by just one residue. Moreover, matches do not necessarily establish a biological relationship or any other related meaning.

For example : Regular expression for tyrosine phosphorylation site:
[RK] – x (2)–[DE]–x (3)–Y

Description: [RK] : an arginine (R) or lysine (K) residue followed by
x (2) : two residues of any type followed by
[DE] : an aspartic or glutamic acid residue and then
x (3) : 3 residues of any type and
Y : a tyrosine residue

The result is interpreted with the help of the given base points.

X residue	–	Any amino acid
X (4)	–	Any residue 4 times
X (2, 6)	–	From 2 to 6 residues of the same type. However, such expressions fail at even single mismatch
A dash '-'	–	Separates one residue from another, it contains no information
[IVL]	–	Any of these three residues, iso leucine, valine or leucine, from the bracket can be at that position.
{PG}	–	Except P and G other residues are allowed here.

Fuzzy regular expressions

These introduce some fuzziness in the pattern or regular expression. It indicates that sometimes regular expression is made by considering all the amino acid residues of the same biochemical properties (for example: amino acids H, K, R are basic and I, L, M, V are hydrophobic). These regular expressions are more relaxed and accept a wider range of residues. This is used in the eMOTIF system.

For example: Sequence 1: G D H R T T C G
Sequence 2: G D K R M M C G
Sequence 3: P D R R M M C G

Fuzzy regular expression for the above sequences is: [GP]–D–[HKR] – R – [TM] – C – G

WW_DOMAIN_1, PS01159; **WW/rsp5/WWP domain signature** (PATTERN)	
Consensus pattern:	**W - x(9,11) - [VFY] - [FYW] - x(6,7) - [GSTNE] - [GSTQCR] - [FYW] - {R} - {SA} - P**
Sequences known to belong to this class detected by the pattern:	ALL
Other sequence(s) detected in Swiss-Prot:	9.

Figure 4.8 *A screenshot from ExPASy Prosite showing the consensus pattern in signature representation*

In Fig. 4.8, amino acid Trp (W) is followed by any character 9–11 times. Then either of the three residues, Val (V), Phe (F) or Tyr (Y), followed by any of these three residues, F, Y, W. Next any residue for 6–7 times followed by residues G/S/T/N/E and then G/S/T/Q/C/R followed by F/Y/W. Next a conserved residue R will be followed by S or A, then finally amino acid P should be present in all the sequences. Any sequence with the above mentioned features would be considered as one from the given pattern.

Rules: The regular expression should not be very short, as very short matches (3–4 residues) cannot give realistic predictions. But these matches may provide information about a certain type of active site present in the sequence. These short patterns are called rules. A ***pattern*** gives the fingerprint of a family. A ***rule*** gives information from a protein sequence that is not a character of only that family. The same rule sequences can be found in the proteins of different families. It is possible to recognise even distantly related sequences.

For example: Rule for N-glycosylation site is: N – {P} – [ST] – {P}

Profile method

A **profile** is a matrix derived from multiple sequence alignment, that is, a column-wise representation of amino acid frequencies. This profile represents distant and common characteristics among those sequences of a multiple sequence alignment. We identify closely and distantly related sequences from a profile. The following example from an MSA gives rise to a position-specific scoring matrix (PSSM), an amino acid scoring matrix.

Example 4.1

A multiple sequence alignment

Sequence 1: G C T A T
Sequence 2: G C _ A T
Sequence 3: G C _ A T
Sequence 4: G G _ A A

	Col1	Col2	Col3	Col4	Col5
A	-	-	-	1	.25
C	-	.75	-	-	-
G	1	.25	-	-	-
T	-	-	.25	-	
-	-	-	.75	-	-

Profile for the MSA

G C _ A T

Consensus string for the given MSA

Consensus sequences derived from multiple sequence alignment reflect the characteristic features common to a set of sequences. The ***consensus symbol*** is one that occurs most frequently in a column.

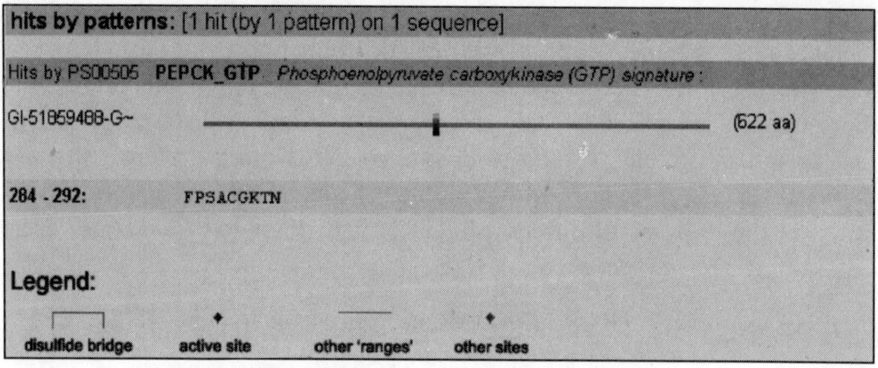

Figure 4.9 *Screenshot from ExPASy: ScanProsite tool for phosphoenolpyruvate carboxykinase 1 of* Rattus norvegicus *(gi|51859488) showing one hit.*

Hidden Markov model

The hidden Markov model (HMM) was described initially by Leonard E Baum and others in the 1960s and was used for speech recognition in the 1970s. During the 1980s, HMM was first applied in the biological arena for DNA sequences. HMM is a probabilistic model with various states connected with one another. The change from one state to another has a certain transition probability. The possibility of changing one state to another may be different giving different transition probabilities. The sum of all transition probabilities is one. For example, change of A to B, C or D: if A to B transition probability is .50, that is, half, and A to C is .25, A to D will be .25, that is, the sum of all the transition probabilities is .50 + .25 + .25 = 1. HMMs use position-specific scoring to provide the output.

The ***Markov model*** is a finite state machine with probabilities for each transition.

A ***Markov process*** is one which moves from one state to another depending (only) on the previous *n* states.

A ***Markov chain*** is a sequence of random values whose probabilities at a time interval depend upon the value of the number at the previous time. Transition probability is the controlling factor in the Markov chain.

States of HMM

There are a finite number of states in an HMM. It can be of any size, which can be listed. Each state is represented as a node. Basically, these can be grouped as hidden and observed states. Hidden states are the true states of a system that may be described by a Markov process, that is, the presumed ancestral sequence from which the sequences in the query set are hypothesised to have descended. Observable states are the visible states of the process, that is, the individual alignment columns. For example, in an HMM of sequence alignment, the match, insert, delete, start and end states are present. This is explained later in this chapter under profile HMM.

Components of HMM

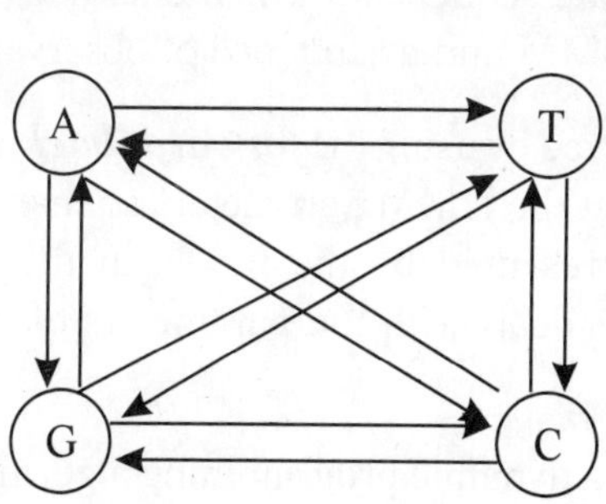

Figure 4.10 *Markov model for DNA sequence*

Output matrix: It is the probability of observing a particular observable state when the hidden model is in a particular hidden state.

Initial distribution: It is the probability of the (hidden) model in a particular hidden state at a particular time $t = 1$.

State transition matrix: It is the probability of a hidden state when the previous hidden state is given.

General features of HMM

- HMM is easy to train.
- It can be easily generated by trained software.
- Use PSSM for matching or substitution of a residue and for introducing a gap.
- It requires a large number of unstructured parameters.

Problems of HMM

There are three problems of interest in HMM:

- The evaluation problem
- The decoding problem
- The learning problem

The evaluation problem (solved by using the ***forward algorithm***): Consider the problem where we have a number of HMMs describing different systems, and a sequence of observations. It evaluates the probability that the observations are generated by the model for a given HMM and a sequence of observations.

The decoding problem (solved by using the ***Viterbi algorithm***): The problem is to find the hidden states that generated the observed output. It decodes the most likely state sequence in the model that has produced the observations for a given HMM and a sequence of observations.

The learning problem (solved by using the ***forward–backward algorithm***): This specifies how to adjust the HMM parameters so that the given training set of observations is represented by the model in the best way for the proposed application. This deals with the parameters of the most probable model.

Viterbi algorithm: This is a dynamic programming algorithm for finding the most likely sequence of hidden states. The path that results in a sequence of observed events is called the Viterbi path. This is used especially in the context of HMMs. It solves HMM's decoding problem.

Forward algorithm: This is similar to the Viterbi algorithm for computing the probability of a sequence of observed events. These algorithms form a subset of information theory. This algorithm solves HMM's evaluation problems using many assumptions such as:

- Observed and hidden states must be in a sequence.
- Each hidden state must correspond to an observed event.
- Up to a certain point the most likely hidden sequence is dependent on the observed event at that point and the most likely sequence at point P-1, that is the position before the current position (defined by first order HMM).

Forward–backward algorithm: Given the current model approximation, it computes the 'forward' probability of arriving at a particular state and the 'backward' probability of generating the final state of the model. It is a very complex algorithm used to solve the learning problem of HMM.

Applications of HMM

- Gene prediction (promoter prediction, TATA box, etc) from gene sequences
- Protein-coding region (ORF) prediction from gene sequences
- Protein secondary structure (motif and domain) prediction from protein primary sequences
- Protein profile analysis
- Multiple sequence alignment from homologous sequences giving phylogenetic predictions
- RNA and tRNA structure prediction from RNA sequence

PROFILE HMM

Profile HMM uses position-specific scoring for match, mismatch or gap opening and extension. It allows position-dependent insertion and deletion penalties. To perform a profile analysis, first an alignment in the HMM form is encoded. As match and insert states emit a residue (every match and insert state is represented by an amino acid character in an HMM of amino acid sequence alignment), we can say that these states have a probability distribution of amino acids. The transition probability from each state adds up to one.

Once an HMM is constructed we can get an alignment as output, based on the HMM score. To get a proper result, we need to give the desired output for a certain kind of input (by changing the parameters) and compute the output probabilities efficiently.

Match states in a profile HMM: Match state means a position in the model for every position in the sequence to be aligned to the model. Each state/node in an HMM model corresponds roughly to a position (column) in the alignment from which it was built. Match states are represented as a square for each residue in the column (Fig. 4.11).

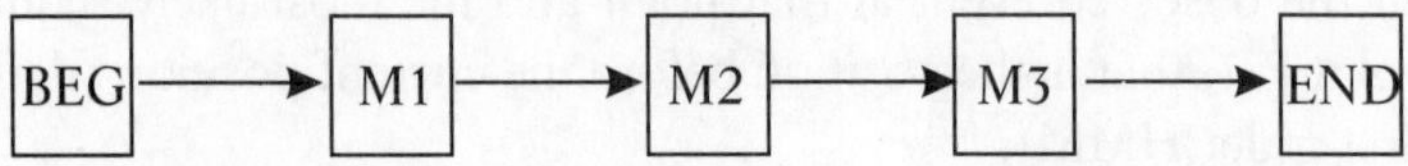

Figure 4.11 *Match states in a profile HMM*

Addition of insert state in profile HMM: The insert state does not change the position in the model; hence it is given in the same column. As insert is performed usually only in one sequence and match and delete states are found in all sequences in a multiple sequence alignment (*see Chapter* 7 for a full explanation), for each subsequent match and delete we move to the next column (Fig. 4.12).

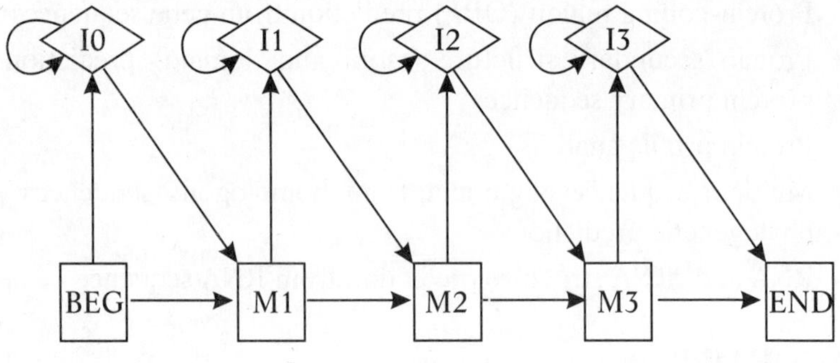

Figure 4.12 *Addition of insert state in profile HMM*

Profile HMM with match insert and delete state: A profile HMM has two types of probabilities: transition and emission. ***Transition probability*** is the probability of the transitioning of one state into another. ***Emission probability*** is the probability of a given residue existing at that position in the alignment. The probability of any sequence generated depends on the transition and emission probabilities of each node.

Dynamic programming algorithm is used here to align a sequence to a profile HMM. This searches for the most probable path that the sequence may take through the model, using the transition and emission probabilities to score each possible path. Profile HMM is used to compare profile HMMs and sequences and with this, the model identifies distant homologs. This model can be trained and used to compare domains and also for multiple sequence alignment.

M= match state represented as a rectangle

I = insert state represented as diamonds

D = delete state represented as circles

In addition to these three states, there are two more states, start and end. The match and insert states output an amino acid residue while the delete state outputs a gap. Self-loops on insert output multiple insertions (Fig. 4.13).

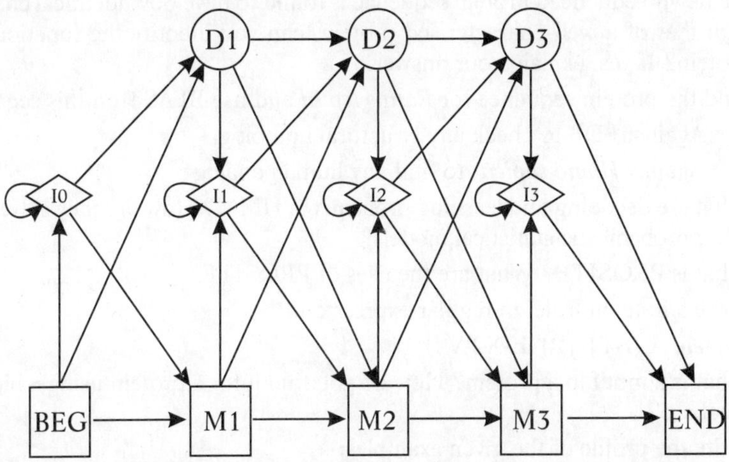

Figure 4.13 *Graphical representation of profile HMM for global alignment*

HMMER: Profile HMM software HMMER is suitable for making and using HMMs of biological sequences. Using profile HMMs, these programs model the primary structure consensus of a family of protein or nucleic acid sequences. (Details at: http://www.psc.edu/htbin/man2html/man2html.pl/general/software/packages/hmmer/man/hmmer).

EXERCISES

1. What are the various parameters for the BLAST search program? What is the effect of changing the parameters on the result? Perform an experiment and verify (*Hint*: Open NCBI BLAST; paste a sequence and view the result after clicking BLAST. Now change the window size and view the difference in result).

2. For what kind of sequences does FASTA work better then BLAST? Give the steps for a FASTA algorithm.
3. What is 'word size'? What is the word size used by BLAST and FASTA in NCBI?
4. While working with the BLASTp search program, what cut-off score will you use:
   a. To know about the availability of a sequence in a database
   b. To locate distant homologs
5. For the same sequence, perform any four BLAST searchs and analyse:
   a. First five hits from each output and compare the result. Why is there a difference?
   b. Change the word length and gap weight and report the difference.
6. If a newly sequenced protein sequence is found to have 60% identical characters with that of a well-characterised protein, can you identify the function of the protein? If yes, explain your answer.
7. Find the protein sequence for *Rattus leptin* and use BLAST on this sequence:
   a. Against PDB to check any structural homolog
   b. Against *Homo sapiens* to find any human analog
8. What are decoding and learning problems in HMM? How are they solved using other probabilistic statistical models?
9. What is PROSITE? What are the uses of PROSITE?
10. Write a note on 'rule' in regular expression.
11. Explain A-[ST]-{P}-L-X2-V.
12. What is a motif in a protein? How do you find it for a protein using a biological database?
13. Write the profile of the given examples:

    ATCYLGGS
    ATVCLGGT
    ATVPLGGS
    ATVRLGGS

14. Write a regular expression for the given MSA. What is a fuzzy regular expression? Write the fuzzy regular expressions for the same:

    ATVYLGGSTD
    ATVCLGGTTD
    ATVPLGGSSD
    ATVRLGGSSE

CHAPTER 5

Scoring Matrices

LEARNING OUTCOME

- Explain distance: Hamming and Levenshtein distance
- Define gaps: constant, affine and convex gap weight
- Describe scoring matrices: PAM and BLOSUM
- Explain the importance of sequence comparison in molecular biology

Sequence alignment is the technique of comparing two or more sequences (pairwise or multiple alignments, respectively). The sequences are placed one above the other in such a way that every character or space of one sequence is placed opposite to the unique character or space of another sequence. If the sequences are very small they can be manually lined up and aligned. But proper alignment programs are required for lengthy and highly variable sequences. The sequences are compared, mainly to confirm the relationship among them. During the course of evolution, mutations occur, creating differences between families of related species.

Similarity and Identity

These are terms that illustrate the relationship between two proteins with one another. The residue position at which both sequences being compared have the same type of residue is called ***identical residue***.

Example 5.1

The residues N and T are identical residues in the given example.

```
A F N T T
    | |
L N N T S
```

The residue positions at which both sequences being compared have amino acids with similar properties are called *similarity residues*.

For example: AL and TS are similar residues. Similar residues are represented with a colon (:)

```
A F N T T
:   | | :
L N N T S
```

To assess similarity, ***scoring matrices*** can be used. Scoring matrices list the percentage similarity for each possible pair of amino acids. The sum of the scores of the alignment for each position is called the ***similarity score***. Similarity (not identity) is probabilistic in nature because biological changes like mutation, recombination and selection are arbitrary events

MUTATIONS

They are permanent, transmissible changes to genetic material. These changes are mostly promptly repaired; if not they result in a mutation. So we can also define mutation as a failure of DNA repair. These changes can be indel (addition and deletion of a residue) or alter (transition and transversion). Indel changes or shifts a reading frame completely so these are also called ***frame shift mutations***. On the basis of function, mutations can be categorised as follows.

Loss of function mutation results in reduced protein function.

Gain of function mutation results in an abnormal activity on a protein.

Single base mutations that alter a base into another can be grouped as follows.

Silent mutations: These mutations do not cause a change in the sequence. Each amino acid can be encoded using several different codons. In the standard genetic code, TCT stands for serine. If it is changed to any one of the other three bases—C, G or A—serine will still be encoded. They are called silent mutations as they cause no change in their product and cannot be detected without sequencing the gene.

Missense mutations*:* These mutations change the codon and hence the sequence. Each amino acid has a codon. If the codon is altered, it refers to another amino acid. For example: GTG is the code for valine. A mutation in the second base to C changes the codon to GCG, which is the codon for glutamic acid.

Nonsense mutations: These mutations change the code to a stop codon. For example, any mutation producing TAA, TAG and TGA (stop codons) is a nonsense mutation.

Chromosome mutations: These occur during meiosis. They change the arrangement or even structure of the chromosome. It can be an inversion, deletion or duplication of a chromosome or exchange of a chromosome segment with another chromosome (translocation).

TRANSLOCATIONS

They are the transfer of a piece of one chromosome to a non-homologous chromosome. Transformation is usually a reciprocal process where two non-homologous chromosomes swap segments. For example, in leukaemia, swapping occurs between chromozomes 9 and 22. Most mutations destroy information about the evolutionary relatedness of the sequences (Fig. 5.1). The amino acid changes that are accepted by natural selection are called ***accepted mutations***. These changes do not significantly change the function of the protein.

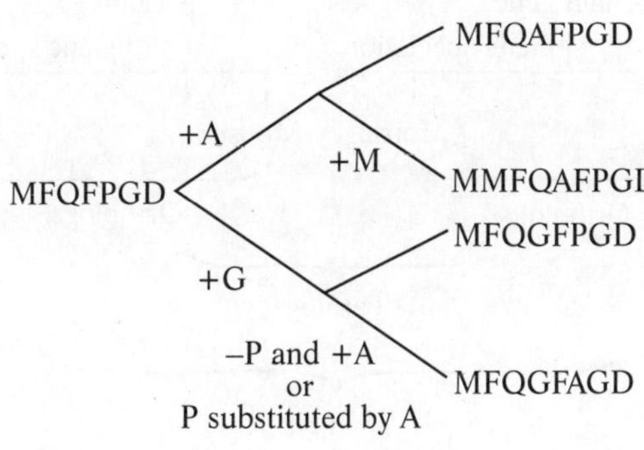

FIGURE 5.1 *A phylogenetic tree showing the phylogenetic relationship and probable amino acid changes during evolution among related protein sequences.*

HOMOLOGY AND ANALOGY

Homology refers to the similarity in sequence due to shared ancestery. It is a hereditary function. ***Analogy*** refers to the similarity which is incidental or due to other reasons. Sequence homology can be reliably inferred from statistically significant similarity over a majority of the sequence length. Sequences with similar structure and function are called ***homologs***. Homology is an evolutionary statement; the homologs share similar ancestry among given sequences—they have descended from a common ancestor. Homologous sequences are predicted to have common 3D structure and function. Wings of birds and bats are analogous as they perform the same function (fly) but their structure is different. Homologous sequences are of two types: paralogous and orthologous.

Orthologous gene sequences

These are sequences that are separated by a speciation event; that is, when a species diverges into two different species, the two different species formed are said to be orthologous. Orthologous genes are genes in different species that are similar to each other because they originated from a common ancestor with a similar function. In Fig. 5.2, the α-globin gene from the mouse and frog are orthologous.

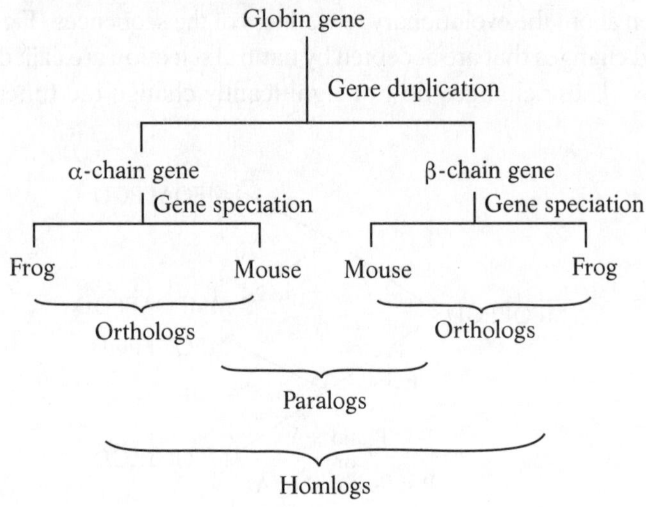

FIGURE 5.2 *Flow chart differentiating various homologs*

Paralogous gene sequences

These gene sequences are formed as a result of a gene duplication event; that is, the gene in an organism is duplicated to occupy two different positions in the same genome. Paralogs typically have the same or similar function but they may have different functions as well, as the duplicate gene is free to mutate and acquire new functions. In Fig. 5.2, the α-globin and β-globin from the mouse are paralogs.

DISTANCE

Sequences can be compared either by distance or similarity calculations. We can measure the relationship between two sequences in two ways. In Ex. 5.2, the sequence is 80% similar or 20% different.

Example 5.2

```
S1 = A C G T A C C G T A
     | | | |     | | | |
S2 = A C G T C A C G T A
```

Two types of distances are discussed here: Hamming and Edit.

Hamming distance: The number of mismatching characters between two strings of the same length is called as the ***Hamming distance*** (HD). This is an upper bound algorithm as it takes less time and space to compute. In Ex. 5.2, there are two mismatches so, HD = 2.

Levenshtein or **Edit distance:** It is possible to change one sequence to another by a series of operations called edit operations. The total number of edit operations required to change one sequence into another is called the *edit distance*. It is not as simple to compute as Hamming distance. During evolution, the changes in a DNA sequence are caused by three common local mutations: insertion, deletion and substitution. Hence the edit distance can be used as a means to approximately measure the number of DNA replications that occurred between two DNA sequences. This is also referred to as ***evolutionary distance***. Edit operations can be either indel (addition or deletion) or alter (transition or transversion).

Indel

Insertion or deletion of a unique character or space in a sequence is called indel. Two given sequences S1= AGT and S2= ACGT can be aligned in two ways: by inserting C at position two in S2 or by deleting C from position two in S1.

$$S1 = A\,G\,T\ldots \xrightarrow{+C} A\,C\,G\,T\ldots = S2$$
$$S2 = A\,C\,G\,T\ldots \xrightarrow{-C} A\,G\,T\ldots = S1$$

Alter

Transition or transversion in a sequence is called alter. ***Transition*** is a mutation that changes one purine to another purine (A to G) and a pyrimidine to another pyrimidine (T to C). The following change is an example of transition.

S1= A C G T --- ⟶ A C **A** T --- = S2

Transversion is a mutation that changes a purine to pyrimidine (A to T) and pyrimidine to purine (G to C). The following change is an example of transversion.

S1= A C G T --- ⟶ A C **C** T --- = S2

In aligning the sequences correctly, one of the major problems is obtaining the edit distance between the two sequences. Dynamic programming algorithm for edit distance can solve this problem.

GAPS

A gap is the maximal consecutive run of spaces in a string (single string) of an alignment. Each operation in a sequence alignment is given a score or weight (insert and delete). These are called indel operations and are given the same score (negative scoring). Various algorithms are used to find out the number of edit operations required to align two sequences. Each algorithm employs a certain matrix carrying a different score for each match (wt_m), mismatch (wt_{mm}) and gap values (wt_g). Values for opening a gap (the first space in a gap) and extending a gap (in case of a gap with more than one space) is also used differently in different matrices and algorithms.

Example 5.3

Sequence 1: A C G T _ _ _ G A _ T
Sequence 2: A _ _ T T A G A C T

For sequence 1: Number of gaps =2 and Number of spaces = 4;

For sequence 2: Number of gaps =1 and Number of spaces = 2

The alignment would be described as having five matches, no mismatch, three gaps and six spaces.

Changes in a DNA sequence take place by point mutation, recombination and insertion and deletion. Mutations, while causing small changes for aligning two sequences, also introduce gaps. Gaps are costly for the overall alignment score. Fewer gaps should be introduced and only when they are really required for an alignment. Each scoring matrix has its own gap opening and gap extension penalties that work best for sequences with a certain similarity percentage.

For example: BLOSUM 62: Gap opening penalty: –11
Gap extention penalty: –1
BLOSUM 50: Gap opening penalty: –12
Gap extention penalty: –2

By default, NCBI BLAST uses $wt_g = -11$, $wt_s = -1$ and FASTA uses $wt_g = -10$, $wt_s = -2$

In Ex. 5.3, if an algorithm using the BLOSUM 62 matrix is used for sequence 1, the first gap will have the gap opening penalty –11 for the first space and the gap extention penalty –1 and –1 for the next two spaces (any subsequent spaces if present in a gap will be given the value –1).

Different gap weights are used by various alignment methods: constant, affine, convex and arbitrary.

Constant gap weight: In this system, the number of spaces in a gap is not taken into account. Once a gap is opened, it is given a certain weight, wt_g, which is independent of the number of spaces (n) in that gap. The number of spaces in a gap is not counted and each gap is given the same penalty irrespective of the number of spaces. Hence, in Ex. 5.3, sequence 1 using the BLOSUM 62 matrix will have the gap value –11 for the first gap (3 spaces) and for the second gap (1 space).

Total constant gap weight = $wt_m - wt_{mm} - wt_g$

where gap initialisation weight or gap penalty = wt_g, match weight = wt_m and mismatch weight = wt_{mm}.

This is the most basic gap weight but is not used by various programs because it is not fair to penalise one space gap and four space gaps equally to get a good alignment score, that is, the total combined score of match, mismatch and gap.

Affine gap weight: This is the most widely used gap model. It is a generalisation of the constant gap weights structure: a gap initialisation or opening weight and a gap extension weight (wt_s) for extending the gap by one or more spaces is allotted. But each extra space is given same value. We can say that a constant gap weight is simply an affine gap weight with n = 0. Ex. 5.3 is an instance of affine gap weight.

Total affine gap weight = $wt_m - wt_{mm} - (wt_g + n \cdot wt_s)$

Convex gap weight: In this method, each additional space is given some lesser value than the previous space in a gap. Some biologists suggest a gap function, where the gap extension penalty first increases to a maximum value and then decreases to near zero. In Ex. 5.3, for Sequence 1, first gap (using FASTA), the first space is given a weight of –10, the second space is given a weight of –2 and the third space is given a weight of –1 (values used in FASTA).

Arbitrary gap weight: It is a very general weight model, where any of the three methods can be used to penalise spaces in a gap. Here the gap weight is an arbitrary function of its length n. Constant, affine and constant gap weight models are the subcases of this model. This model takes into account that the two sequences can be aligned in three ways: gap at the beginning of the alignment, in the middle of an alignment or at the end of an alignment. The position of a gap in a sequence also changes the overall score of an alignment. As given in the figure below, the first alignment sequence S1 (i) is aligned strictly to the right of the sequence S2 (j); that is, all the characters on the left are not aligned while they are aligned on the right, so an alignment starts with a gap in S1.

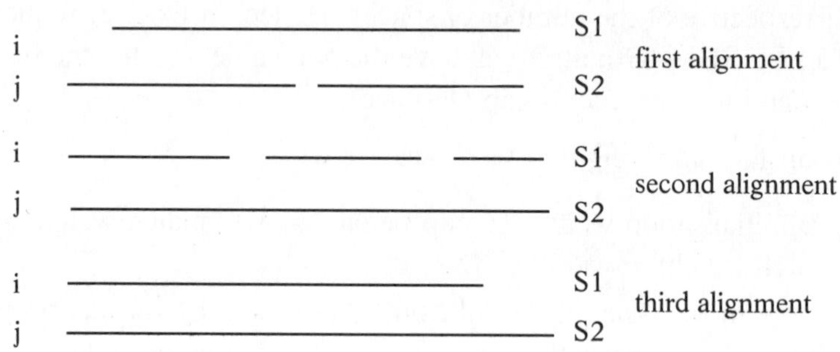

In the second alignment, S1 and S2 are aligned opposite each other so that there is no gap either at the start or the end of a sequence. Gaps in this alignment in the middle of the sequences. The third alignment S1 (i) is aligned to the left of the alignment S2 (j), so the alignment ends with a gap in S1.

Scoring matrices

Sequence alignment of related protein sequences can determine amino acid changes. It helps us know if the two sequences have come from the same ancestor through the process of evolution. If the relationships among a group of proteins is known, the amino acid changes that have occurred during evolution can be predicted. Amino acid substitution matrices are used for this purpose. Margaret Dayhoff initiated this study and Dayhoff amino acid substitution matrices came into existence in 1978.

Scores are given for each match or mismatch. For any alignment, a number is assigned to each position in the sequence depending on the match, mismatch or gap at that position. The scores for all positions in the alignment are then added to give the total score, called ***alignment*** or ***similarity score***. This score is used to select the optimal alignment among alternative alignments. An ***amino acid scoring matrix*** is a two-dimensional array that lists scores with all possible pairs of amino acids. There are three types of scoring matrices:

- Identity matrices
- Genetic matrices
- Scoring matrices

When two amino acids residues are not identical but similar, the replacement of one residue by another does not affect the biological function of the sequence. These two residues have high similarity scores. A very small score (sometimes negative) is given to those replacements that affect biological function. Conservative mutations or substitutions are given a higher score than non-conservative substitutions.

DAYHOFF AMINO ACID SUBSTITUTION MATRICES

These matrices are also known as PAM (point or percent accepted mutation). They list the probability of changing one amino acid to another in homologous protein sequences during evolution. According to Dayhoff, each change in an amino acid at a particular site is supposed to be independent of previously verified mutational events at that site.

In the 1970s, Margaret Dayhoff made an extensive study of the frequency with which amino acids substitute each other during evolution. The proteins in several families of proteins were aligned and the phylogenetic trees for each family were constructed. This led to a table of relative frequencies with which amino acids replaced each other over an evolutionary period. This table and the relative frequency of occurrence of amino acids in the proteins studied were combined in computing the PAM scoring matrices.

This matrix has weights that are derived based on how often different amino acids replace other amino acids in evolution. Based on a database of 1,572 changes in 71 groups of closely related proteins, the PAM matrix was created. This way a 20 × 20 mutation probability matrix was generated by using all possible amino acid changes. In this matrix, all twenty amino acids are written on both the X and Y axes. Then the matrix is filled with the score each amino acid is provided to replace another. From Fig. 5.3(a), the alanine to alanine match score is 13 while the mismatch value for alanine to arginine is 3 and for arginine to alanine is 6. The alignment score for the amino acid sequences S1= ADRT and S2= ADCT by using the PAM 250 matrix will be 13 + 11 + 1 + 11= 36.

		Ala	Arg	Asn	Asp	Cys	Gln	Glu	Gly	His	Ile	Leu	Lys	Met	Phe	Pro	Ser	Thr	Trp	Tyr	Val
		A	R	N	D	C	Q	E	G	H	I	L	K	M	F	P	S	T	W	Y	V
Ala	A	13	6	9	9	5	8	9	12	6	8	6	7	7	4	11	11	11	2	4	9
Arg	R	3	17	4	3	2	5	3	2	6	3	2	9	4	1	4	4	3	7	2	2
Asn	N	4	4	6	7	2	5	6	4	6	3	2	5	3	2	4	5	4	2	3	3
Asp	D	5	4	8	11	1	7	10	5	6	3	2	5	3	1	4	5	5	1	2	3
Cys	C	2	1	1	1	52	1	1	2	2	2	1	1	1	1	2	3	2	1	4	2
Gln	Q	3	5	5	6	1	10	7	3	7	2	3	5	3	1	4	3	3	1	2	3
Glu	E	5	4	7	11	1	9	12	5	6	3	2	5	3	1	4	5	5	1	2	3
Gly	G	12	5	10	10	4	7	9	27	5	5	4	6	5	3	8	11	9	2	3	7
His	H	2	5	5	4	2	7	4	2	15	2	2	3	2	2	3	3	2	2	3	2
Ile	I	3	2	2	2	2	2	2	2	2	10	6	2	6	5	2	3	4	1	3	9
Leu	L	6	4	4	3	2	6	4	3	5	15	34	4	20	13	5	4	6	6	7	13
Lys	K	6	18	10	8	2	10	8	5	8	5	4	24	9	2	6	8	8	4	3	5
Met	M	1	1	1	1	0	1	1	1	1	2	3	2	6	2	1	1	1	1	1	2
Phe	F	2	1	2	1	1	1	1	1	3	5	6	1	4	32	1	2	2	4	20	3
Pro	P	7	5	5	4	3	5	4	5	5	3	3	4	3	2	20	6	5	1	2	4
Ser	S	9	6	8	7	7	6	7	9	6	5	4	7	5	3	9	10	9	4	4	6
Thr	T	8	5	6	6	4	5	5	6	4	6	4	6	5	3	6	8	11	2	3	6
Trp	W	0	2	0	0	0	0	0	0	1	0	1	0	0	1	0	1	0	55	1	0
Tyr	Y	1	1	2	1	3	1	1	1	3	2	2	1	2	15	1	2	2	3	31	2
Val	V	7	4	4	4	4	4	4	4	5	4	15	10	4	10	5	5	5	72	4	17

FIGURE 5.3(a) The PAM 250 matrix

		Ala	Arg	Asn	Asp	Cys	Gln	Glu	Gly	His	Ile	Leu	Lys	Met	Phe	Pro	Ser	Thr	Trp	Tyr	Val
		A	R	N	D	C	Q	E	G	H	I	L	K	M	F	P	S	T	W	Y	V
Ala	A	9867	2	9	10	3	8	17	21	2	6	4	2	6	2	22	35	32	0	2	18
Arg	R	1	9913	1	0	1	10	0	0	10	3	1	19	4	1	4	6	1	8	0	1
Asn	N	4	1	9822	36	0	4	6	6	21	3	1	13	0	1	2	20	9	1	4	1
Asp	D	6	0	42	9859	0	6	53	6	4	1	0	3	0	0	1	5	3	0	0	1
Cys	C	1	1	0	0	9973	0	0	0	1	1	0	0	0	0	1	5	1	0	3	2
Gln	Q	3	9	4	5	0	9876	27	1	23	1	3	6	4	0	6	2	2	0	0	1
Glu	E	10	0	7	56	0	35	9865	4	2	3	1	4	1	0	3	4	2	0	1	2
Gly	G	21	1	12	11	1	3	7	9935	1	0	1	2	1	1	3	21	3	0	0	5
His	H	1	8	18	3	1	20	1	0	9912	0	1	1	0	2	3	1	1	1	4	1
Ile	I	2	2	3	1	2	1	2	0	0	9872	9	2	12	7	0	1	7	0	1	33
Leu	L	3	1	3	0	0	6	1	1	4	22	9947	2	45	13	3	1	3	4	2	15
Lys	K	2	37	25	6	0	12	7	2	2	4	1	9926	20	0	3	8	11	0	1	1
Met	M	1	1	0	0	0	2	0	0	0	5	8	4	9874	1	0	1	2	0	0	4
Phe	F	1	1	1	0	0	0	0	1	2	8	6	0	4	9946	0	2	1	3	28	0
Pro	P	13	5	2	1	1	8	3	2	5	1	2	2	1	1	9926	12	4	0	0	2
Ser	S	28	11	34	7	11	4	6	16	2	2	1	7	4	3	17	9840	38	5	2	2
Thr	T	22	2	13	4	1	3	2	2	1	11	2	8	6	1	5	32	9871	0	2	9
Trp	W	0	2	0	0	0	0	0	0	0	0	0	0	0	1	0	1	0	9976	1	0
Tyr	Y	1	0	3	0	3	0	1	0	4	1	1	0	0	21	0	1	1	2	9945	1
Val	V	13	2	1	1	3	2	2	3	3	57	11	1	17	1	3	2	10	0	2	9901

FIGURE 5.3(b) The PAM 1 matrix

The matrix is designed to give an alignment score between sequences that have diverged by a particular degree of evolutionary distance. Altshul et al developed a statistical theory for sequences and have examined how well the PAM matrices can distinguish diverged proteins (more or less) when aligned locally. Each PAM matrix is designed to compare two sequences, which are a specific number of PAM units apart. PAM 1 is the matrix calculated from the comparison of sequences with no more than 1% divergence or Accepted Point Mutation per 100 residues (Fig. 5.3(b)). PAM 1 is 1 Accepted Point Mutation per 100 amino acids (to simplify the appearance, the elements are shown multiplied by 10,000); it gives the same Cys to Cys replacement score of 9973. (Figure 5.3(a) shows the PAM 250 matrix and Fig. 5.3(b) shows the PAM 1 matrix adapted from Figure 82. Atlas of Protein Sequence and Structure, Suppl 3, 1978, M.O. Dayhoff, ed. National Biomedical Research Foundation, 79.). The PAM 120 score matrix is designed to compare sequences that are 120 PAM units apart. The choice of matrix can strongly influence the result of the study. Some important considerations and problems in the PAM approach are:

1. At any site, the replacement is dependent only on the amino acid at that site and the probability given by the table (Markov model).
2. All the positions in the amino acids are not the same.
3. Each position has a unique environment that changes over evolutionary time.
4. As PAM matrices are based on a small set of closely related proteins, it has been criticised and compared with that of other scoring matrices.

Steps to construct PAM matrices

1. Select a few sequences that are at least 85% identical.
2. Align them in such a way that you get minimum mutations, that is, mismatches and gaps.
3. To construct PAM matrices, 71 trees containing 1,572 exchanges are used. It signifies that 1572 mutations are checked to create a matrix, i.e., to assign a value for the mutation of one amino acid into another. Mutations that are more common in nature do not change function much and are hence given more weight, while rare changes are given less weight.
4. In all pairwise comparisons, compute replacements that are accepted by natural selection.
5. Compute amino acid mutability or the probability of a given amino acid to be replaced.
6. Join data from steps 4 and 5 to produce a *Mutation Probability Matrix* for PAM 1, according to the following formula:

   $$M_{ij} - m_j A_{ij} / \Sigma A_{ij}, \text{ i.e., } M_{ij} = 1 - m_j$$

   where A_{ij} is the number of times amino acid j was replaced by amino acid i in all comparisons, m_j is the mutability or the probability of a given amino acid, j, to be replaced and M_{ij} is the mutation probability matrix (a unit of evolutionary change).
7. Now divide each element of the mutation probability matrix by the frequency of occurrence of each residue to compute the *Log Odds Matrix (S)* for similarity scoring. The *Log Odds Matrix* is created by taking all log values to base 10: a value of +1 would mean that the corresponding pair has been observed 10 times more frequently than expected by chance.

   $$S_{ij} = \log R_{ij} \text{ and } R_{ij} = M_{ij} / F_i$$

   where, R_{ij} = Relatedness Odds Matrix, and f_i =the frequency of residue i.

8. Finally, a 20 × 20 mutation probability matrix is generated using all possible amino acid changes.

The PAM 250 mutation matrix is a mutation probability matrix for the evolutionary distance of the 250 PAMs score multiplied by 100 for simplification. In comparing two sequences of average amino acid frequency at this evolutionary distance, there is a 52% probability that the position containing Cys in the first sequence will also have Cys in the second sequence. It means that in nature if it is seen that a sequence has a Cys at any position in sequence one, 52% of the time, a homologous sequence will be seen with Cys at the same position.

BLOSUM (BLOCKS Amino Acid Substitution Matrices)

Steven and Jorja Henikoff developed BLOSUM 62 for scoring sequence alignment. It is one of the newly developed log odds scoring matrices. The Dayhoff PAM matrices are of limited value as their substitution rates are derived from alignments of sequences that are at least 25% similar. So PAM does not work to obtain a relationship between very distantly related species. These matrices were derived from blocks of aligned sequences in the BLOCKS database. Compared to PAM matrices, they have a very large data set (Table 5.1).

Table 5.1 Comparison of PAM and BLOSUM matrices

SNo.	PAM	BLOSUM
1.	Based on explicit evolutionary model	Implicit evolutionary model
2.	Based on mutations observed throughout regions in a global alignment	Based only on highly conserved series of alignments
3.	Based on less data	Based on more data than PAM matrices
4.	Substitutions are counted along the branches of an evolutionary tree	Substitutions are counted within the columns of a multiple sequence alignment
5.	Higher numbers in the PAM matrix naming scheme denote greater evolutionary distance	Larger numbers denote higher sequence similarity and hence smaller evolutionary distance
6.	Example: PAM 250 is used for more distant sequences than PAM 120	Example: BLOSUM 80 is used for closer sequences than BLOSUM 45

Depending on the percentage of identity of the clustered sequences, different BLOSUM matrices are used. For example, the BLOSUM 80 matrix is used for sequences clustered at equal to or greater than 80% of identity and the BLOSUM 45 matrix for 45% or greater clustering percentage (Fig. 5.4).

	A	R	N	D	C	Q	E	G	H	I	L	K	M	F	P	S	T	W	Y	V
A	5	−2	−1	−2	−1	−1	−1	0	−2	−1	−1	−1	−1	−2	−1	1	0	−2	−2	0
R	−2	7	0	−1	−3	1	0	−2	0	−3	−2	3	−1	−2	−2	−1	−1	−2	−1	−2
N	−1	0	6	2	−2	0	0	0	1	−2	−3	0	−2	−2	−2	1	0	−4	−2	−3
D	−2	−1	2	7	−3	0	2	−1	0	−4	−3	0	−3	−4	−1	0	−1	−4	−2	−3
C	−1	−3	−2	−3	12	−3	−3	−3	−3	−3	−2	−3	−2	−2	−4	−1	−1	−5	−3	−1
Q	−1	1	0	0	−3	6	2	−2	1	−2	−2	1	0	−4	−1	0	−1	−2	−1	−3
E	−1	0	0	2	−3	2	6	−2	0	−3	−2	1	−2	−3	0	0	−1	−3	−2	−3
G	0	−2	0	−1	−3	−2	−2	7	−2	−4	−3	−2	−2	−3	−2	0	−2	−2	−3	−3
H	−2	0	1	0	−3	1	0	−2	10	−3	−2	−1	0	−2	−2	−1	−2	−3	2	−3
I	−1	−3	−2	−4	−3	−2	−3	−4	−3	5	2	−3	2	0	−2	−2	−1	−2	0	3
L	−1	−2	−3	−3	−2	−2	−2	−3	−2	2	5	−3	2	1	−3	−3	−1	−2	0	1
K	−1	3	0	0	−3	1	1	−2	−1	−3	−3	5	−1	−3	−1	−1	−1	−2	−1	−2
M	−1	−1	−2	−3	−2	0	−2	−2	0	2	2	−1	6	0	−2	−2	−1	−2	0	1
F	−2	−2	−2	−4	−2	−4	−3	−3	−2	0	1	−3	0	8	−3	−2	−1	1	3	0
P	−1	−2	−2	−1	−4	−1	0	−2	−2	−2	−3	−1	−2	−3	9	−1	−1	−3	−3	−3
S	1	−1	1	0	−1	0	0	0	−1	−2	−3	−1	−2	−2	−1	4	2	−4	−2	−1
T	0	−1	0	−1	−1	−1	−1	−2	−2	−1	−1	−1	−1	−1	−1	2	5	−3	−1	0
W	−2	−2	−4	−4	−5	−2	−3	−2	−3	−2	−2	−2	−2	1	−3	−4	−3	15	3	−3
Y	−2	−1	−2	−2	−3	−1	−2	−3	2	0	0	−1	0	3	−3	−2	−1	3	8	−1
V	0	−2	−3	−3	−1	−3	−3	−3	−3	3	1	−2	1	0	−3	−1	0	−3	−1	5

FIGURE 5.4 The BLOSUM 45 matrix

Steps to construct BLOSUM matrices

BLOSUM matrices are used to align sequences that are distantly related. So only the part of the sequence that is similar is taken into account.

1. The starting data is conserved blocks from the BLOCKS database, i.e., aligned ungapped sequences.
2. The observed frequency of each pair of residues in the blocks is examined.
3. Clustering is done for similar sequence segments in a block. All identities above a threshold similarity percentage are considered for clustering.

Equivalent PAM and BLOSUM matrices:

PAM 100 ==> Blosum 90
PAM 120 ==> Blosum 80
PAM 160 ==> Blosum 60
PAM 200 ==> Blosum 52
PAM 250 ==> Blosum 45

More divergent ⟷ Less divergent

More divergent	Less divergent
PAM 250	PAM 1
BLOSUM 45	BLOSUM 100

IMPORTANCE OF SEQUENCE COMPARISON IN MOLECULAR BIOLOGY

1. To identify unknown sequences found in lab experiments
2. To compare new genes to known ones
3. To obtain information about the evolution of genes
4. To guess the functions for entire genomes full of new gene sequences

EXERCISES

1. What is the Hamming distance between SEASON and REASON?
2. 'Gaps are of immense biological importance'. Explain in brief. How are they different from space?
3. 'When the gap is only one space long, the affine gap weight is same as the constant gap weight'. Explain.
4. What are absolute and normalised gap penalty?
5. On what basis did Henikoff and Henikoff develop the scoring matrices? List the salient features of the PAM and BLOSUM matrices.
6. What is PAM? List the different matrices of PAM.
7. State the importance and limitations of PAM matrices.
8. When can a mutation be accepted in a protein by evolution?
9. What is PAM? Explain with an example.
10. For sequences with a similarity of at least 80%, which matrix would you prefer to use and why?
11. Which scoring matrices would you use to compare distantly related sequences and closely related sequences? Substantiate your answer.

Assignment

Using a protein sequence from the protein database for human beings, run the Psi BLAST program with default parameters. Now change the nr (non-redundant: as default in menu) parameter to the pdb parameter and get the result. Next change any organism to a vertebrate and report the result. Explain the difference in results due to change in parameter. Perform InterproScan from EBI. Search for the same sequence and report the domains and regular expression for the sequence.

Section III

SEQUENCE ALIGNMENT

Chapter 6: Pairwise Sequence Alignment
Chapter 7: Multiple Sequence Alignment
Chapter 8: Phylogenetic Analysis

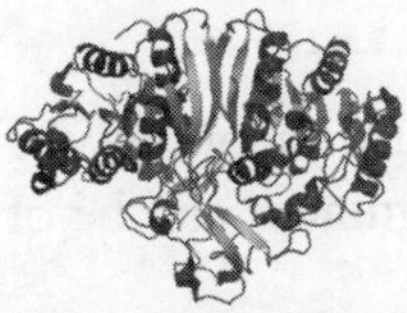

CHAPTER 6

Pairwise Sequence Alignment

LEARNING OUTCOME

- Define global alignment
- Define local alignment
- Explain the methods for aligning two sequences
    - Dot plot method
    - Dynamic programming
        - Edit distance dynamic programming
        - Needleman–Wunsch algorithm
        - Smith–Waterman algorithm
- Explain heuristic algorithms

Pairwise sequence alignment is the comparison of two sequences for a pattern common to both the sequences. Why do we need to compare sequences? Since we believe that gene sequences may have common ancestors, sequence alignment can help us trace the evolutionary history, that is, the number of mutations, insertions and deletions of bases that have taken place to transform one DNA sequence into another. The two sequences to be aligned are written across a page in two rows by keeping one character above the other. They are aligned in such a way that identical characters (match) fall in one column. The non-identical characters can be placed in the same column (mismatch) or opposite a space (gap). Higher scores are given to matches and lower scores to mismatches, while gaps are penalised. The alignment with the maximum score (more matches and least gaps) is the **optimal alignment**. An alignment signifies the changes that might have occurred during evolution between the two homologous sequences. Two sequences can be aligned over their entire length or only for the portion common to both the sequences. Pairwise alignment can be of two types: local and global.

Global alignment

Global alignment is done across the entire length of the sequence, including matched characters, gaps and mismatches. Choosing different mismatch and gap penalties (that is, different scoring matrices) may produce different alignments for the same sequences. It is important to choose the perfect scoring matrix for aligning two sequences. One of the most basic algorithms to align two sequences was developed by Needleman and Wunsch in 1970.

Example 6.1

Global alignment of two sequences S1 and S2

```
S1= G P R D L S S V S _ F E G P
        | | | | | |     |     |
S2= N _ R D L S S V I T F _ _ P
```

Local alignment

If the two given sequences are not so similar and it is difficult to align the two sequences across the full length, then local alignment can be used to align the sequences. Local alignment provides information about conserved regions or domains. From these conserved regions it is possible to get an idea of the evolutionary history. Given a scoring matrix based on the sequence similarity, the Smith–Waterman algorithm finds the best local alignment between two sequences.

Example 6.2

Local alignment of two sequences, S1 and S2

```
S1= _ G P R D L S S V S S F E _
          | | | | | |
S2= _ _ _ R D L S S V _ _ _ _ _ _
```

These two sequences are aligned locally. Here, alignment of a conserved domain of six characters in length is achieved. The vertical bars represent the alignment of identical characters.

Local alignment is more meaningful than global alignment as it can achieve some alignment even with sequences that are not so similar. It can also be used to align sequences of unequal length or when only a conserved domain is found in two sequences.

Methods for aligning two sequences

Various methods are used to align two sequences. These methods differ in their approach and accuracy of result. Some algorithms are slower but more accurate. Some algorithms may give faster results, but at the cost of accuracy of the result. Since sequence similarity is an indicator of evolutionary relationship, we need to use appropriate methods to envisage evolutionary changes between two homologous sequences. There are three different methods for pairwise sequence alignment:

- Dot plot method
- Heuristic method
- Dynamic programming

DOT PLOT METHOD

Dot plots have a long history. In this method, the sequences are visually compared for regions of similarity. Initially, Jevons (1884) used dot plots to graph the weight of British Sovereign coins. Since then it has been used in various fields. It was first described by Gibbs and McIntyre in 1970, to compare two DNA or protein sequences. The characters of the two sequences to be aligned are placed along the x- and y-axes and a dot is placed wherever the characters match. A diagonal line indicates an aligned stretch. A complete diagonal indicates a good match, while many short diagonals indicates alignments in short stretches. This comparison is performed not just by a one-to-one comparison of characters but also of words (a string of characters; fixed length sections of 5 or 7 characters). The dot plot method provides a useful way to visualise the sequences being compared, though it does not provide an exact alignment, which is best done by dynamic programming algorithms.

The three important parameters to construct a dot plot are scoring scheme, cut-off score and window size.

Scoring system in dot plot

DNA sequences are compared by alphabetical matching, ACGT which indicates similarity. For example, A–A is a match and A–C is a mismatch.

Some tools give a score of 1 for each match and 0 for a mismatched pair. (EMBOSS package: +5 for a match and –4 for a mismatch).

Protein sequences need more complex scoring schemes, as dissimilar amino acids does not necessarily mean a mismatch. Biochemically similar residues are also considered as a match, but are given a lesser score than identical matches. The choice of a correct scoring scheme (reward matches and penalise mismatches) affects the cut-off score.

Cut-off score

The value of the cut-off score can be set low or high, depending on the level of agreement sought between the sequences. Dotter programs (by Eric Soth Hammer) allow adjustment of the cut-off score dynamically. More dots are plotted with lower cut-off scores, which may be due to chance matches. This introduces noise to the dot plot. To reduce the noise, the cut-off score is increased (word size can also be increased to reduce noise). Higher cut-off scores produce less dots and hence the dot plot will be less noisy; the chance of such dots will be more significant. A higher cut-off score gives significant though fewer number of dots.

Window or word size

It is important to choose the correct window size for certain features. Smaller features or matches need a smaller window size for detection, while larger features need a larger window size. Though a smaller window size gives a detailed plot, it also gives a noisy picture, that is, crowding of dots/diagonals. A larger word size helps to reduce the noise, but it can miss small matches. Features can be missed when plotting with a word size that is significantly larger than the feature. Changes in window size can be made to produce different types of results by using the Dotlet program.

Algorithm

1) Obtain two sequences (or the same sequence in opposite order to find repeats, inverted repeats and loops) to be compared along the Cartesian axis. Refer the FASTA algorithm on page 55 for details of plotting a dot on a matrix.
2) Choose a certain word size (say 11 characters). Word size is the most important part of a dot plot. Word size changes depending on the features to be detected. The smaller the word size, the smaller the features to be detected and the more detailed the plot.

3) Compare the two sequences for that word size starting from character 1 to 11, then 2 to 12, 3 to 13, and so on. Now assign values for matches and mismatches according to the scoring system (say 2 for a match and 0 for a mismatch) to obtain the alignment score.
4) Starting with the first character at the x-axis, place a dot where the character on the y-axis is the same, that is, if the alignment score is more than cut-off score, place a dot close to the middle of the group for the given word size.

   If the cut-off score is ten, and from step 3, if the alignment score is 12 (that is, more than cut-off score), a dot will be introduced to the plot.
5) Place all the dots in this manner. The diagonal runs of dots indicate similar regions.
6) Continue this process until the graph is filled with dots representing all possible matches.

   A long run of matches appears as diagonals. Isolated dots represent random matches that do not provide any significant alignment.

   Larger window size is used for filtering. Filtering removes random matches.

   For DNA sequences, generally larger window size than for protein sequences is used. DNA sequences produce more random matches due to only four DNA symbols (protein sequence compares 20 amino acid symbols).

   Typically DNA sequences use a window size of 15, with a stringency, that is, cut-off score, equal to 10 (that is, a dot is placed if a match is found between 10 and 15 characters, for a window size of 15). For protein sequences that are not so similar but have some small portion of similarity (like active sites), a large window size (say 20) and small stringency (say 5) is used to detect the similarity among long dissimilar regions.
7) Search for the dots that give a continuous diagonal line (or the longest among all possible diagonal lines). The diagonal shows that the corresponding characters on the x-and y-axis are aligned. This way we get a comprehensive overview of the two sequences though we do not get proper alignment.

Some codes used in this method

A - adenine	C - cytosine	G - guanine	T/U - thymine/uracil
R - purine/A/G	Y - pyrimidine	M - amino	W - weak/A/T
S - strong/G/C	V - not T/A/C/G	D - not C/A/T/G	B - not A/C/G/T
H - not G/A/C/T		N - any/A/T/C/G	

Repeats can be detected by comparing the sequence against itself. Matching repeat regions generate dots parallel to the leading diagonal (Fig. 6.1(a)). Multiple repeats can also be detected in this manner.

Inverted repeats are found distributed on the plot as parallel lines to the trailing diagonal. However, they are not found very close to the trailing diagonal as in the stem loop (Fig. 6.1(b)).

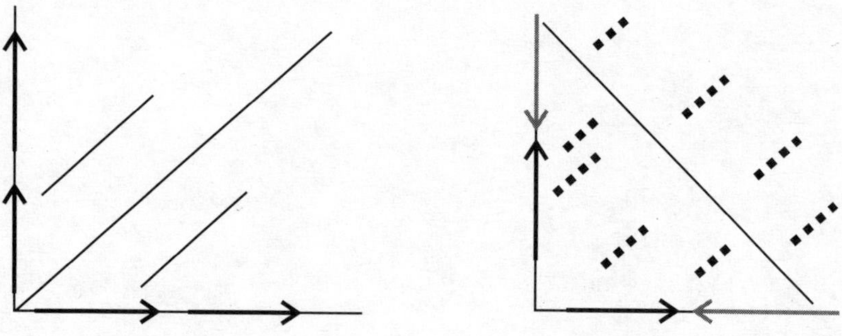

(a) Repeats (b) Inverted repeats

FIGURE 6.1 *Repeats in a sequence*

A **stem loop** is a lollipop-shaped structure formed when a single-stranded nucleic acid molecule loops back on itself to form a complementary double helix (stem) topped by a loop.

The following is an example of a stem loop.

G C C G C G G G C C G A A A A A A
C G G C G C C C G G C C C C C C

It can be detected by comparing the sequence with its reverse and complement. Comparing the stem loop sequence with itself produces a leading diagonal (Fig. 6.2(a)). Now reverse the order of sequence on the y-axis; we will get a trailing diagonal of dots (Fig. 6.2(b)). If the loop region is present in that sequence, parallel lines very close to the trailing diagonal will be found (Fig. 6.2(c)).

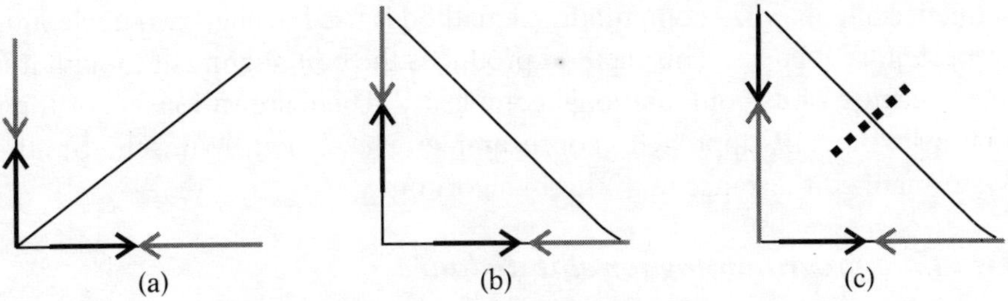

FIGURE 6.2 *(a) Comparing the sequence with itself; (b) Reverse order of the y-axis sequence; (c) Loop region close to the trailing diagonal*

A **low complexity region (LCR)** is a run of the same amino acids or repeat of the same amino acid pattern in protein sequences. These sequences produce high scoring alignment artificially and hinder sequence alignment. This region is detected by analysing the dot matrix of a sequence against itself (Fig. 6.3). The LCR is seen as horizontal or vertical rows of dots representing repeated matches of one residue position. This region is usually filtered while performing database searches as it hinders the database result.

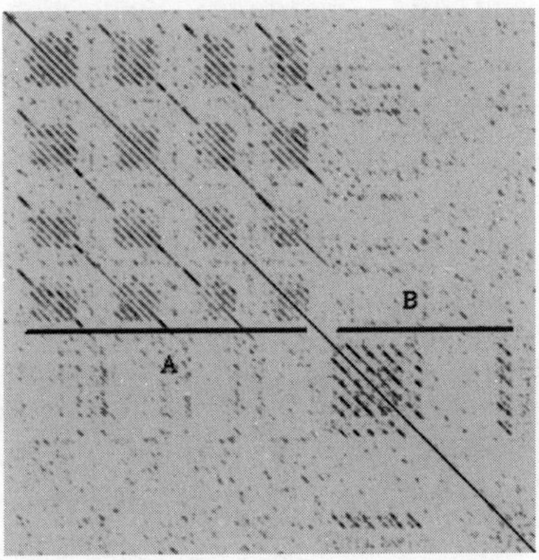

FIGURE 6.3 *A screenshot from the Dotlet program showing repeated domains*

DYNAMIC PROGRAMMING

Dynamic programming (DP) is a method (not a computer program) of solving problems, usually with optimal path or overlapping problems. In dynamic programming the subproblems are first solved. Then these solutions are remembered for later use and finally at the end all the subanswers are put together to find a solution to the main problem. For sequence alignment, a computational method is used to align two nucleotide or protein sequences. This method produces the best alignment though it is slow because of its computational complexity. There are various algorithms that use the DP approach. For example: Needleman–Wunsch, Smith–Waterman, edit distance and Viterbi algorithms.

Dynamic programming for edit distance

This algorithm searches for the cheapest way to transform one string of characters (source) into another string (output). To do so at any point, copy the current character of the source into the output or delete the existing character in the source string.

Example 6.3

Edit operations for changing the string S1= ROAD to S2 = RODE will be: copy (R-R),

copy (O-O), delete A, copy (D-D), insert E.

Assuming that copying costs 2, insertion 3 and deletion 1.

Cost of changing string S1 into string S2 will be 2 + 2 + 1 + 3= 8.

The above is a simple example and by following the rules of copy, insert and delete, it can be easily solved. This will not be possible if the sequence string is very long. To do so, we use the edit distance algorithm for dynamic programming.

Algorithm

Perform dynamic programming calculation of edit distance in sequences S1 and S2 and return the best alignment possible.

Input: Two sequences S1 and S2 and values for match, mismatch and gaps

Output: Aligned sequence(s).

The characters i and j belong to sequence S1 and S2, respectively. Here i ranges from 0 to n and j ranges from 0 to m. If D is assigned for distance, D(i, j) will be the values of edit distance. To obtain edit distance there are three steps in the dynamic programming approach: recurrence relation, tabular computation and trace back.

1. **Recurrence relation:** It is a recursive method. In this step, values for the base condition are assigned. The base conditions for the edit distance problem are:

   D(0, 0) = 0, that is, no edit operations if no characters are there in both the sequences.

   D(i, 0) = i, that is, to change i characters of S1 to 0 characters of S2, the only way is to delete i characters of S1.

   D(0, j) = j, that is, to change 0 characters of S1 to j characters of S2, the only way is to add j characters to S1.

   D(i, j) = Minimum {D(i – 1, j) + 1, D(i, j) + D(i, j), D(i, j – 1) + 1 }

   Here D(i, j) = 1 if S1≠ S2 and D(i, j) = 0 if S1= S2 (that is, if there is a match, there is no edit operation and for a mismatch, one edit operation will be performed).
2. **Tabular computation:** The bottom-up approach is used to compute D(i, j). For this, a table of size (m + 1) × (n + 1) is created, where S1 corresponds to the vertical axis of the table with m characters and S2 corresponds to the horizontal axis of the table with n characters. This table is filled with values obtained from the recurrence relation step.

Example 6.4

Compute the edit distance for the given sequences: S1= ACGT and S2= AGGT.

The table given below shows each character's position in the computation table.

j

N columns

M Rows

	0	1	2	3	4
X	X	A	C	G	T
X	(0,0)	(0,1)	(0,2)	(0,3)	(0,4)
A	(1,0)	(1,1)	(1,2)	(1,3)	(1,4)
G	(2,0)	(2,1)	(2,2)	(2,3)	(2,4)
G	(3,0)	(3,1)	(3,2)	(3,3)	(3,4)
T	(4,0)	(4,1)	(4,2)	(4,3)	(4,4)

i

a_{ij}

Compute the values from formulae written in the recurrence relation step.

D(0,0) = 0

D(1,0) = 1, D(2, 0) = 2 as D (i,0)=i and likewise other positions till (4,0) and (0,4) are calculated and tabular computation is completed for the first row and the first column.

X	X	A	C	G	T
X	0	1	2	3	4
A	1				
G	2				
G	3				
T	4				

Now the inner positions are filled using another formula: D(i, j) = Minimum {D(i – 1, j) + 1, D(i, j) + D(i, j), D(i, j – 1) + 1}

D(1,1)= Minimum{1+1, 0+0, 1+1}= {2,0,2}; as 0 is minimum we will put 0 at (1,1) in bold for future reference, that is, for next step.

Now compute the values from the formulae used in the recurrence relation step and fill the table. Similarly, other positions are computed until (4,4).

X	X	A	C	G	T
X	0	–1	2	3	4
A	1	2 0 2			
G	2				
G	3				
T	4				

In the next table an arrow is placed, showing the position from where the minimum value (required by the formulae) has been obtained for easy understanding and for ease in the trace back step. Finally, the table will look as follows:

X	X	A	C	G	T
X	0	1	2	3	4
A	1	2 0 2	3 2 1	4 3 2	5 4 3
G	2	1 2 3	2 1 2	3 1 2	4 3 2
G	3	2 3 4	2 2 3	2 1 3	3 2 2
T	4	3 4 5	3 3 4	2 3 4	3 1 3

In this table, the top value in each box is obtained from top {D (i – 1, j) + 1 (that is, i – 1 row and j or same column); the centre value from the diagonal {D (i – 1, j – 1) + D (i, j)} and the last value from the left {D (i, j – 1) + 1}. The arrows make the path in the trace back step easy to search because we know that the top value is obtained from the box above, the middle value from the diagonal box and the value below these two from the side box.)

3. **Trace back:** This step traces back from the right bottom corner to the top left corner, checking where the next value has come from. The next value can be computed in three ways: to the right, down and diagonally down.

While tracing back moving towards the top, a gap is introduced to S1 and the jth character (corresponding to that position at left) to S2 (that is, in the sequence above, i.e. S1). We do not have such a case in this example, but in Example 6.5 in alignment 1, the arrow moves from the right bottom corner character towards top. Here a gap is inserted in S1 and S2 will have the corresponding character from the sequence at the y-axis. When we trace back to the left side, we give the corresponding i^{th} character on top to

S1 and a gap in S2. While tracing back diagonally, we give both the i and j characters to S1 and S2. In the given example, all the positions are traced back diagonally, so no gap is found.

X	X	A	C	G	T
X	0	1	2	3	4
A	1	0	2	2	3
G	2	1	1	1	2
G	3	2	2	1	2
T	4	3	3	2	1

In the given example, only one alignment is possible as the trace back takes place diagonally:

S1 = ACGT

S2 = AGGT

For the given example, the similarity matrix is:

	A	**G**	**C**	**T**
A	**10**	–1	–3	–4
G	–1	**7**	**–5**	–3
C	–3	–5	9	0
T	–4	–3	0	**8**

The score for the above alignment based on the similarity matrix is (All the values here are copy value. As no insert or delete is found in this example, there is no need to give insert and delete values) 10 + (–5) + 7 + 8= 20. In case of more than one alignment, the best alignment is the one which gives the minimum score, i.e., minimum edit operations.

Needleman–Wunsch algorithm

The Needleman–Wunsch (NW) algorithm is a dynamic programming algorithm for global alignment. It was proposed by Saul Needleman and Christian Wunsch in 1970. The objective of the NW algorithm is to find the best alignment (global alignment) in two sequences and give its similarity. This is similar to the edit programming algorithm, but provides values for match, mismatch and gaps using various scoring matrices. A good alignment has few mismatches, very few gaps and maximum matches. So the higher value is given to matches, and mismatches and gaps are penalised. A gap is penalised more than a mismatch as gaps are usually not allowed in the alignment.

Taking all the basic string definitions to be the same as in dynamic programming of edit distance (instead of distance, here similarity 'S' is computed), two sequences can be aligned using the NW algorithm along their entire length. The NW algorithm can be explained in three steps: initialisation, matrix computation and trace back.

1. **Initialisation:** Create a table of size (m + 1) × (n + 1) where the sequence P corresponds to the vertical axis of the table with m characters, and L corresponds to the horizontal axis of the table with n characters. With S as the similarity value, the base condition here is:

   S(0, 0) = 0, S(i, 0) = i + gap value, S(j, 0) = j + gap value

2. **Tabular computation:** As in edit distance, this step is calculated using the formula:

   S(i, j) = Maximum S(i – 1, j) + gap value, S(i, j –1) + gap value, S(i – 1, j – 1) + (i, j)

   S(i,j) is equal to a match or a mismatch value, that is, by moving right in a row and down in a column, the gap value is added to i – 1 and j – 1 values, and by moving diagonally, the match or mismatch value is added to i – 1, j – 1 value.

Example 6.5

Align S1 = GCA and S2 = GCCT globally using the NW algorithm. Given values: match +2, mismatch –1 and gap –2.

Compute the values from the formulae written in the initialisation step.

S(0,0) = 0 and S(1,0) = –2, S (2, 0) = –2 + (–2)= –4 and likewise.

In the same way, values for all the positions are calculated and tabular computation is performed for the first row and first column as in edit distance algorithm.

Now the inner positions are filled using another formula:

S(1,1)= Max {–2 + (–2), 0 + 2, –2+ (–2)}= {–4, 2, –4}. Here 2 is maximum so we will insert a diagonal arrow for 2 at (1,1). In this manner all the other positions are computed till (4,3). An arrow is placed showing the place from where the maximum value is obtained. The table will now look as follows:

X	X	G	C	A
X	**0**	**–2**	**–4**	**–6**
G	**–2**	–4 **2** –4	–6 –3 **0**	–8 –5 **–2**
C	**–4**	**0** –3 –6	–2 **4** –2	–4 –1 **2**
C	**–6**	**–2** –5 –8	**2** **2** –4	0 **3** 0
T	**–8**	**–4** –7 –10	**0** –3 –6	**1** **1** –2

3. **Trace back:** This step traces back from the right bottom corner to the top left corner, tracing the arrows from where the maximum value is obtained. The next value can be achieved as discussed in edit programming by three ways: from left to right, top to down and diagonally down. So check for all three positions while tracing back. This step is similar to that explained in the Smith–Waterman algorithm.

X	X	G	C	A
X	0	**–2**	**–4**	**–6**
G	**–2**	–4 **2** –4	–6 –3 0	–8 –5 **–2**
G	**–4**	**0** –3 –6	–2 **4** –2	–4 –1 **2**
C	**–6**	**–2** –5 –8	**2** **2** –2	0 **3** 0
T	**–8**	**–4** –7 –10	**0** –3 –6	**1** **1** –2

Three alignments are possible.:

S1 = GCA– Alignment 1
S2 = GCCT

S1 = GC–A Alignment 2
S2 = GCCT

S1 = G–CA Alignment 3
S2 = GCCT

Smith–Waterman algorithm

This is a well-known algorithm for performing local alignment. It was first proposed by Temple Smith and Michael Waterman in 1981. It compares two sequences and returns similar regions in the two sequences. This algorithm is guaranteed to find the optimal local alignment with respect to the scoring system used. Unlike the NW algorithm, here the position with negative scoring matrix is given a value zero and tracing back starts at the position with the highest scoring matrix until a position with score zero is encountered. This fragment produces an alignment with the highest score. Being an extensive computational algorithm, the Smith–Waterman (SW) algorithm is fairly demanding of time [O(n,m) time for two sequences of length n and m] and space. That is why it has been replaced by the BLAST and the FASTA methods (though it does not guarantee finding an optimal solution) in practical use. SSEARCH, in FASTA (ftp://ftp.virginia.edu/pub/fasta) sequence analysis package uses the SW algorithm (Fig. 6.4).

As in the Needleman–Wunsch algorithm, the D(i,j) matrix is generated but generation and interpretation of the matrix is slightly different. It can be explained with the following example.

Example 6.6

Align S1= CCAG and S2= CAGT. Values for match, mismatch and gap are 1, 0 and – 2, respectively.

Step 1: Initialisation: As with the NW algorithm, create a table of size (m + 1) × (n + 1) where sequence P corresponds to the vertical axis of the table with m characters, and L corresponds to the horizontal axis of the table with n characters. Taking S as the similarity value, the base conditions are: S(0,0) = 0, S(i,0) = 0 and S(j,0) = 0.

It means that a local alignment of a string with an empty string gives a score zero. This algorithm searches for an ungapped alignment. All non-positive values are considered as zero here, as in the first row and first column we add a gap value that is mostly negative and hence zero.

Step 2: Tabular computation: The matrix is populated with values of (i,j).

S(i,j) = Maximum {S(i–1,j) + gap value, S(i,j–1) + gap value, S(i–1,j–1) + S(i,j)} where S(i,j) is equal to match or mismatch value.

The values are calculated as for the NW algorithm and the matrix is filled with only positive values; for all other negative values, zero is entered and for convenience the pointer is drawn at the same time.

S(0,0) = 0; S(0,1) = 0 + (–2) = –2. As it is negative, the value is zero. Similarly, values for all other positions are calculated based on the formula specified and the table is computed.

X	X	C	C	A	G
X	0	0	0	0	0
C	0	1	1	0	0
A	0	0	0	2	0
G	0	0	0	0	3
T	0	0	0	0	1

Step 3: Trace back: In this step, as in the last two algorithms, one can trace back from the box with maximum value to the top left corner, checking from where the next value has come (checking pointers in the previous step). As in the SW algorithm, a gap is usually not allowed; while tracing back it moves diagonally (as you know; moving to the top gives a gap in the first or top sequence, and moving to the left gives a gap in the second or down sequence).

X	X	C	C	A	G
X	0	0	0	0	0
C	0	1	1	0	0
A	0	0	0	2	0
G	0	0	0	0	3
T	0	0	0	0	1

Alignment: As we are always tracing back diagonally we get one possible alignment here without a gap: S1 CAG

S2 CAG

Scoring: 1 + 1 + 1 = 3

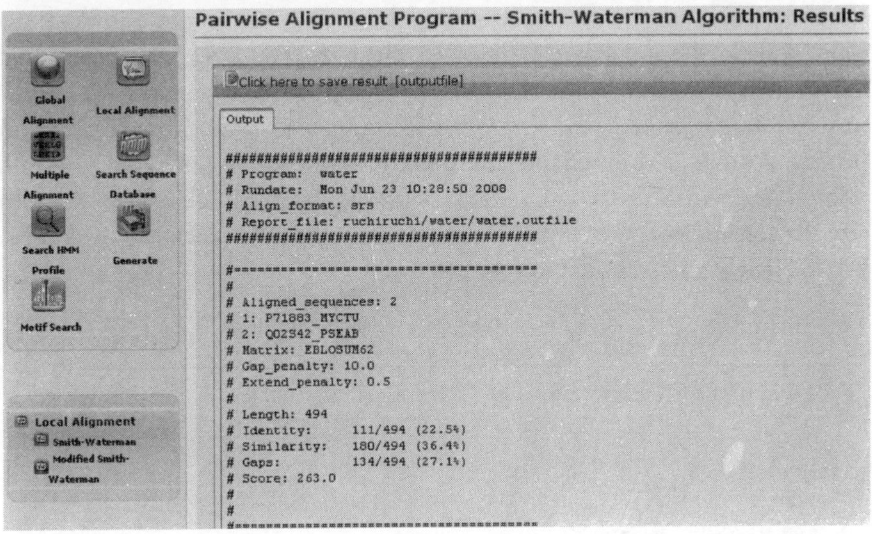

FIGURE 6.4 *A snapshot from EXOME Horizon software package showing local alignment result for P71883_MYCTU and Q02S42_PSEAB*

HEURISTIC ALGORITHM

BLAST or FASTA use the heuristic database search method, which is the most used method. It is also one of the most important methods for

- aligning a query sequence with a sequences in the database (BLAST and FASTA program
- aligning two bacterial sequences (bacterial BLAST)
- aligning two given sequences (BLAST2 seq)

As dynamic programming is computationally intensive and hence slow, dynamic programming methods are not used for database searches. Instead, heuristic methods, which are fast though approximate, are used. The important characteristics of heuristic algorithms are that they are fast, ungapped (though we have some gapped programs) and local (for a part of the sequence).

A DNA sequence comprises only four nucleotides, while a protein sequence is made up of twenty amino acids. Hence it is easier to search for similar patterns in proteins than in DNA. To perform a database search, it is better to translate the DNA sequence for encoding proteins into a protein sequence for a more reliable result.

FASTA

Given a query sequence, FASTA searches for local alignment with the sequences in the database. Originally, the FASTP program was designed for protein sequence similarity. Now the FASTA package has programs for protein to protein, DNA to DNA, protein to translated DNA (with frameshifts), and ordered or unordered peptide searches. This program initially performs word to word matches (ktups), where by changing the word size the sensitivity and speed of the program is controlled. The algorithm for FASTA has been discussed in *Chapter 4*.

TABLE 6.1 Types of FASTA: Basic FASTA programs

Program name	Query sequence	Database sequence	Algorithm used
Nucleotide BLAST	Nucleotide	Nucleotide	DNA/RNA FASTA, FASTM, FASTS
Protein BLAST	Protein	Protein	FASTA, SSEARCH, FASTS, FASTF
FASTX/FASTY	Translated DNA (with frame shifts)	Protein	
TFASTX/ TFASTY	Protein	Translated DNA (with frame shifts)	
TFASTs	Peptides	Translated DNA	

BLAST

It is a simplification of the Smith–Waterman algorithm and is faster than the FASTA program. It looks for similar regions in two sequences without allowing a gap, though now there is gapped BLAST (WU-BLAST). This is the algorithm that is most commonly used for database search and sequence alignment. The algorithm and other properties of BLAST are discussed in *Chapter 4*.

TABLE 6.2 Basic BLAST programs (E)

Program name	Query sequence	Database sequence	Algorithm used
Nucleotide BLAST	Nucleotide	Nucleotide	BLASTN, MEGABLAST
Protein BLAST	Protein	Protein	BLASTP, PSI-BLAST and PHI-BLAST
BLASTX	Translated nucleotide	Protein	BLASTP
TBLASTN	Protein	Translated nucleotide	BLASTP
TBLASTX	Translated nucleotide	Translated nucleotide	BLASTP

Specialised BLAST programs

- GEO BLAST: Searches sequences for gene expression data.
- bl2seq: Aligns two sequences using BLAST.
- Ig BLAST: Searches for immunoglobins by using BLAST.
- SNP BLAST: Searches for single nucleotide polymorphisms (SNPs).
- Microbial BLAST: Aligns two microbial sequences.
- Genome BLAST: Aligns genome sequences from various organisms.
- WU-BLAST2: Gapped BLAST program developed at Washington University.

At NCBI-BLAST, three BLAST searches are available: web MEGABLAST EST analysis tool, standalone BLAST executables, BLAST Network Client 'BLASTcl3'

Web MEGABLAST EST analysis tool is used for aligning nucleotide sequences that to some extent differ as a result of sequencing or any other 'errors'.

Standalone BLAST executables is a command line program that uses local downloaded copies of the NCBI-BLAST databases for BLAST searches. The executables are available at ftp://ftp.ncbi.nih.gov/blast/executables/.

BLAST Network Client 'BLASTcl3' server is used to submit a single file of FASTA sequences to NCBI-BLAST databases without downloading the database locally.

Tools for pairwise sequence alignment

Dotlet and Dotter: Based on the dot plot method.

Bl2seq: Based on the BLAST algorithm.

ALION and LALIGN: Based on the dynamic programming algorithm.

EMBOSS: A package for sequence alignment.

LAGAN: A set of programs used for alignment and visualisation. It is available at the Vista server.

The Accelrys GCG Wisconsin Package: It is a commercial software package for sequence alignment and analysis.

EXOME™-Horizon Package: A commercial software package with integrated, multi-user work environment for bioinformatics research, data management and training.

Exercises

1. What is 'word size'? What is the word size used by BLAST and FASTA in NCBI?
2. Write a note on 'threshold values'.
3. For a big size sequence, which BLAST algorithm is preferred?
4. How will you decide between BLAST and the Smith–Waterman algorithm for aligning two sequences locally?
5. What is a dot plot? Discuss the advantages and disadvantages of dot plot analysis.
6. How can you identify repeats using dot plot? Can you find relatively longer repeats by increasing stringency? Other than finding repeats, what else is dot plot used for?
7. Explain the concept of the Smith–Waterman algorithm. How does this result in a local alignment?
8. Align the given strings locally using the dynamic programming algorithm: (match value= +1, mismatch= –1 and gap= –2).

   Sequence 1 = LPMNPS

Sequence 2 = LPMNNK

9. Change the values for match to + 4, mismatch to 0 and gap to –4 and compute the alignment for the same strings.
10. Compute edit distance for the given strings using dynamic programming:

    Sequence 1 = SUPPOSE

    Sequence 2 = DISPOSE

    Report how many alignments are produced and which is the best alignment using the BLOSUM 62 matrix.
11. Align the given strings locally using the dynamic programming algorithm (value for match = +1, for mismatch = –1 and for gap = –2).

    Sequence 1= PAINTER

    Sequence 2= CLAINTON

    Confirm your answer by giving the score for the given alignment.
12. Build a complete DP table and compute the edit distance and global alignment for the given sequences: (match= +1, mismatch= –1 and gap = – 2).

    Sequence 1= WISE

    Sequence 2= NISSE
13. Align the sequences of *Human leptin* and *Rattus leptin* and report the number of identical residues, using the Alion and Lalign pairwise sequence alignment tools. Change the parameters (scoring matrix, word length or gap weight) and find out the difference in the two results.
14. Perform LALIGN search for HBB_HUMAN - LGB1_PEA.
    a. Why is there a difference in result for local and global alignment?
    b. Why are several alignments displayed when performing local alignment?
    c. What does '% identity' mean? How is it computed?
    d. What do the symbols':' and '.' stand for?
    e. Modify the gap penalties. Examine more closely how these parameters influence the occurrence and the length of gaps ('-').
    f. Modify the scoring matrices used, that is, BLOSUM 35 and BLOSUM 80, and examine more closely how these parameters influence the scores and the alignments.

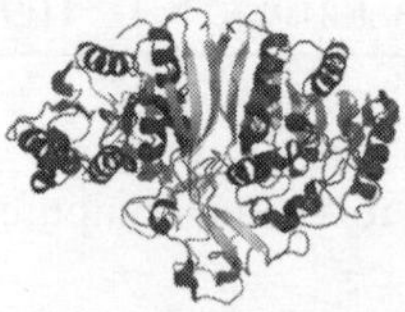

CHAPTER 7

Multiple Sequence Alignment

LEARNING OUTCOME

- Explain how to score a multiple sequence alignment
- Explain the sum of pair method
  - o Progressive alignment algorithms: Feng–Doolittle algorithm
  - o Iterative algorithm: Barton–Sternberg algorithm
- Describe multiple sequence alignment by HMM
- List the software tools for multiple sequence alignment

Unlike pairwise alignments that involve two sequences (nucleotide or protein), more than two sequences (nucleotide or protein) are required for generating multiple sequence alignments. A database search usually reveals many homologous sequences. The residues of the homologous sequences are aligned together in columns for multiple sequence alignment. While aligning, wherever a sequence does not possess an amino acid in a particular position, it is denoted by a dash. Highly identical sequences are used to give some meaningful results. Ideally, a column of aligned residues occupies similar three-dimensional structural positions and they diverge from a common ancestral residue. These multiple alignments can be used to establish phylogenetic relationships.

Coloured results from multiple sequence alignment tools enable easy interpretation of the result (Table 7.1):

TABLE 7.1 *Colour as a multiple sequence alignment tool*

Colour	Residue type	Amino acid
Yellow	Small nonpolar	Ala, Gly, Ser, Thr
Green	Hydrophobic	Cys, Ile, Leu, Met, Phe, Pro, Trp, Tyr, Val
Magenta	Polar	Asn, Gln, His
Red	Negatively charged	Asp, Glu
Blue	Positively charged	Arg, Lys

Scoring in multiple sequence alignment (MSA)

The score in MSA is the sum of the scores for all pairwise alignments induced by the MSA. The optimal alignment is the alignment with the maximum score. To score an MSA, two things should be kept in mind:

1. Some positions are more conserved than others.
2. The sequences are correlated (can be represented by a phylogenetic tree).

Conserved positions are important as they provide important biological information. So they are given a higher score than non-conserved ones.

SUM OF PAIR METHOD

The sum of pair or SP method scores a multiple sequence alignment by adding the scores for all possible combinations of amino acid pairs in a column of a multiple sequence alignment using a substitution matrix. Here, columns are assumed to be statistically independent. This is the most common method used to find the score of an MSA. For each column, the SP score between two residues is taken from the PAM or BLOSUM matrix. A gap against a residue is given a gap penalty while a gap against a gap is given a zero value.

It is an extension of the dynamic programming approach. But here, three or more sequences are aligned simultaneously. The SP method scores each position in the protein in an MSA. The number of combinations of pairs in a column is $n(n-1)/2$, where n is the total number of sequences in a column. In the SP method, each sequence is scored as if it is derived from its previous sequence and not from one common ancestor sequence. SP scoring grows exponentially with the length of the sequences and the number of sequences to be aligned.

There are two types of alignment algorithms for MSA: first progressive alignment and second iterative alignment.

Progressive alignment

In this technique, the first two most related sequences are taken and aligned by the pairwise alignment program. This method uses the dynamic programming method to build an MSA. It is important to align the most similar pairs of sequences first. A guide tree can be used to efficiently model this in the progressive alignment algorithm. Once done, the alignments will be fixed and cannot be changed later. The third nearest sequence is chosen next and aligned with the first two aligned sequences. This process is repeated for all unaligned sequences till all the sequences are aligned. The Feng–Doolittle algorithm uses the progressive alignment method to produce an MSA.

Feng–Doolittle algorithm

1. Compute all possible pairwise alignments. For N sequences, a diagonal matrix of N(N – 1)/2 is calculated for all pairs using standard pairwise alignment. So for three sequences S1, S2 and S3, 3(3–1)/2= 3 possible combinations of pairwise alignment is possible, i.e., S1–S2, S1–S3 and S2–S3.
2. The raw alignment scores are taken as approximate pairwise distances. Usually PAM substitution matrix and affine gap penalty are used to convert alignment scores to distances.
3. A guide tree is constructed by using the clustering algorithm of Fitch and Margoliash (this will be discussed in detail in the next chapter).
4. From best paired sequences, start alignment as in progressive alignment. Starting from the first node added to the tree, the child nodes are aligned. The two most similar sequences are aligned first. Following the guide tree, add the next sequence, aligning to the existing alignment and insert gaps as necessary.
5. Once a gap is introduced in the alignment at any step (denoted as X), its position cannot be changed ('once a gap, always a gap').
6. The above steps are repeated for all other nodes—from most similar pairs to least similar pairs—in the order in which they were added to the tree, until all the sequences are aligned.

Alignment scores are converted to distance values using the formula:

$$D = -\log S_{eff} = -\log \frac{S_{obs} - S_{rand}}{S_{max} - S_{rand}}$$

where S_{obs} is the observed pairwise alignment score; S_{max} is the maximum score.

S_{rand} is the score of a random alignment, S_{eff} is the normalised percentage similarity. Here log function is used to compute distance more linearly.

ClustalW

This is a tool for MSA based on progressive strategy. Selection of different substitution matrices, depending on the similarity of the sequences, and selection of position-specific gap opening and gap extension penalty are the parameters used to obtain the best result. The MSA from ClustalW cannot be modified once we have gone from one step to the next because of the 'once a gap, always a gap' rule. Once a gap is introduced in an alignment; it cannot be changed in subsequent steps as in the iterative alignment method. Some important properties of ClustalW are:

1. It works on progressive alignment strategy.
2. Neighbour joining algorithm is used to build the tree.
3. It works by the 'once a gap, always a gap' rule.
4. Sequence–sequence, sequence–profile and profile–profile alignment is done progressively.

Algorithm

Input: Multiple protein sequences S1, S2, . . ., Sn (may be of same or various lengths).

Output: Aligned sequences showing conserved and unconserved regions.

Step 1: Pairwise alignment: Align the given multiple sequences by dynamic programming method for each pair. Calculate the score using the formula discussed in the pairwise alignment method.

For example, in the three sequences S1, S2, S3

S1: A B B C....... B C C D A
S2: A _ B C ....B C C D A
S3: A A B C ....B C _ D _

Sequence (S1:S2) aligned score (say) = 10
Sequence (S2:S3) aligned score (say) = 17
Sequence (S1:S3) aligned score (say) = 7

Step 2: Phylogenetic tree construction: Create a binary tree with the scores obtained from Step 1, using the neighbour joining algorithm (*see Chapter 8*) for the first pair with least distance.

As in the given example above, S1 and S3 will be aligned first to build the tree:

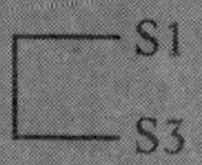

Step 3: Extend the alignment progressively: Extend the alignment progressively by adding other pairs to the tree in order of less to more distant sequences. This method progressively aligns the nodes in order of decreasing similarity, using sequence–sequence, sequence–profile and profile–profile alignment.

As we have only three sequences here, S2 will join next.

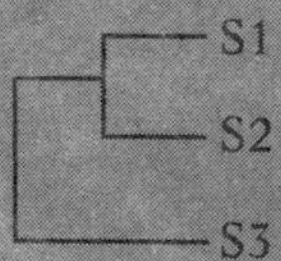

Step 4: Obtain final output of aligned sequences: For the given example, the above tree is final. For sequence (1, 2: 3) the score is say 16. If more than three sequences are present, it will give a corresponding tree. In the case of four sequences, if the score for 4,2:3 is less than 16, it will be joined first. Different types of trees and their construction are explained in detail in *Chapter 8*.

Important characteristics of a ClustalW output: Many options are available for a ClustalW output. The different formats used here are ALN, GCG, PHYLIP, PIR and GDE.

By default some symbols denote the degree of conservation observed in each column:

* Means the residues or nucleotides in that column are identical in all sequences in the alignment.

: Means conserved substitutions.

. Means semi-conserved substitutions.

Coloured results aid easy interpretation at a glance. (*Source:* EBI ClustalW server)

AVFPMILW	Red	Small [small + hydrophobic (incl. aromatic-Y)]
DE	Blue	Acidic
RHK	Magenta	Basic
STYHCNGQ	Green	Hydroxyl + Amine + Basic – Q
Others	Grey	

CLUSTALW (1.82) multiple sequence alignment

```
HBB_HUMAN     --------VHLTPEEKSAVTALWGKVN--VDEVGGEALGRLLVVYPWTQRF
              FESFGDLST
HBB_HORSE     --------VQLSGEEKAAVLALWDKVN--EEEVGGEALGRLLVVYPWTQR
              FFDSFGDLSN
HBA_HUMAN     ---------VLSPADKTNVKAAWGKVGAHAGEYGAEALERMFLSFPTT
              KTYFPHF-----
HBA_HORSE     ---------VLSAADKTNVKAAWSKVGGHAGEYGAEALERMFLGFPT
              TKTYFPHF-----
MYG_PHYCA     ---------VLSEGEWQLVLHVWAKVEADVAGHGQDILIRLFKS HPETLE
              KFDRFKHLKT
GLB5_PETMA    PIVDTGSVAPLSAAEKTKIRSAWAPVYSTYETSGVDILVKFFTSTP
              AAQEFFPKFKGLTT
LGB2_LUPLU    ----------GALLTESQAALVKSSWEEFNANIPKHTHRFFILVLEIAPAA
              KDLFSFLKG--T
                           *: : : * . : .: * : * :
HBB_HUMAN     PDAVMGNPKVKAHGKKVLGAFSDGLAHLDN-----LKGTFATLSELH
              CDKLHVDPENFRL
HBB_HORSE     PGAVMGNPKVKAHGKKVLHSFGEGVHHLDN-----LKGTFAALSEL
              HCDKLHVDPENFRL
HBA_HUMAN     -DLSHGSAQVKGHGKKVADALTNAVAHVDD-----MPNALSALSDLH
              AH KLRVDPVNFKL
HBA_HORSE     -DLSHGSAQVKAHGKKVGDALTLAVGHLDD-----LPGALSNLSDLH
              AH KLRVDPVNFKL
MYG_PHYCA     EAEMKASEDLKKHGVTVLTALGAILKKKGH-----HEAELKPLAQSH
              ATKHKIPIKYLEF
GLB5_PETMA    ADQLKKSADVRWHAERIINAVNDAVASMDDT--EKMSMKLRDLSGK
              HAKSFQVDPQYFKV
LGB2_LUPLU    SEVPQNNPELQAHAGKVFKLVYEAAIQLQVTGVVVTDATLKNL
              GSVHVSKGVAD-AHFPV
                           . ..:: *. : . : *. * . : .
HBB_HUMAN     LGNVLVCVLAHHFGKEFTPPVQAAYQKVVAGVANALAHKYH------
HBB_HORSE     LGNVLVVVLARHFGKDFTPELQASYQKVVAGVANALAHKYH------
HBA_HUMAN     LSHCLLVTLAAHLPAEFTPAVHASLDKFLASVSTVLTSKYR------
HBA_HORSE     LSHCLLSTLAVHLPNDFTPAVHASLDKFLSSVSTVLTSKYR------
MYG_PHYCA     ISEAIIHVLHSRHPGDFGADAQGAMNKALELFRKDIAAKYKELGYQG
GLB5_PETMA    LAAVIADTVAAG---------DAGFEKLMSMICILLRSAY-------
LGB2_LUPLU    VKEAILKTIKEVVGAKWSEELNSAWTIAYDELAIVIKKEMNDAA---

                               : : .: ... . :
```

FIGURE 7.1 *A result from the multiple sequence alignment tool ClustalW server, aligning seven different sequences*

```
(
(
(
(
HBB_HUMAN:0.08080,
HBB_HORSE:0.08359)
:0.23578,
(
HBA_HUMAN:0.06516,
HBA_HORSE:0.05541)
:0.19444)
:0.07579,
GLB5_PETMA:0.37023)
:0.02699,
MYG_PHYCA:0.37220,
LGB2_LUPLU:0.47094);
```

FIGURE 7.2 *ClustalW (dnd) result from the example shown in Fig. 7.1*

The result from the ClustalW dnd format can be saved in notepad with a .nj extension and can be opened in Phylodraw software (can be downloaded from the internet) to show the phylogenetic relationship.

Iterative algorithm

The iterative method attempts to improve the weak points of the progressive alignment method, that is, its dependence on initial pairwise alignments. The scoring method used assigns an initial global alignment and then realigns sequence subsets. The realigned subsets are aligned to produce the next iteration.

Algorithm

1. Generate an initial multiple alignment by using any one of the algorithms for MSA.

   For example:
   ```
   S1: A B B C B _ _ B C C D A
   S2: A B _ C A B D B C C D _
   S3: A _ B C _ _ D B C C D A
   S4: A A B C A B D B C _ D _
   ```
   Profile: A . b C . b d B C c D a
2. Take one or more sequences out of the group and change the profile. In this example, S1 is taken out of the profile.

For example: S2: A B _ C A B D B C C D _
S3: A _ B C _ _ D B C C D A
S4: A A B C A B D B C _ D –

Changed Profile: A . b C a b D B C c D A

Realign the sequence(s) taken out (i.e. S1 here) to the changed profile of the remaining aligned sequences.

Realigned S1: A B B C – B – B C C D A

Changed Profile: A . b C a b D B C c D A

3. Steps 2 to 4 are repeated till the overall score improves and stopped when the alignment does not improve anymore.

Barton–Sternberg multiple alignments

1. The first two sequences with the highest pairwise similarity are searched and aligned by using standard pairwise dynamic programming alignment.
2. Search the sequence that is most similar to the profile of the alignment of the first two by profile sequence alignment.
3. Repeat Step 2 until all sequences have been included in the multiple alignments.
4. Realign the first sequence to the profile of the other aligned sequences.
5. Repeat Step 4 for all the sequences.
6. Repeat steps 2 to 5 till the alignment scores stop converging.

MULTIPLE SEQUENCE ALIGNMENT BY HIDDEN MARKOV MODEL (HMM)

As discussed in *Chapter 4*, HMM for MSA has almost the same architecture of match, insert and gaps as that of profile HMM. It can be explained by the following steps (Fig. 7.3):

1. The HMM model is initialised with prior information (transition probabilities and state of amino acids). A guess is made at this point through prior information for the expected variation in MSA. The success of MSA is very dependent on the correct initial guess and prior conditions. For example: MSA of initial sequences shows amino acid D in any column; it is more probable that the same column in the query sequence will have D. If any column shows character A in some sequences and B in some, it is more likely that the column in the query sequence will have either A or B and so on. But it is always a guess only,

which is usually found to be correct (for homologous sequences) but not always. These are the prior conditions guessed for those columns.

2. The HMM model is then trained by the sequence data to check if at any place a character or gap is present (using approximately 20–100 sequences). This trained model is used to produce an alignment.
3. The possible path in the model for each sequence is computed. Forward–backward algorithm helps to reduce the computations to the number of steps in the model times the total length of the training sequences. This results in the probability of finding a particular path in the sequence.
4. Training steps are repeated to check if that position has a character or gap by changing the sequences and profile, as it was done in the MSA algorithm, until no significant change in parameters is found. This trained model gives the most probable path for each sequence by using the Viterbi algorithm.
5. This results in an MSA of the sequences with the corresponding match, insert or delete states for each sequence.

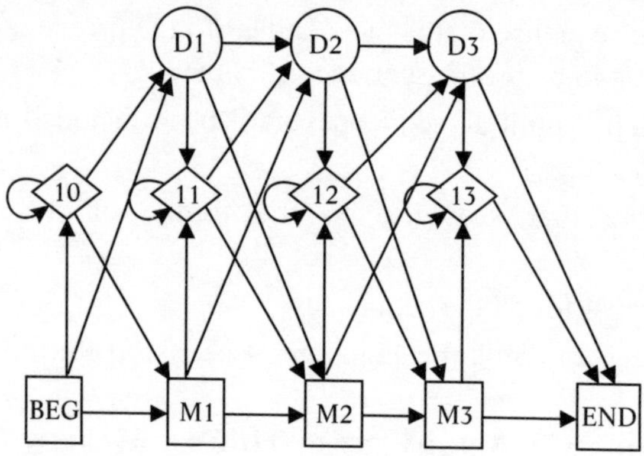

FIGURE 7.3 *Graphical representation of profile HMM, where match state is represented by M, I is insert state and delete state is represented by D.*

Match and insert states output an amino acid residue while the delete state outputs a gap. Self-loops on insert outputs multiple insertions.

Example 7.2

A multiple sequence alignment showing 4 sequences aligned with each other.

S1: P – F P G
S2: P M F P G
S3: P – F – G
S4: P – F P G

Path in HMM for generating sequence 1 and 4: In the above example, S1 and S4 take a path in HMM with all match states. These two sequences do not have either a delete or an insert state. A gap at the second position is caused by an insert in S2 and is the property of only S2 so that is not considered as a gap and we can read it directly as PFPG, as it is better to have one edit operation than many for one change.

Start → M1 → M2 → M3 → M4 → END

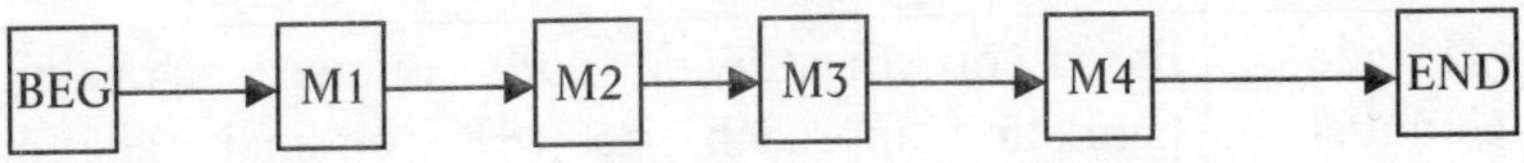

Path in HMM for generating sequence 2: In the S2 sequence at position two (but considered as column 1), character M is an insert as it is not found in all other sequences but only in S2. Hence it is considered as an insert, instead of a delete in all other sequences:

Start → M1 → I1 → M2 → M3 → M4 → END

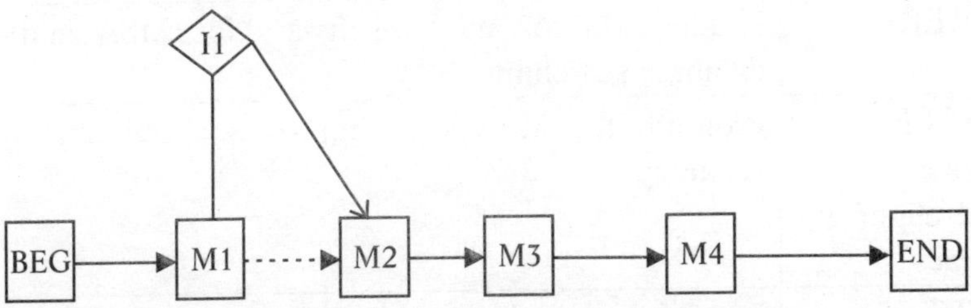

Path in HMM for generating sequence 3: In S3, column 4 has a delete as all other sequences except S3 have a character P there. So it is taken into account that character P was deleted from that position in S3:

Start → M1 → M2 → delete → M3 → END

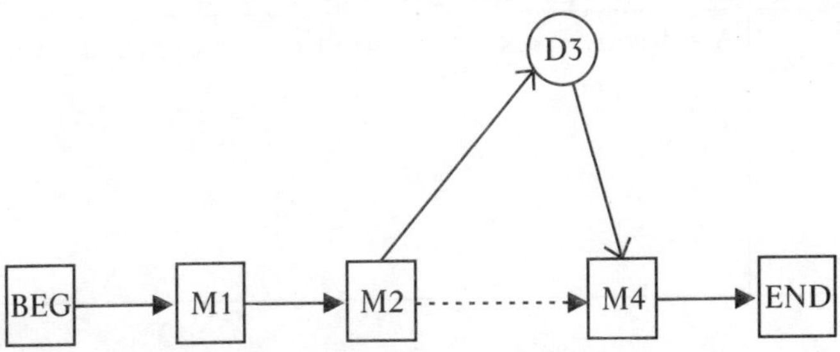

SOFTWARE TOOLS FOR MSA

ClustalW	General purpose multiple sequence alignment program.
Multalin	Multiple alignment with hierarchical clustering.
MSA	Multiple sequence alignment.
DIALIGN	Fragment-based alignment program for finding local similarity by MSA.
DCA (Divide-and-Conquer Multiple Sequence Alignment)	Based on the divide and conquer algorithm, a heuristic approach to SP optimal alignment. Multiple alignment by randomised iterative strategy (Gotoh's RIW/DNR methods).
T-Coffee	Compares all sequences two by two, producing global alignment and many local alignments and then combines all these alignments into a multiple sequence alignment.
HMMER	Hidden Markov model software for MSA and for database searching.
MUSCLE-improved speed/alignment accuracy	Program for MSA with improved speed alignment accuracy.
MAFFT	Fast Multiple Alignment Program for amino acid or nucleotide sequences.
STRAP	An interactive program for producing and analysing multiple sequence alignments.
MACAW	A software package for locating, analysing and editing blocks of localised sequence similarity and linking them into a composite alignment.
CINEMA (Colour INteractive Editor for Multiple Alignments)	A software package for multiple sequence alignment.

EMBOSS (European Molecular Biology Open Software Suit)	Has a list of sequence alignment programs.
Accelrys GCG 11.0	Formerly the GCG Wisconsin Package, it provides new and upgraded algorithms for sequence alignment.
EXOME™-Horizon Package	Commercial software package that has an integrated, multi-user work environment for bioinformatics research, data management and training.

Exercises

1. What is the sum of pairs rule?
2. Differentiate between the progressive and iterative algorithms.
3. What do the different colours given for amino acids mean in ClustalW?
4. Perform multiple sequence alignment using the ClustalW server for the numbers 6981148, 40646783 and 46854679, and report the most conserved portion.
5. Describe the Feng–Doolittle method and the Barton–Sternberg alignment.
6. Write in brief about the basic concept behind HMM for multiple sequence alignment. Draw the path for each sequence in HMM for the given MSA.

   S1= A B – C D E

   S2= A B G C D E

   S3= A B – C – E

6. Compare the alignment of the sequences from exercise 4 above, produced by ClustalW, T-Coffee and Multalin.
7. Colour the residues of different classes in different colours as used in ClustalW from EBI for exercise 4.

CHAPTER 8

Phylogenetic Analysis

LEARNING OUTCOME

- Define phylogenetic trees
- Explain the steps to construct an evolutionary tree
- Explain distance-based tree construction
- Explain unweighted paired group with arithmetic mean method
- Describe the Fitch and Margoliash method
- Explain the neighbour joining method
- Define clustering algorithms
- Define hierarchical clustering
- Define K-means clustering
- Define self-organising maps
- Explain character-based methods: MP, ML

The publication of Darwin's work, *On the Origin of Species,* in 1859 changed the way biological science was understood. After Darwin, it was realised that organisms could indeed change and all current forms of living things had arrived at that form by change and natural selection—the mechanism of evolution. This showed a conduit to the construction phylogenies, lists or diagrams that showed the evolutionary paths from populations of organisms in the course of many generations. Though an enormous amount of sequence data is available to scientists, sequence analysis or even pairwise alignments do not answer many questions. Queries regarding evolution and the relationship among various organisms are answered by multiple sequence alignment and phylogenetic analysis.

A **phylogenetic tree** is a graphical representation of the evolutionary relationship between taxonomic groups. **Phylogenetic systematics** is the name given for this biology-related field that reconstructs evolutionary history and studies the pattern of relationships among organisms. In phylogenetics, we use clues from evolutionary events to try to reconstruct evolutionary history.

Phylogeny is the study of patterns of similarity among living organisms.

Phylogenetics can be defined as the field of biology dealing with the characterisation of relationships among various live components on earth. This study starts with collecting data and analysing them, and extends to the interpretation of those results to give a new meaning.

Phylogenetic systematics deals with identifying and understanding the evolutionary relationships among extant (living) and extinct (dead) organisms on earth.

Cladistics is the study of the pathway of evolution.

Phenetics is the study of the relationships among a group of organisms on the basis of the degree of similarity between them (molecular, phenotypic and anatomical).

Topology is the branching pattern of the tree.

Molecular evolution involves the process of evolution at the scale of DNA, RNA and proteins. Mutations occurring in a sequence are the basis of molecular evolution. Mutations give information about the conserved and diverged sequence positions. Evolution is a continuous process without any clear boundaries. Variation within the gene pool results in the genetic variations required for evolution. Somatic mutations have no significant effect, but mutations in germ cells can be transferred from one generation to another.

Phylogenetic trees

The graphical representation of the evolutionary relationship of genes/taxa/ sequences is called a phylogenetic tree (Fig. 8.1). A phylogenetic tree is constructed by nodes representing the taxonomic unit, branches representing the relationship between the taxonomic units and roots representing the ancestor sequence.

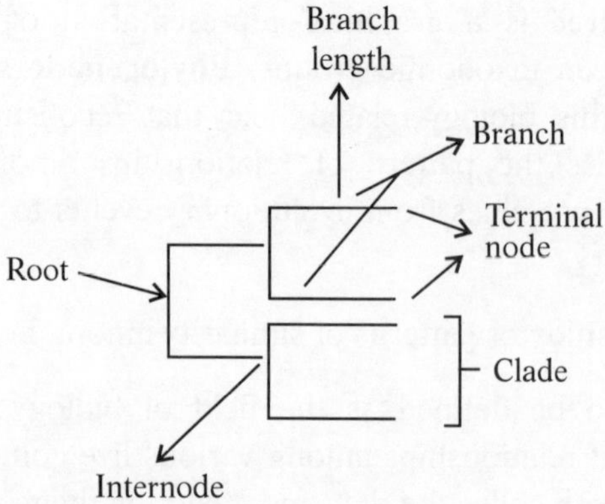

FIGURE 8.1 *A phylogenetic tree*

Rooted tree: It is a tree where a node is defined as the root (Fig. 8.2(a)). A rooted tree is based on the molecular clock and provides both the evolutionary path as well as the relationship among the species. The resultant tree is called a *cladogram*.

Unrooted tree: It specifies the relationship among species without identifying a common ancestor or evolutionary path (Fig. 8.2(b)). The resultant tree is called a *phenogram*.

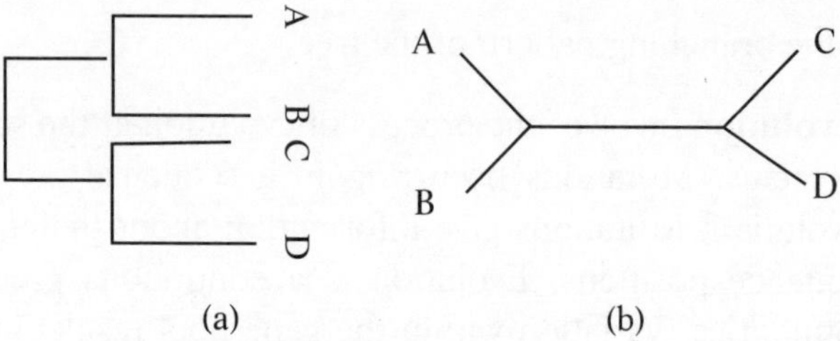

FIGURE 8.2 *(a) Rooted tree and (b) Unrooted tree with four leaves*

TABLE 8.1 *Possible number of rooted and unrooted trees for a number of OTUs*

Number of operational taxonomic units (OTUs)	Number of possible rooted trees	Number of possible unrooted trees
2	1	1
3	1	3
4	3	15
5	15	105
8	10395	$135{,}135 \times 10^6$

TERMINOLOGY RELATED TO PHYLOGENETIC TREES

Node is the taxonomic unit (existing species or an ancestor), also called operational taxonomic unit (OTU).

Distance scale represents the number of differences between the sequences.

Clade can be explained as a group of two or more taxonomic units coming from the same common ancestor.

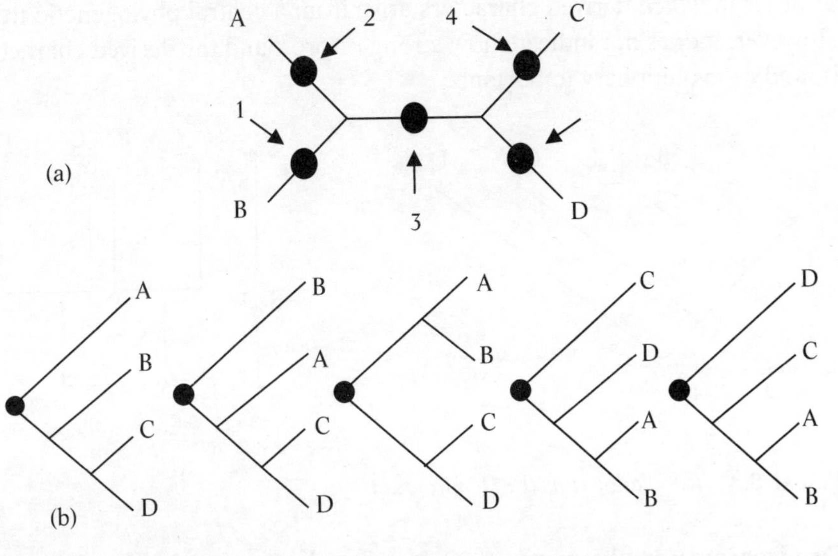

FIGURE 8.3 *(a) An unrooted tree with four taxan. The unrooted tree from (A) can produce five rooted trees(b)*

Branch describes the relationship between the trees in terms of descent and ancestory. A branch can be scaled (calibrated to represent the passage of time) or unscaled (branch length not proportional to the number of changes that have occurred).

Degree is the number of adjacent branches present in an internal node.

Branch length suggests the number of changes that have occurred in the branch.

Phenogram is classified as a tree-like representation expressing phenetic relationships.

Cladogram is defined as the topology of a rooted phylogenetic tree. Evolutionary trees represent clade, a group of organisms that includes an ancestor and all descendents of that ancestor. The simplest statement about an evolutionary relationship cladogram is a tree formed using cladistic methods. This type of tree only represents a branching pattern, that is, its branch lengths do not represent time. At the 'Y' junction, that is, at the new branch, novel characters of evolutionary origin are used to split one group from the rest. While constructing a cladogram, many hundreds of characters should be considered and sorted out with the help of a computer for the best fit between the branches. Cladograms emphasise the sequence or order in which derived characters arise from a central phylogenetic tree. However, it does not indicate how strong or profound the derived character is, and its evolutionary importance.

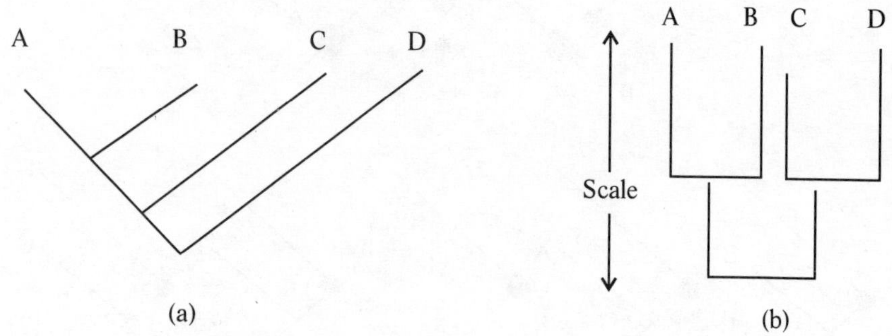

FIGURE 8.4 *(a) Cladogram; (b) Dendrogram*

Dendrogram (or ultrametric tree) is a broad term for the diagrammatic representation of a phylogenetic tree. It is an additive tree, a generalisation of ultrametric trees, where the tips of the trees are equidistant from the root of the tree. We can explain it as the number of mutations in the additive tree and is assumed to be proportional to the chronological distance of a node to the ancestor; it is also assumed that the mutations take place with the same rate in all paths. An additive tree contains information about branch lengths. The direction along the Y axis in additive trees represents the amount of change or time.

Phylogram is a phylogenetic tree that explicitly represents the number of mutations or character changes through its branch lengths.

Chronogram is a phylogenetic tree that explicitly represents evolutionary time through its branch lengths.

Polytomy is classified as a node with a degree greater than three (one ancestor having more than two immediate descendants). A fully resolved tree does not have polytomy.

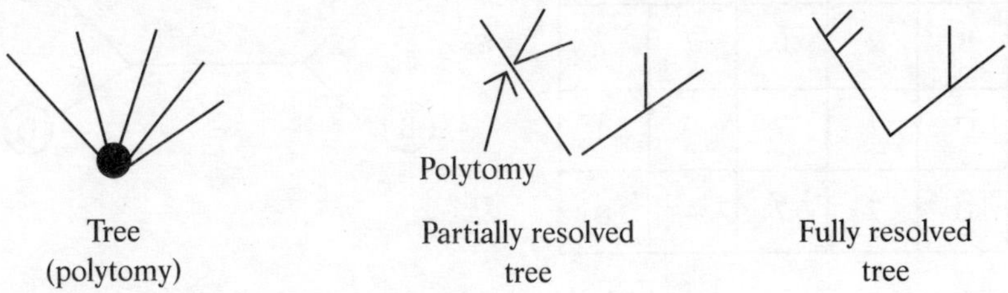

FIGURE 8.5 *Polytomy*

Polytomy can represent two different cases. First, it can represent the literal hypothesis that a common ancestral population split through speciation into multiple lineages. Such an internal node is referred to as a hard polytomy and it represents simultaneous divergence. On the other hand, the polytomy depicted in a cladogram can represent that the same ancestor may not have given rise to all daughter taxa, but is unclear which resolved pattern is the best hypothesis; such a node is referred to as a soft polytomy. Soft polytomy does not provide the actual order of divergence and is actually the more commonly intended meaning of polytomy.

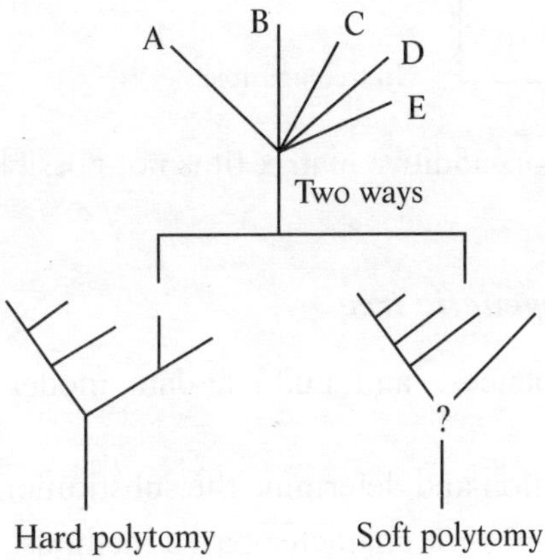

FIGURE 8.6 *Hard and soft polytomy. The figure representing hard polytomy can be represented in shorthand notation* {*[(A, B), C], (D, E)*}.

Additive and **non-additive matrix**: In an unrooted binary tree with n leaves, an additive matrix can generate a tree with a given matrix with properly defined weights, while a non-additive matrix cannot produce a tree.

	A	B	C	D
A	0	2	7	7
B	2	0	7	7
C	7	7	0	4
D	7	7	4	0

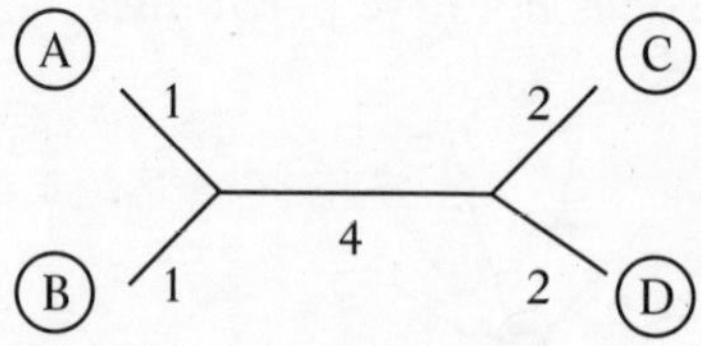

The above table shows additive matrix and the corresponding tree. Here the distance between each node in the tree corresponds to the matrix. For example, the distance between A and B is 1 + 1=2, between A and D is 1 + 4 + 2 = 7 and so on.

	A	B	C	D
A	0	4	6	6
B	4	0	2	2
C	6	2	0	3
D	6	2	3	0

No tree possible

The above table shows a non-additive matrix (it is not possible to make a tree with the given matrix).

Steps to construct a phylogenetic tree

1. Extract a dataset (sequences) and build a data model (alignment method).
2. Consider sequence variation and determine the substitution model.
3. Build the tree using distance- or character-based methods.
4. Construct the resultant tree by character evaluation.

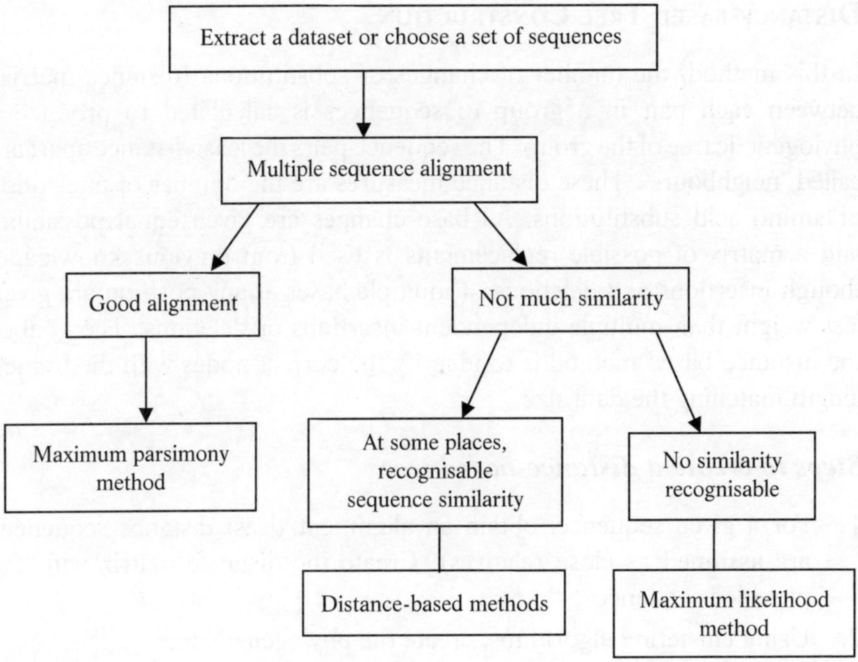

FIGURE 8.7 *A flow chart illustrating the steps for the selection of a method to build a tree depending on the type of dataset available.*

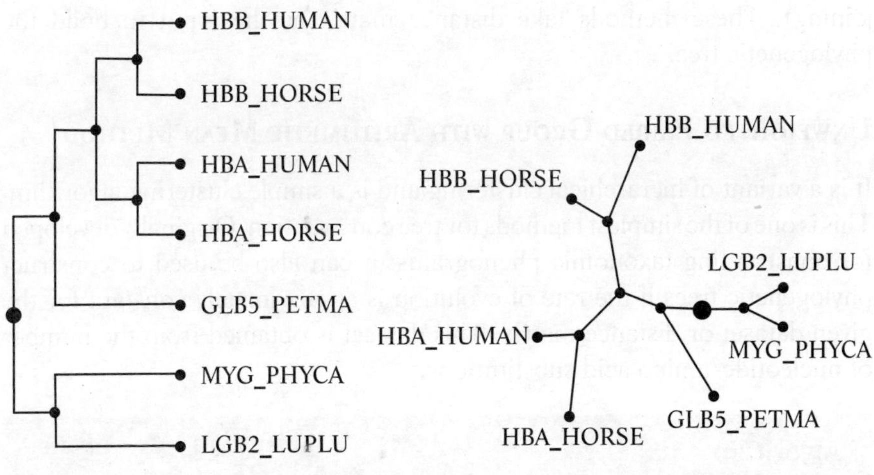

FIGURE 8.8 *A rooted and an unrooted phylogenetic tree using the Phylodraw drawing tool for seven different sequences.*

DISTANCE-BASED TREE CONSTRUCTION

In this method, the number of changes or substitutions (distance matrix) between each pair in a group of sequences is calculated to produce a phylogenetic tree of the group. The sequence pairs the least distance apart are called 'neighbours'. These distance measures are the number of nucleotide or amino acid substitutions. All base changes are given equal possibility and a matrix of possible replacements is used from previous knowledge, though insertions and deletions of multiple bases at any position are given less weight than multiple independent insertions or deletions. The goal of the distance-based method is to identify the correct nodes with the branch length matching the data size.

Steps to create a distance-based tree

1. For a given sequence, obtain an alignment (least distance sequences are assumed as close relatives). Create the distance matrix with the provided sequences.
2. Using clustering algorithms, create the phylogenetic tree.
3. To construct the tree, first join two least distant pairs of sequences followed by successive sequences with more distance, one by one.

The various distance-based methods include UPGMA (unweighted paired group with arithmetic mean), FM (Fitch–Margoliash) and NJ (neighbour joining). These methods take distance matrix as the input to build the phylogenetic tree.

UNWEIGHTED PAIRED GROUP WITH ARITHMETIC MEAN METHOD

It is a variant of hierarchical clustering and is a simple clustering algorithm. This is one of the simplest methods for tree construction. Originally developed for constructing taxonomic phenograms, it can also be used to construct phylogenetic trees if the rate of evolution is approximately constant for the given dataset or distance matrix. This dataset is obtained from the number of nucleotide/amino acid substitutions.

Algorithm

Consider a distance matrix of five different sequences or organisms (A, B, C, D and E). Choose the most closely related sequences. Here, A and B are only two mutations or least distant apart.

	A	B	C	D
B	2			
C	4	4		
D	8	6	6	
E	8	8	8	10

1. Cluster the sequences with the smallest distance, that is, the most similar. Here A and B are the least distance (2 substitutions) apart so they will be joined first. As it is a method that takes the arithmetic mean to give its branch distance, A and B individually will be: Dist (AB)/2 = 2/2 =1 or 1 substitution distance from the common node:

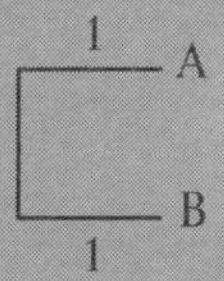

2. Now a new distance matrix will be created with AB as the composite node, and by obtaining the distances of AB with C, D and E. The second cycle of calculations will start with a new distance matrix:

Dist (AB, C) = Dist AC + Dist BC/2 = (4+ 4)/2= 4
Dist (AB, D) = Dist AD + Dist BD/2= (8+ 6)/2= 7
Dist (AB, E) = Dist AE + Dist BE/2 = (8+ 8)/2= 8

	AB	C	D
C	4		
D	7	6	
E	8	8	10

3. Now the least distance is 4 between AB and C, so they will get clustered. The distance from the internal node to AB and C will be: 4/2 = 2.

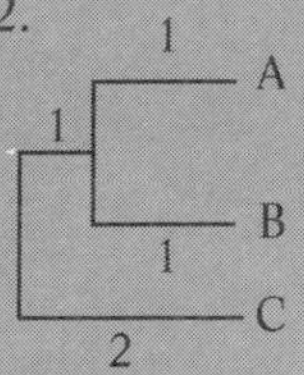

4. As in Step 3, the distances will be calculated and the new distance matrix will be created with ABC as the composite node and the distances of ABC with D and E.

	ABC	D
D	6.5	
E	8	10

5. Now ABC to D is clustered as they have the least distance. The distance from the internal node to ABC and D will be: 6.5/2 = 3.25.

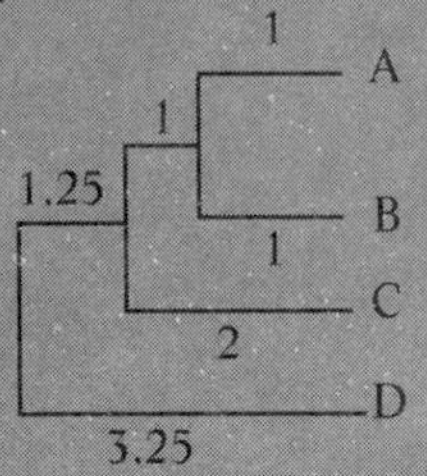

6. Distances will again be calculated and the new distance matrix will be created with ABCD as the composite node and the distance of ABCD with E.

	ABCD
E	9

7. The distance from the internal node to the composite unit ABCD and to E will be: 9/2= 4.5. This way the last unit can finally be clustered with the composite unit and the final phylogenetic tree is achieved.

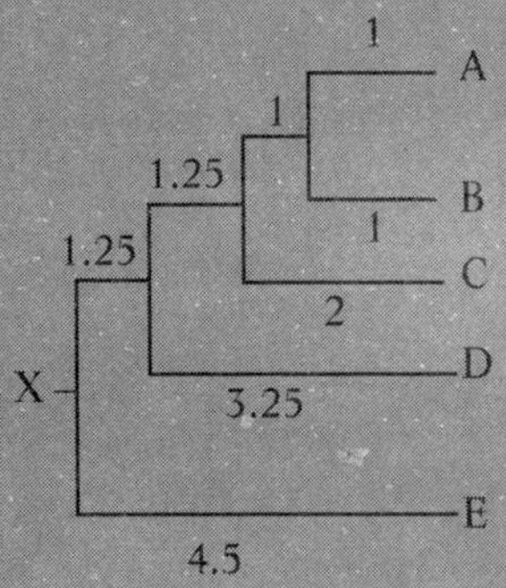

As UPGMA assumes equal rate of mutations along all the branches, the theoretical root (here X) will be equidistant from all the OTUs. Usually we do not get such an equal mutation rate at both the branches, so this algorithm gives only a basic understanding of the clustering algorithm and is not used in phylogenetic tree prediction software tools (usually FM and NJ are used).

FITCH AND MARGOLIASH METHOD

This method was first used by Fitch and Margoliash (FM) in 1987. In this algorithm, the sequences are combined in threes to calculate length of the branches and produce the phylogenetic tree. For short branches (less substitution), this algorithm gives fairly accurate trees. This algorithm can be best explained by taking two examples: one with just three sequences and another with more than three sequences.

Algorithm

Steps for three sequences:

1. First an unrooted tree is drawn with three branches from a common ancestor node from the given distance matrix.

	A	B
B	20	
C	40	45

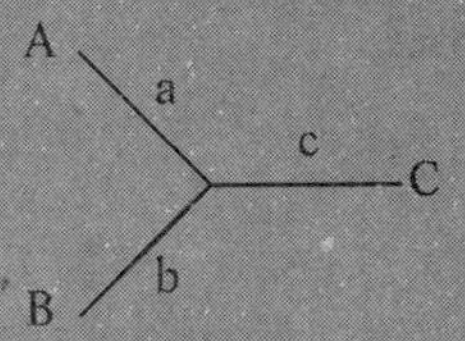

2. Calculate the length of the branches algebraically.

   Distance from A to B = a + b = 20 -------- Equation 1

   Distance from B to C = b + c = 45 -------- Equation 2

   Distance from C to A = c + a = 40 -------- Equation 3

3. Subtract Equation 3 from Equation 2 to get Equation 4

   b – a = 5 -------- Equation 4

4. Add Equation 1 and Equation 4 to get values for a, b and c individually.

   (a + b) + (b – a) = 20 + 5; b = 12.5

5. Substitute the value of b in Equation 1 and get a = 20 – 12.5 = 7.5

6. Substitute place the value of a in Equation 3 and get c = 40 – 7.5 = 37.5

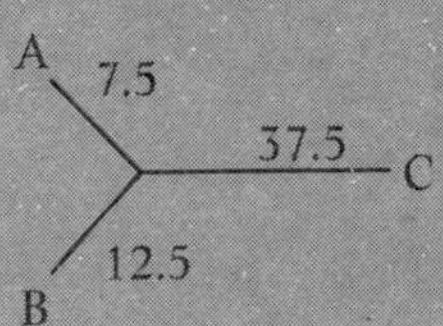

This method calculates the branch lengths of each sequence from its common ancestor. As in the given example, this length is different for each sequence; we can say that a, b and c diverge at different rates.

For more than three sequences, this algorithm works somewhat differently. Here the most closely related sequences are kept separate and all other sequences are combined as a single OTU to create a new distance matrix with three rows and three columns and this is then solved.

NEIGHBOUR JOINING METHOD

Here the initial tree is a star tree and the algorithm is a special case of star decomposition method. In the case of separate lineage, the rate of evolution varies. This method works well in such conditions and gives the most reliable phylogenetic tree.

Steps in creating a tree

1. Raw data is provided as a distance matrix, as in all distance-based methods.
2. The method of choosing the two sequences to decompose the star tree is different from the Fitch–Margoliash method. The sequences are paired based on the effect of the pairing on the sum of the branch lengths of the tree.
3. A modified matrix is created and the tree is constructed by linking the least distant pair of nodes in this modified matrix.
4. When two nodes are linked, their common ancestral node is added to the tree and the OTUs are removed from the tree.
5. A tree of reduced size is arrived at by decomposing two branches into one.
6. This process is repeated until two nodes remain, separated by a single branch.

This method is fast and is therefore used for large datasets. Using this method, the distance matrix of highly branched (multiple substitutions) trees can be calculated. It gives only one possible tree and is dependent on the model of evolution used.

Example 8.1

Create a new distance matrix from the provided distance matrix:

	A	B	C	D
B	4			
C	5	3		
D	6	7	5	
E	7	8	8	9

Step 1: Calculate the net divergence r (i) for each OTU from all other nodes:

r(A) = d(AB) + d(AC) + d(AD) + d(AE) = 4 + 5 + 6 + 7 = 22
r(B) = d(BA) + d(BC) + d(BD) + d(BE) = 4 + 3 + 7 + 8 = 22
r(C) = d(CA) + d(CB) + d(CD) + d(CE) = 5 + 3 + 5 + 8 = 21
r(D) = d(DA) + d(DB) + d(DC) + d(DE) = 6 + 7 + 5 + 9 = 27
r(E) = d(EA) + d(EB) + d(EC) + d(ED) = 7 + 8 + 8 + 9 = 32

Step 2: Calculate the new distance matrix (m) for each pair of nodes.

M(i, j) = d(i, j) – [r(i) + r(j)] / (N – 2)
m(AB) = d(AB) – [r(A) + r(B)]/(5 – 2) = 4 – 44/3 = –10.67
m(AC) = d(AC) – [r(A) + r(C)]/(5 – 2) = 5 – 14.33 = –9.33
m(AD) = d(AD) – [r(A) + r(D)]/(5 – 2) = –10.33
m(AE) = d(AE) – [r(A) + r(E)]/(5 – 2) = –11
m(BC) = d(BC) – [r(B) + r(C)]/(5 – 2) = –11.33
m(BD) = d(BD) – [r(B) + r(D)]/(5 – 2) = –9.33
m(BE) = d(BE) – [r(B) + r(E)]/(5 – 2) = –10
m(CD) = d(CD) – [r(C) + r(D)]/(5 – 2) = –11
m(CE) = d(CE) – [r(C) + r(E)]/(5 – 2) = –9.66
m(DE) = d(DE) – [r(D) + r(E)]/(5 – 2) = –10.66

The new distance matrix is

	A	B	C	D
B	–10.67			
C	–9.33	–11.33		
D	–10.33	–9.33	–11	
E	–11	–10	–9.66	–10.66

Step 3: Select the least value. Here it is –11.33. This is the distance between B and C. Hence, first cluster B and C.

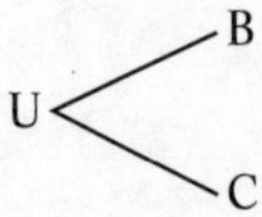

Now the distance from the new node 'U' to B and C is calculated.

d(BU) = d(BC)/ 2 + r(A) – r (B)/2(N – 2) = 3/2 + 22 – 22/ 2(3) = 1.5

d(CU) = d(BC) – d(BU) = 3 – 1.5 = 1.5

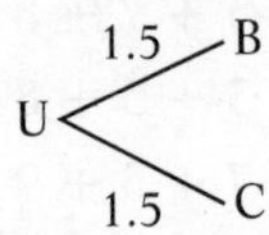

In UPGMA, the distance of both the nodes from the new node was equal (just half), but here another formula (given above) is used to obtain the distance of both the nodes from the new node and it may or may not be equal.

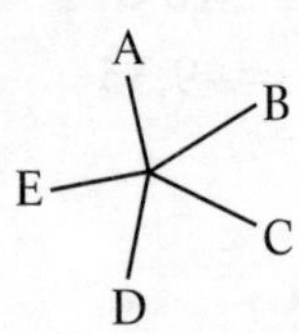

Initial star tree

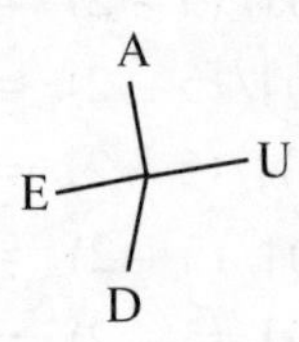

Tree after first clustering

Step 4: New distance matrix with BC as single node 'U':

d(UA) = d(BA) + d(CA) – d(BC)/2 = 4 + 5 – 3/2 = 7.5

d(UD) = d(BD) + d(CD) – d(BC)/2 = 4.5

d(UE) = d(BE) + d(CE) – d(BC)/2 = 6.5

	A	U	D
U	7.5		
D	6	4.5	
E	7	6.5	9

Step 1 to Step 3 will again be repeated, the least distant nodes will be searched and joined to the existing tree, and a new matrix is calculated as in

Step 4. This process is repeated till one branch with two nodes is achieved. The final tree will look like two nodes separated by a branch.

X ———— Z

Final NJ tree

CLUSTERING ALGORITHM

It is a distance-based method for gene prediction. Genes with the same type of expression patterns are grouped by using the clustering algorithm. The grouping has to satisfy the following conditions:

1. ***Homogeneity***: Only very similar genes are clustered in a group with each other. If d(i, j) is the distance between two genes i and j, then d(i, j) should be small.

2. ***Separation***: Different genes must go to separate clusters. Here d(i, j) should be large.

How closely the genes are related depends on two factors:

- The kind of distance measure used
- The principle used to construct the clusters

Clustering is implemented by using two approaches:

- ***Top-down/Divisive approach***: Starts with a single gene and gradually other related genes are joined to form one cluster—that is, it builds a hierarchy of clusters. Example: Hierarchical clustering
- ***Bottom-up agglomerative approach***: A big cluster with all the data is separated to create smaller clusters with related data: it breaks up a hierarchy of clusters. Example: K-means clustering.

Hierarchical clustering

This is a bottom-up approach. Hierarchical clustering is an agglomerative method which starts from a single gene and finally produces a single hierarchical tree. It is a multi-variant tool often used in phylogenetic and comparative genomics. There is an ordered way or hierarchy by which the variables are brought together.

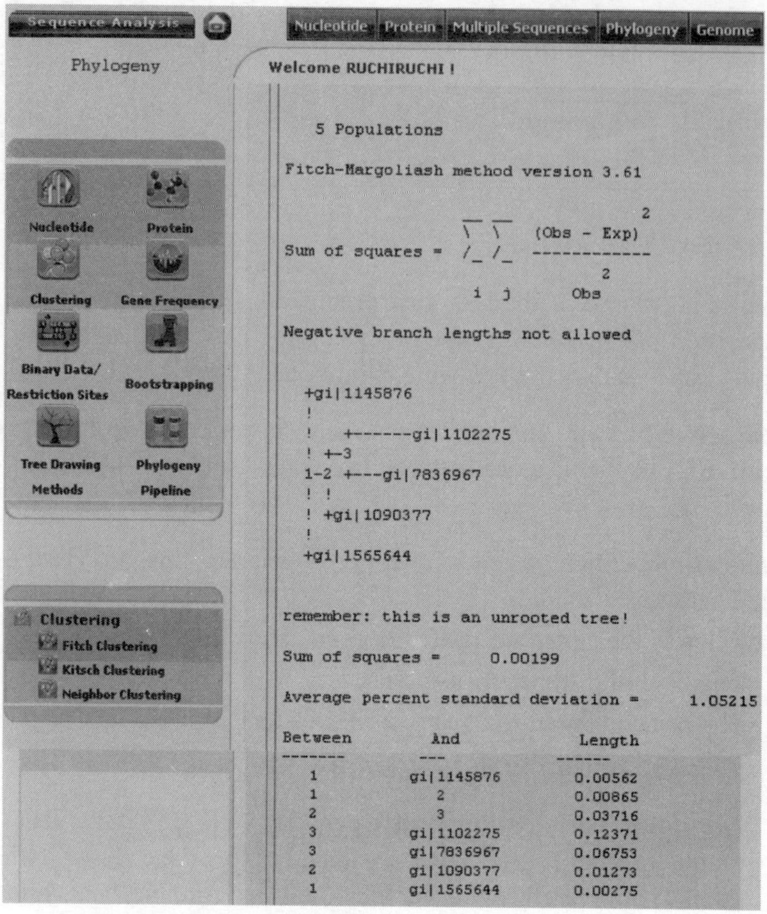

FIGURE 8.8 *A snapshot from the EXOME–Horizon software showing clustering using the Fitch–Margoliash algorithm*

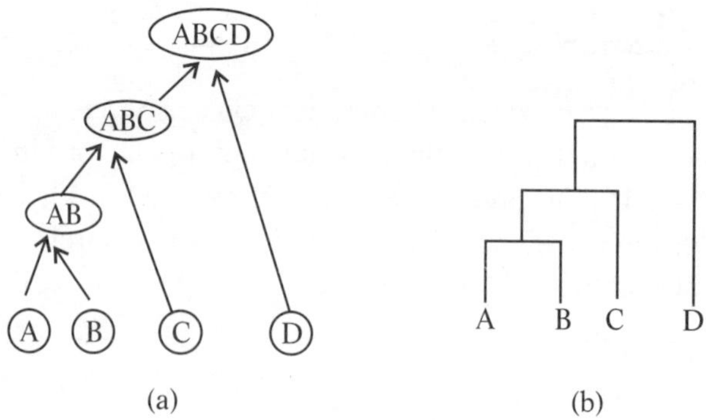

FIGURE 8.9 *(a) Hierarchical clustering approach for four genes and (b) the corresponding graph*

Algorithm

Input: A distance matrix d for n * n elements.

Output: A hierarchical tree where the edges of the trees are assigned lengths, and the distance between leaves (length of the path in the tree that connects two leaves) is the distance matrix.

1. Create a distance matrix with n * n elements with distance d.
2. Locate the nearest genes or cluster of genes in the matrix.
3. Join the nearest genes to form a new cluster.
4. Create a new distance matrix for the existing cluster with the new cluster.
5. Repeat these steps till all the genes are clustered. Simultaneously make a graph for the gene clustering as in Fig. 8.9(b).

There are three types of hierarchical clustering:

1. **Complete linkage clustering:** When a new gene is joined to an existing node and if that distance is the largest from the new cluster, we get the maximum separation of clusters using this method (Fig. 8.10(a)).
2. **Single linkage clustering:** When a new gene is joined to an existing node and if the distance is the smallest from the new cluster, minimum separation of clusters is achieved. This approach reveals the most similar clusters (Fig. 8.10(b)).
3. **Average linkage clustering:** If the distance of the new gene from the node is the average distance from the new gene to all other genes in that node, average linkage clustering is achieved. This approach gives a balance between separation of dissimilar clusters and union of similar clusters (Fig. 8.10(c)).

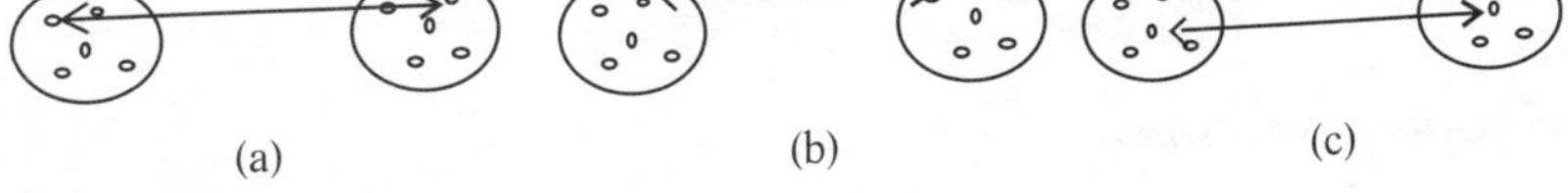

FIGURES 8.10 *Various hierarchical clustering of genes where genes joining the new node are at the largest distance (a) smallest distance (b) or average distance (c).*

K-means clustering

Similar to hierarchical clustering, in this type a number of clusters are prespecified by a prespecifier. This method is very sensitive to the value of k. The bootstrap method is used to validate the clusters.

1. Prespecify 'k', that is, the number of clusters.
2. Assign all data, that is, all genes or sequences to any one cluster.
3. Compute the average expression (for each cluster, termed as *centroid*).
4. Each gene is now compared with all the centroids and moved to the centroid with minimum distance.
5. Recompute centroids after the genes have changed their groups.
6. This movement of genes is performed till the genes are assigned to the clusters with the closest distance.

Self-organising maps (SOM)

It is based on the neural network and is a top-down approach, like K-means clustering.

1. The genes are assigned to a series of grid-like partitions.
2. The centroid for each partition is computed.
3. For each gene the reference centroid is selected (closest one) and then adjusted such that it is similar to the centroid of the genes assigned to that cluster iteratively.
4. The genes are now mapped to the nearest node.
5. Finally, all the genes are mapped to the closest node.

CHARACTER-BASED METHODS

These methods work on a score based on the number of evolutionary changes or substitutions that occur among various sequences. The score for a character-based tree construction comes from the number of mutations required to explain all the observed character sequences.

There are two major character-based methods: maximum parsimony and maximum likelihood.

Maximum parsimony

It is also called the minimum evolution method, as it infers a phylogenetic tree by minimising the total number of steps required to construct the tree. This method searches for the most parsimonious tree from all possible phylogenetic trees. Each tree here represents a hypothetical model of the evolutionary events. The most parsimonious tree among all possible models will be one that has the least number of evolutionary changes. This method holds good for only a small number of sequences, as for four sequences only three phylogenetic trees are possible. But for more number of sequences (say 20), the number of possible trees will increase dramatically.

Important characteristics

- Branch-and-bound method helps to find the optimal tree.
- It is a cladistic method on shared and derived characters.
- Searches for the most parsimonious tree from all possible phylogenetic trees.
- Only informative sites are analysed.
- It is used for quite similar sequences, as the most parsimonious tree with the least evolving changes is checked.
- It holds good for only a small number of sequences.
- It returns only tree topologies; branch lengths are not found.

Algorithm

Input: Multiple homologous sequences S_1, S_2... S_n.

Output: A phylogenetic tree.

1. Obtain somewhat similar sequences.
2. Construct the trees with all possible tree topologies.
3. Calculate the number of evolutionary changes at each branch point in the sequences.
4. Select informative sites, that is, sites that have the same sequence character in at least two taxa.
5. Only informative sites are analysed to produce the most parsimonious trees.
6. The most parsimonious trees will be the one with the least number of changes.

This algorithm finds the best possible tree. But the method is time-consuming and useful only for a small dataset (fewer number of sequences).

Programs using this method

Paup: In a Macintosh environment.

Phylip package: Here the score is based on the minimum number of mutations required to change a codon for the first amino acid into a codon for the second amino acid, and accepts only that path which actually changes the amino acid.

For nucleic acid sequences, the Phylip package has DNAPARS (treats gaps as a fifth nucleotide state) and DNACOMP (finds the tree with largest number of sites). For protein sequences, this program uses PROTPARS (does not count silent mutations as they are not considered to have any evolutionary significance).

A computer program package called MEGA (Molecular Evolutionary Genetics Analysis) for estimating evolutionary distances, reconstructing phylogenetic trees and computing basic statistical quantities from molecular data has been developed based on the maximum parsimony method. It computes statistical quantities like nucleotide and amino acid frequencies, transition/transversion biases, codon frequencies and the number of variable sites in specified segments in nucleotide and amino acid sequences to produce the result.

Advantages

- It is based on both shared and derived characters; so it performs better than distance methods for a small number of sequences.
- It outputs many 'parsimonious trees'.

Disadvantages

- It is a cladistic approach and only gives tree topologies; it does not give branch lengths as in the phonetic approach.
- It is slower than the distance-based methods, as it searches for all possible tree topologies for the given sequence.
- It uses only informative sites to give the score.
- It gives many parsimonious trees.
- It may give an incorrect prediction when there is more sequence variation.

Maximum likelihood

This algorithm uses all informative sites and evaluates all possible trees. It then checks the likelihood of each tree using an explicit model of evolution. This model produces the most probable tree for the given sequences. It is similar to the maximum parsimony method for returning the trees with the least number of changes as the most likely tree. This method can produce relevant results among more diverse sequences.

Important characteristics

1. It produces the most probable tree for the given sequences.
2. It uses all informative sites to produce the possible trees.

3. It uses an explicit model of evolution to produce the most probable tree.
4. It can produce a tree from even very diverse sequences.

Algorithm

1. Multiple sequences are taken as input.
2. A list of all possible trees is generated.
3. Characters from MSA are placed on the outer leaves of the trees. This gives the first tree.
4. All patterns of change at the inner nodes are found.
5. The probability of change at each branch is taken from probability tables (for the chosen evolutionary model).
6. The probability of each pattern of change is calculated (with all combinations of branch probabilities).
7. The probability total is found for the first tree at the first site.
8. This procedure is repeated for all other possible trees with sequences from the first site.
9. Now the second site in MSA is analysed using the same list of trees, and a second set of characters is placed on the outer branches.
10. The procedure is repeated for all the sites in MSA.
11. The tree with the highest probability at all the sites found will represent the most likely tree.

Advantages

- It gives branch lengths along with tree topologies.
- It produces a statistical estimate of significance for each branch.
- It uses all informative sites.
- It can produce a tree even when the sequences vary a lot.
- It evaluates different tree topologies.
- Compared to other tree building methods, the result is least affected by sampling errors.

Disadvantages

- It is very slow as it is a computationally intense method.
- It works well with a fewer number of sequences.
- The results differ, depending on the model of evolution used.

Programs using this method

The Phylip package includes DNAML (without molecular clock) and DNAMLK (with molecular clock) for nucleic acid sequence (DNA and RNA).

PROTML, a PASCAL program for inferring evolutionary trees from amino acid sequences, also uses this method.

Exercises

1. What are OTUs and what is a composite OTU?
2. What is branch length? What does it signify?
3. For a dataset of five numbers, calculate the number of possible rooted and unrooted trees.
4. What are the steps in molecular phylogenetic analysis?
5. Show that any binary tree with 'n' vertices has '2n – 3' edges.
6. What are the different ways of representing a phylogenetic tree?
7. Name some multiple sequence alignment tools and phylogenetic software.
8. Define cladistics and phenetics. Explain in detail a cladogram and a phenogram.
9. What is a phylogenetic tree? Discuss the concept of mutation with reference to phylogenetic studies. Write in brief about the different ways of representing a phylogenetic tree.
10. Explain distance-based algorithms for producing rooted and unrooted trees.
11. Explain the UPGMA method and solve the given problem using the UPGMA algorithm.

	A	B	C
B	4		
C	4	2	
D	8	8	6

Assignments

1. Take a protein sequence from a microbe and BLAST it. Choose a homologous sequence from the BLAST result and perform a pairwise sequence alignment using any dynamic programming software (for example, NeedleP for global alignment and WaterN for local alignment at EBI, LALIGN or ALION). Report similarity, identity and gap values for both local and global alignment. Now change various parameters and note the changes in alignment.

2. From the BLAST results, choose five sequences and perform a multiple sequence alignment using any MSA software tool (for example, ClustalW at EBI, T-Coffee or MultAlign). Now copy the distance from the result (after alignment starts with '('and ends with')') in a notepad and save it as a .nj extension. Download the Phylodraw software from the internet. In the software, click Open link from the Menu bar. Now open the .nj file. This will show the relationship among five sequences as a tree. Draw both rooted and unrooted trees.
3. Take the same sequences as in the second assignment and perform phylogenetic analysis using the Phylip package.

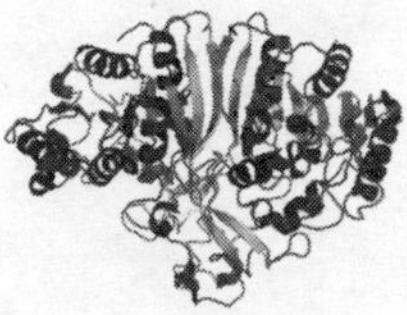

Section IV

OTHER BIOINFORMATICS ALGORITHMS

Chapter 9: Basic Algorithms
Chapter 10: Graph Algorithm
Chapter 11: String Algorithm

CHAPTER 9

Basic Algorithms

LEARNING OUTCOME

- Explain exhaustive search
- Explain branch and bound
    - o Travelling salesman problem
- Explain divide and conquer
    - o Merge sort
    - o Quick sort
- Explain the greedy algorithm

Exhaustive search

For discrete problems for which no efficient solution method is known, it might be necessary to test each possibility sequentially to determine if it is the solution. It is usually applied for optimisation problems. Here the algorithm checks for all possible ways to solve the problem and picks the optimum solution. Obviously, it is not an efficient algorithm, because, if the number of possible ways to solve a problem is very large, it might take a long time. It is used only for small problems.

For example, while preparing for an examination, one has a number of topics to learn. Each topic will fetch a certain score and each will take a fixed time to prepare. If the time to prepare for the exam is limited, then the topics that fetch the maximum can be selected for study in the limited time. To solve this problem using exhaustive search, the time needed and the score are calculated for all possible combinations. This is feasible for a small value of n but as the value of n increases, it becomes a massive task. As the search is guaranteed to generate all reachable states before it terminates with failure, this is said to be an exhaustive search. In bioinformatics, this method is used in whole-genome tandem repeats.

In the travelling salesman problem (discussed later in this chapter), if the number of cities is 3, the total number of possible routes is 3! or 6. Hence, exhaustive search is feasible. But as the number of cities increases, the total number of possible routes increases exponentially, as for 10 it will be 10! or 3628800. Exhaustive search is not a good solution here. Exhaustive search can use depth first search (DFS) or breadth first search (BFS). In BFS we first check all the siblings and then the children, while in depth first search (DFS) we first check the children and then the siblings.

Example 9.1

Consider a tree with root A. This indicates that A is the starting state for our search. It has two children B and C. B has two children D and E whereas C has only one child F.

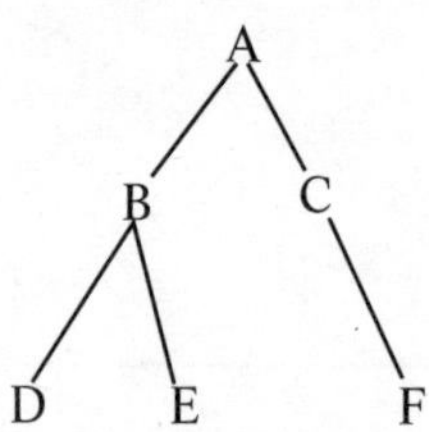

In BFS, when the goal node is 'E', start from the root A. Since it has no siblings, go to its child B, then sibling C, then children of B which are D and E. Since E is found, the search is over. The traversed nodes are darkened in the figure below.

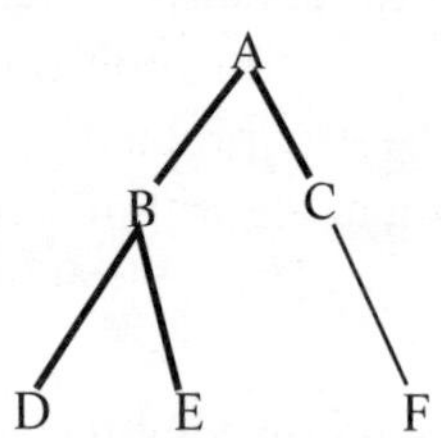

BFS: ABCDE

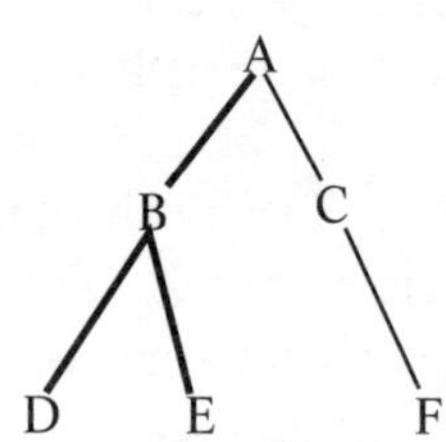

DFS: ABDE

The maximum depth of our tree is only three. In DFS, when this limit is reached and if the solution has not been found, the search backtracks to the previous level and explores any remaining alternatives at this level. If we use DFS, and our goal node is 'E', we start from root A, go to its child B, then the children of B, which are D and E. Now, since E is found, the search is over. The traversed paths are darkened in the figure.

Motif search: Exhaustive search is also used for motif finding, as described below.

Let the DNA string be an array of size m and the motif be another array of size n; m>n. We need to know whether the sequence motif is available in the DNA string, and at which position. The solution is simple in the exhaustive method.

Example 9.2

DNA string of 100 characters' length

Motif of length 20

First, search from 1 to 20 in the DNA string for the motif. If the motif does not match, then search from 2 to 21, then 3 to 22 and so on till 81 to 100 or the motif is found. So this algorithm searches for m – n + 1 in the worst case. In the given example, it is 100 – 20 + 1= 81 searches. If we succeed in finding the pattern in the third try, it means the motif is present from 3 to 22 characters in the given sequence. The steps can be explained by an algorithm.

Algorithm

Let K and Max be variables.

Step 1: (Initialisation) Set K = 1 , Max = m – n + 1

Step 2: Repeat Steps 3 to 5 while K < Max

Step 3: Repeat for i = 1 to n

If motif[i]!= DNASequence[K + i –1] then go to Step 5

(End of inner loop)

Step4 : Set Index = K & Exit (Success)

Step5 : Set K = K+1

(End of Step 2 outer loop)

Step 6 : Set Index = 0 (Failure)

Step 7 : Exit

Here Index is a variable. If, after execution, Index has a value i, this means the motif is present from i to (i + n – 1)th character locations.

Branch and bound algorithm

This is a general algorithmic method to find the optimal solution of various optimisation problems proposed to solve global optimisation models. All child nodes are generated before any live node can become the parent node. This is called branching. Then it is bound by finding the upper and lower bounds for the optimal solution within a feasible sub-region. It is slow and often leads to exponential time complexities in the worst case. We will see how the Branch and Bound algorithm is used to solve the travelling salesman problem.

TRAVELLING SALESMAN PROBLEM

A salesman regularly spends his time visiting n cities/nodes. On every tour, he visits each city only once, and ends up where he started. To minimise the distance travelled by him, the order of the places to visit can be computed. The travelling salesman problem aims to arrive at a plan that joins all the nodes by travelling a minimum distance. Here we assume that every tour starts and ends at the same node, say vertex one.

Travelling salesman problem (TSP) using branch and bound

Problem: Sort out the shortest path using the branch and bound algorithm from the given cost matrix of five nodes. These 5 nodes represent the 5 cities that the salesman has to visit. The numbers in a specific row or column represent the cost of travel from the row city to the column city. For example, at the third row, the first column number is 5; it means that the cost to travel from Chennai to Mumbai is 5 units. Here infinity (α) is used for nil distance (as zero is used for a different purpose). The TSP problem is an optimisation problem, as we are searching for the lowest cost to complete a simple tour.

	Mumbai(1)	Goa(2)	Chennai(3)	Delhi(4)	Mysore(5)
Mumbai(1)	α	12	30	14	10
Goa(2)	3	α	16	2	7
Chennai(3)	5	5	α	7	12
Delhi(4)	15	9	18	α	3
Mysore(5)	19	7	16	4	α

Step 1: Reduce the given cost matrix. First, reduce row 1; while reducing, it should have at least one zero in each row and each column. The smallest entry in row 1 is the cheapest way to leave to Mumbai.

A row is reduced by taking the smallest entry in the row, 10 in this case, and subtracting it from every other entry in the row. The smallest entry, 10 in this case, is also added to the lower bound.

$$\begin{vmatrix} \alpha & 2 & 20 & 4 & 0 \\ 1 & \alpha & 14 & 0 & 5 \\ 0 & 0 & \alpha & 2 & 7 \\ 12 & 6 & 15 & \alpha & 0 \\ 15 & 3 & 12 & 0 & \alpha \end{vmatrix} \text{ reduced by } \begin{matrix} (-10) \\ (-2) \\ (-5) \\ (-3) \\ (-4) \end{matrix}$$

There is no zero in column three so again reduce the matrix. The remaining columns are already reduced as they have a zero.

$$\begin{vmatrix} \alpha & 2 & 20 & 4 & 0 \\ 1 & \alpha & 14 & 0 & 5 \\ 0 & 0 & \alpha & 2 & 7 \\ 12 & 6 & 15 & \alpha & 0 \\ 15 & 3 & 12 & 0 & \alpha \end{vmatrix} \Rightarrow \begin{vmatrix} \alpha & 2 & 8 & 4 & 0 \\ 1 & \alpha & 2 & 0 & 5 \\ 0 & 0 & \alpha & 2 & 7 \\ 12 & 6 & 3 & \alpha & 0 \\ 15 & 3 & 0 & 0 & \alpha \end{vmatrix} = A$$

$$(-12)$$

Total reduced cost $C_R = 10 + 2 + 5 + 3 + 4 + 12 = 36$ (sum of smallest entries in each row and column which is used to reduce the matrix).

Step 2: Obtain the reduced cost matrix for each node. Assume that the salesman is at Mumbai, i.e., node 1, and he has to visit Goa (node 2), Chennai (node 3), Delhi (node 4) and Mysore (node 5) in such a way that the travelling cost is minimum.

Path 1:2 will give the cost of travel from node 1 to node 2: To compute that, set all entries of row 1 and column 2 (of matrix A) to α and set a_{ji} to α, i.e., a_{21} to α.

$$\begin{vmatrix} \alpha & \alpha & \alpha & \alpha & \alpha \\ \alpha & \alpha & 2 & 0 & 5 \\ 0 & \alpha & \alpha & 2 & 7 \\ 12 & \alpha & 3 & \alpha & 0 \\ 15 & \alpha & 0 & 0 & \alpha \end{vmatrix}$$

All rows and all columns have a zero so there is no need to reduce them again.

Cost for a path i:j is => $C_P = C_R + A_{ij} + r\,A_{ij}$

where C_P = Cost of path 1:2

C_R = Total reduced cost

A_{ij} = Matrix value at (ij) position

r = Reduced matrix (if any) at this particular step

Cost of path 1:2

$(C_P) = (C_R) + A_{12} + r\,[A_{12}] = 36 + 2 + 0 = 38$

Path 1:3 will give the cost of travel from node 1 to node 3. To compute this, set all entries of the first row and the third column of matrix A to α and set a_{ji} to α, i.e., a_{31} to α.

As the first column does not have a zero, reduce it again by subtracting 1 from it.

$$\begin{vmatrix} \alpha & \alpha & \alpha & \alpha & \alpha \\ 1 & \alpha & \alpha & 0 & 5 \\ \alpha & 0 & \alpha & 2 & 7 \\ 12 & 16 & \alpha & \alpha & 0 \\ 15 & 3 & \alpha & 0 & \alpha \end{vmatrix} \Rightarrow \begin{vmatrix} \alpha & \alpha & \alpha & \alpha & \alpha \\ 0 & \alpha & \alpha & 0 & 5 \\ \alpha & 0 & \alpha & 2 & 7 \\ 11 & 16 & \alpha & \alpha & 0 \\ 14 & 3 & \alpha & 0 & \alpha \end{vmatrix}$$

(–1)

Cost of path 1:3

$C_P = C_R + A_{ij} + r\,[A_{ij}] = 36 + 8 + 1 = 45$

Path 1:4 will give the cost of travel from node 1 to node 4. To compute. set all entries of the first row and the fourth column of matrix A to α, i.e., (1,4) to α, and set a_{ji} to α, i.e., a_{41} to α. As there is no zero in the second row, reduce it again by subtracting 1 from it.

$$\begin{vmatrix} \alpha & \alpha & \alpha & \alpha & \alpha \\ 1 & \alpha & 2 & \alpha & 5 \\ 0 & 0 & \alpha & \alpha & 7 \\ \alpha & 16 & 3 & \alpha & 0 \\ 15 & 3 & 0 & \alpha & \alpha \end{vmatrix} \begin{matrix} (-1) \\ \Rightarrow \end{matrix} \begin{vmatrix} \alpha & \alpha & \alpha & \alpha & \alpha \\ 0 & \alpha & 2 & \alpha & 5 \\ 0 & 0 & \alpha & \alpha & 7 \\ \alpha & 16 & 3 & \alpha & 0 \\ 15 & 3 & 0 & \alpha & \alpha \end{vmatrix}$$

Cost of path 1:4 is

$(C_P) = (C_R) + A_{ij} + r\,[A_{ij}] = 36 + 4 + 1 = 41$

Path 1:5 will give the cost of travel from node 1 to node 5. To compute, set all entries of the first row and the fifth column of matrix A to α, i.e., (1,5) to α and set a_{ji} to α, i.e., a_{51} to α.

$$\begin{vmatrix} \alpha & \alpha & \alpha & \alpha & \alpha \\ 1 & \alpha & 2 & 0 & \alpha \\ 0 & 0 & \alpha & 2 & \alpha \\ 12 & 16 & 3 & \alpha & \alpha \\ \alpha & 3 & 0 & 0 & \alpha \end{vmatrix} \underset{(-3)}{\Rightarrow} \begin{vmatrix} \alpha & \alpha & \alpha & \alpha & \alpha \\ 1 & \alpha & 2 & 0 & \alpha \\ 0 & 0 & \alpha & 2 & \alpha \\ 9 & 13 & 0 & \alpha & \alpha \\ \alpha & 3 & 0 & 0 & \alpha \end{vmatrix}$$

As there is no zero in the fourth row, reduce it again by subtracting 3 from it.

Cost of path 1:5 is

$C_P = C_R + A_{ij} + r\,[A_{ij}] = 36 + 0 + 3 = 39$

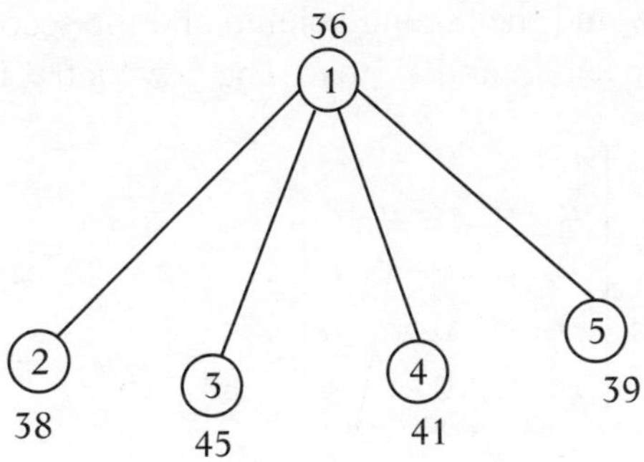

Path 1 → 2 has minimum cost. So the salesman will travel from 1 to 2 first, i.e., Mumbai to Goa.

After 1 to 2 we have to choose between paths (1,2,3), (1,2,4) and (1,2,5). Again we compute the cost of these paths to obtain the minimum cost.

Path (1:2:3) Set the first row and the second column and the second row and the third column to α. Also set a_{21} and a_{31} to α. The new matrix is:

$$\begin{vmatrix} \alpha & \alpha & \alpha & \alpha & \alpha \\ \alpha & \alpha & \alpha & \alpha & \alpha \\ \alpha & \alpha & \alpha & 2 & 7 \\ 12 & \alpha & \alpha & \alpha & 0 \\ 15 & \alpha & \alpha & 0 & \alpha \end{vmatrix} \begin{matrix} \\ \\ (-2) \\ \Rightarrow \\ \\ \end{matrix} \begin{vmatrix} \alpha & \alpha & \alpha & \alpha & \alpha \\ \alpha & \alpha & \alpha & \alpha & \alpha \\ \alpha & \alpha & \alpha & 0 & 5 \\ 0 & \alpha & \alpha & \alpha & 0 \\ 3 & \alpha & \alpha & 0 & \alpha \end{vmatrix}$$

(−12)

As there is no zero in the third row and the first column, reduce it again.

Cost of path (1:2: 3) is

$C_P = C_R + A_{ij} + r\,[A_{ij}] = 36 + 2 + 2 + 12 + 2 = 54$

(Here A_{ij} is $A_{12} + A_{13}$.)

Path (1:2:4) Set the first row and the second column, and the second row and the fourth column to α. Also set a_{21} and a_{41} to α. The new matrix is:

$$\begin{vmatrix} \alpha & \alpha & \alpha & \alpha & \alpha \\ \alpha & \alpha & \alpha & \alpha & \alpha \\ 0 & \alpha & \alpha & \alpha & 7 \\ \alpha & \alpha & 3 & \alpha & 0 \\ 15 & \alpha & 0 & \alpha & \alpha \end{vmatrix}$$

Cost of path (1:2: 4) is

$$C_P = C_R + A_{ij} + r\,[A_{ij}] = 36 + 2 + 0 + 0 = 38$$

Path (1:2:5) Set the first row and the second column and the second row and the fifth column to α. Also set a_{21} and a_{51} to α. The new matrix is:

$$\begin{vmatrix} \alpha & \alpha & \alpha & \alpha & \alpha \\ \alpha & \alpha & \alpha & \alpha & \alpha \\ 0 & \alpha & \alpha & 2 & \alpha \\ 12 & \alpha & 3 & \alpha & \alpha \\ \alpha & \alpha & 0 & 0 & \alpha \end{vmatrix} \underset{(-3)}{\Rightarrow} \begin{vmatrix} \alpha & \alpha & \alpha & \alpha & \alpha \\ \alpha & \alpha & \alpha & \alpha & \alpha \\ 0 & \alpha & \alpha & 2 & \alpha \\ 9 & \alpha & 0 & \alpha & \alpha \\ \alpha & \alpha & 0 & 0 & \alpha \end{vmatrix}$$

Cost of path (1:2:5) is

$$C_P = C_R + A_{ij} + r\,[A_{ij}] = 36 + 2 + 5 + 3 = 46$$

Cost of (1:2:4) is minimum. Now the minimum cost path is 1 to 2 to 4 and the new tree is given below.

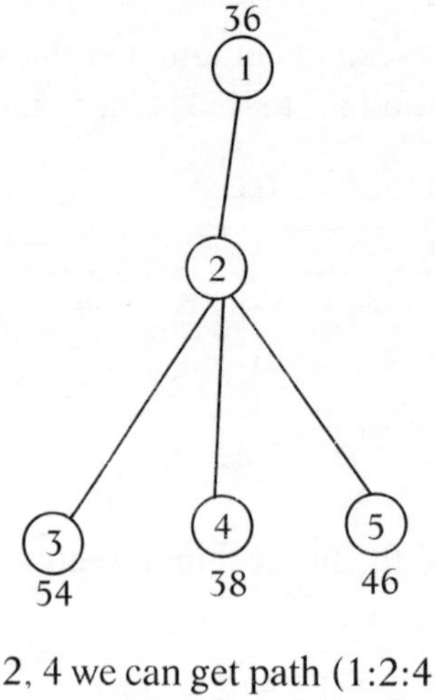

From 1, 2, 4 we can get path (1:2:4:3) node 9 and path (1:2:4:6) node 10. Again in the same way, we can compute these paths to obtain the minimum cost.

Path (1:2:4:3) to node 9: Set the first row and the second column, second row and the fourth column and the fourth row and the third column to α. Also set a_{21}, a_{41} and a_{31} to α. The new matrix is

$$\begin{vmatrix} \alpha & \alpha & \alpha & \alpha & \alpha \\ \alpha & \alpha & \alpha & \alpha & \alpha \\ \alpha & \alpha & \alpha & \alpha & \alpha \\ \alpha & \alpha & \alpha & \alpha & 7 \\ \alpha & \alpha & \alpha & \alpha & \alpha \\ 15 & \alpha & \alpha & \alpha & \alpha \end{vmatrix} \begin{matrix} \\ \\ \Rightarrow \\ (-7) \\ \\ \\ \end{matrix} \begin{vmatrix} \alpha & \alpha & \alpha & \alpha & \alpha \\ \alpha & \alpha & \alpha & \alpha & \alpha \\ \alpha & \alpha & \alpha & \alpha & \alpha \\ \alpha & \alpha & \alpha & \alpha & 0 \\ \alpha & \alpha & \alpha & \alpha & \alpha \\ 0 & \alpha & \alpha & \alpha & \alpha \end{vmatrix}$$

(-15)

As there is no zero in the third row and the first column, reduce it again. Cost of path (1:2:4:3) is

$$C_P = C_R + A_{ij} + r\,[A_{ij}] = 36 + 2 + 0 + 3 + 15 + 7 = 63$$

(Here A_{ij} is A_{12}, A_{14} and A_{13})

Path (1:2:4:5) to node 10: Set the first row and the second column, the second row and the fourth column and the fourth row and the fifth column to α. Also set a_{21}, a_{41} and a_{51} to α. The new matrix is:

$$\begin{vmatrix} \alpha & \alpha & \alpha & \alpha & \alpha \\ \alpha & \alpha & \alpha & \alpha & \alpha \\ 0 & \alpha & \alpha & \alpha & \alpha \\ \alpha & \alpha & \alpha & \alpha & \alpha \\ \alpha & \alpha & 0 & \alpha & \alpha \end{vmatrix}$$

Cost for path (1:2:4:5) is

$$C_P = C_R + A_{ij} + r\,[A_{ij}] = 36 + 2 + 0+0+0 = 38$$

Cost for (1:2:4:5) is minimum.

Now the minimum cost path is 1 to 2 to 4 to 5 and the new tree is given beside.

The minimum cost matrix is 38, so the minimum cost path is 1 to 2 to 4 to 5.

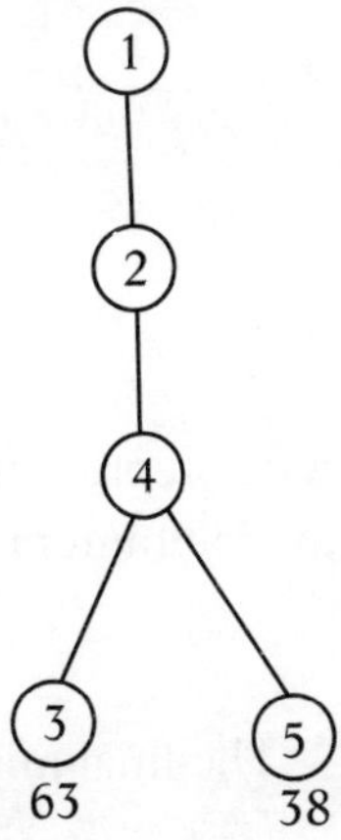

Path 1:2:4:5:3 to node 11: Set the first row and the second column, the second row and the fourth column, the fourth row and the fifth column and the fifth row and the third column to α. Also set a_{21} a_{41}, a_{51} and a_{31} to α. The new matrix is:

$$\begin{vmatrix} \alpha & \alpha & \alpha & \alpha & \alpha \\ \alpha & \alpha & \alpha & \alpha & \alpha \\ \alpha & \alpha & \alpha & \alpha & \alpha \\ \alpha & \alpha & \alpha & \alpha & \alpha \\ \alpha & \alpha & \alpha & \alpha & \alpha \\ \alpha & \alpha & \alpha & \alpha & \alpha \end{vmatrix}$$

Cost of path (1:2:4:5:3) is

$$C_P = C_R + A_{ij} + r\,[A_{ij}] = 36 + 2 + 0 + 0 + 0 = 38$$

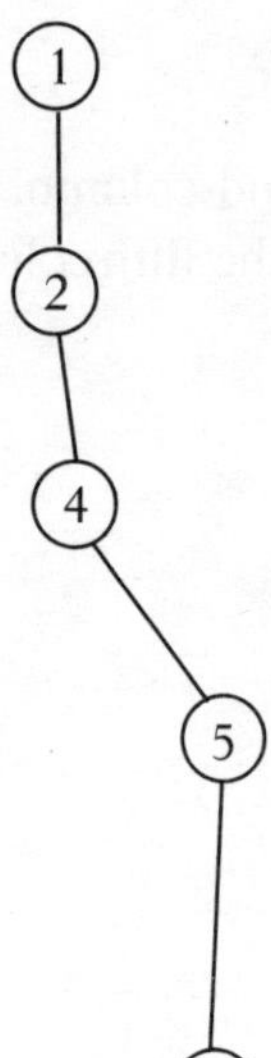

A tree representation of the final minimum cost path

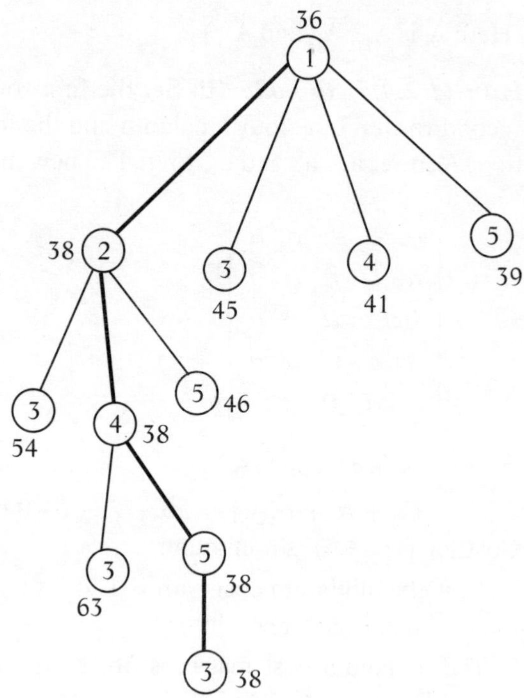

Complete tree showing final path

The final minimum cost path is: 1 → 2 → 4 → 5 → 3

Divide and conquer algorithm

If a problem is computationally difficult to solve, it can be divided into small subproblems and solved to obtain the solution to the bigger problem by using the divide and conquer algorithm. This is a top-down approach in solving a problem because we start from the main problem (top) and move towards the subproblems (down). The divide and conquer algorithm splits or divides a difficult problem into smaller subproblems which are solved independently and recursively. The solutions of the subproblems are combined to get the answer for the whole problem. Divide and conquer algorithms are implemented as recursive procedures. Slow recursion is a disadvantage here and is also not suitable for smaller problems where iterative algorithms are faster. Dividing the problem into subproblems so that the subproblems can be combined to obtain the answer for the problem is the main complexity in designing this algorithm. This algorithm is solved in two phases: a divide phase and a conquer phase.

Divide phase: Divides the bigger problem into smaller subproblems.

Conquer phase: Combines the solutions to the subproblems to obtain the solution of the bigger problem. The steps are given below:

1. The problem can be broken down into two related subproblems mostly from the centre.
2. This is again divided into two related subproblems. This step is repeated until the subproblems are small enough to be solved directly.
3. Combine the solutions of the subproblem two at a time.
4. Finally all the solutions are joined together to provide the solution to the original problem.

The merge sort and quick sort algorithms follow the divide and conquer technique.

MERGE SORT

In this method, the list of solutions of the subproblems is divided into sublists. These sublists are sorted and merged together thereafter to obtain the final sorted list.

Example 9.3

Sort numbers 8, 5, 2 and 14 using the divide and conquer phase algorithm:

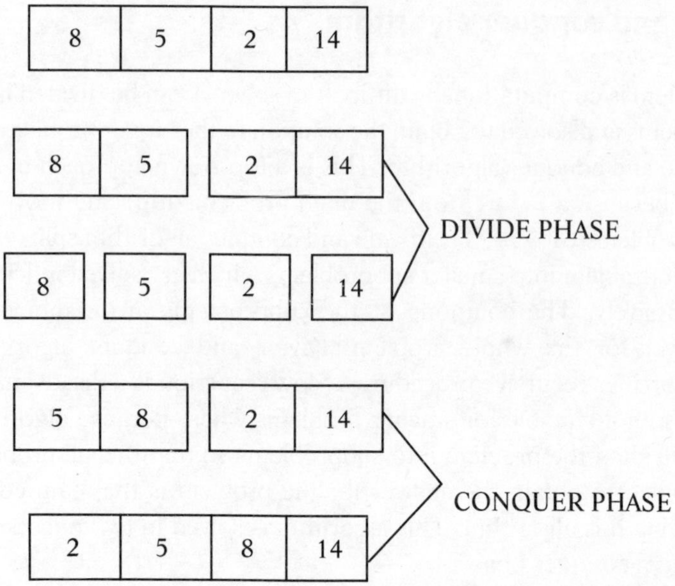

QUICK SORT

Quick sort operates much faster than other sorting techniques; it does not require a large amount of extra memory space, whereas merge sort does require additional arrays (an extra array is required during the conquer phase to store the subarrays).

The broad strategy followed by quick sorting is to divide an array into parts and recursively sort each in the same manner as merge sort. In this method, the following steps are used:

1. Divide the list of input elements into two parts by choosing a partition element called ***pivot***. (Usually the first element of the list is taken as the partition element or pivot element.)
2. One list contains elements that are less than or equal to the partitioning element and the other list has elements that are greater.
3. These two lists are recursively partitioned in the same way till the list is sorted properly.

Example 9.4

Sort the numbers 2, 7, 8, 1, 10, 5 using the quick sort method.

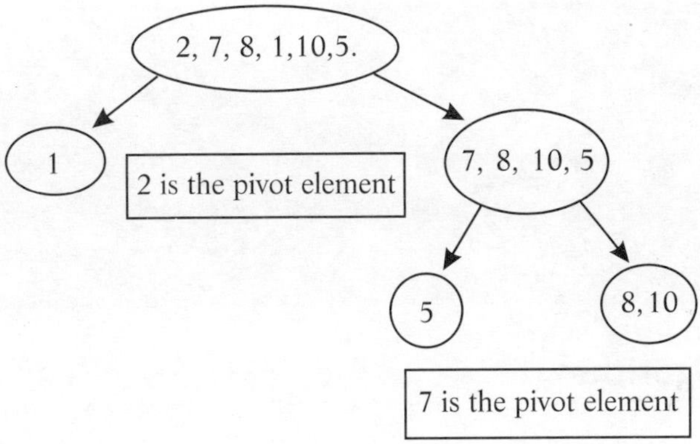

Final output: 1, 2, 5, 7, 8, 10

Algorithm

```
Quicksort(a[0.....n-1],x,y) //x:lower bound and y:upper bound.
//a[0...n–1]-input array to be sorted.

{
if(x < y)
{
z = divide(a,x,y); //divide list into two segments.
Quicksort(a,x,z); //for sorting segment 1.
Quicksort(a,z+1,y); // for sorting segment 2.
}
}
Algorithm: (divide)

divide(a[x...y],x,y)
{
pivot=a[x];
i=x;
j=y+1;
while true do
{
repeat i=i +1 until a[i]>pivot;
repeat j=j –1 until a[j]<pivot;
```

```
if i < j
swap(a[i],a[j]);
else
return j;
}
}
```

Greedy algorithm

Greedy algorithms are simple and straightforward algorithms for solving optimisation problems. They check for a locally optimum solution at each step to produce the globally optimal solution. But they fail to produce the globally optimal solution most of the time as they do not use all the data provided.

As the name suggests, these algorithms are greedy or shortsighted in their approach. They take their decisions on the basis of the information in hand without thinking about the consequences. For any step, the greedy algorithm makes the decision that seems most optimum at that stage and never reconsiders that decision even if it proves to be a wrong move afterwards. Therefore, in certain cases, an incorrect algorithm is given. This algorithm can be explained with Dijkstra's algorithm, explained in *Chapter 10*.

Reversal sort: The genome rearrangement problem can be solved using the reversal sort algorithm—a greedy procedure. In a broad sense the human genome and the mouse genome are similar but are arranged in different orders. If we cut the mouse genome into 300 large fragments (synteny blocks) and compare them with human genome synteny blocks, we can see that there is a shuffling of synteny blocks which produces a completely different genome. This rearrangement in the genome sequence order is the result of evolutionary events; reversal is an important event in rearrangement. At the chromosome level, mutations can occur because of inversion or translocation. In the list below, a reversal sort produces:

1,2,3,4,5,6,7,8,9 → 1,2,3,7,6,5,4,8,9.

Many break points and other events have taken place to change the mouse genome into the human genome. This simple reversal can be sorted using the greedy algorithm, as in the following example.

6512347 → 1562347 → 1256347 → 1235647 → 1234567

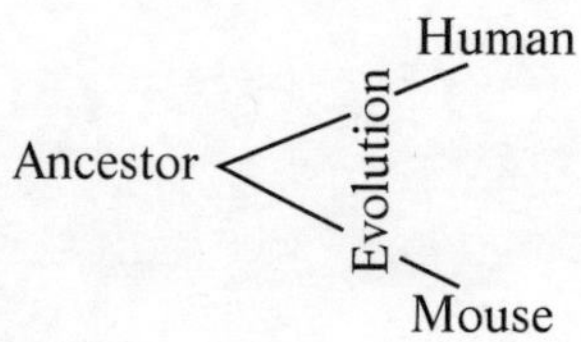

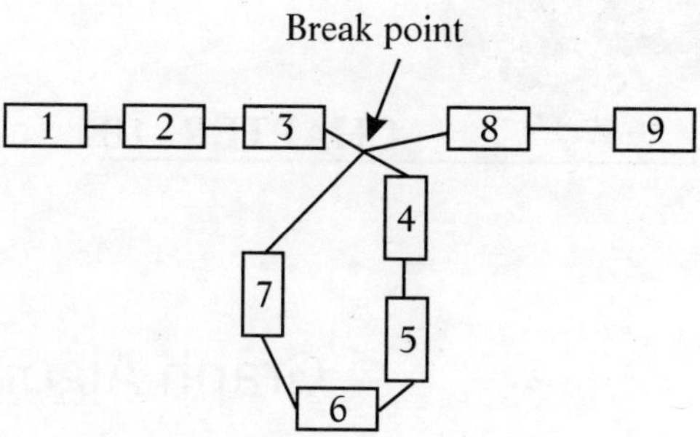

Reversal sort requires four steps to sort the given list.

Exercises

1. Explain the exhaustive search method in brief.
2. What is the branch and bound method? Explain with an example.
3. Sort the string 7, 25, 14, 3, 8, 5, 33, 28 using the divide and conquer algorithm. Which is the more time-efficient algorithm? Specify the running time taken by both the algorithms (Hint: big O notation).
4. Write an algorithm for the quick sort technique.
5. Explain the greedy algorithm with an example.

CHAPTER 10

Graph Algorithm

LEARNING OUTCOME

- List the different types of graphs
- Explain graph theory
  - o Konigsberg bridge problem
  - o Eulerian cycle problem
- Explain the shortest path problem
  - o Dikjistra's algorithm
- Describe the minimum cost spanning tree
  - o Prim's algorithm
  - o Kruskal's algorithm

Graph

Graphs provide visual information about content. A graph is made of nodes called ***vertices*** and internodes called ***edges***. A graph can also be defined as a diagram of points connected by lines.

A graph is denoted by G; an edge by E and the vertex by V.

For example:

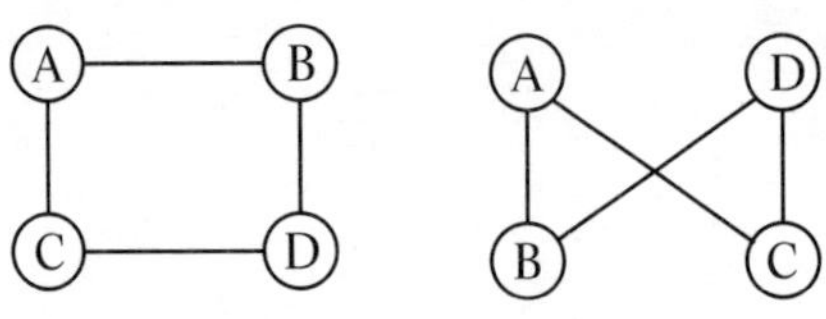

In the above graph, G= VE

where V= {A, B, C, D} and
E= {(A, B), (B, D), (D, C), (C, A)}

On the basis of how V and E are connected with each other, a graph is represented differently even for the same number of V and E.

Degree: The number of edges incident to a vertex is called the degree of a node. In the graph given above, each vertex has a degree of two.

Pendent vertex: A vertex with degree one is called a pendant vertex.

Different types of graphs

Type of graph	Example	Description
Connected graphs	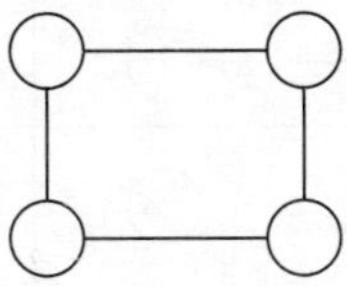	For any two vertices V_i and V_j, there is a path from V_i to V_j.
Disconnected graphs	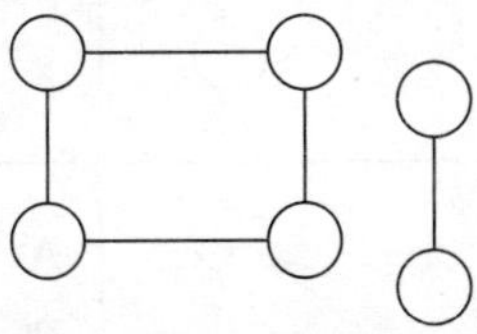	There exists at least one pair of vertices, V_i and V_j, such that a path does not exist between V_i and V_j.
Complete graphs	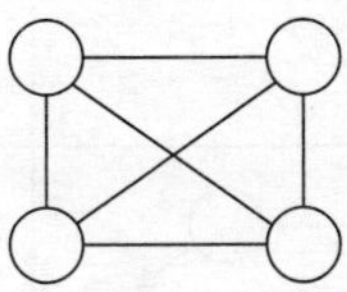	For any two vertices V_i and V_j, there is an edge from V_i to V_j.
Incomplete graphs	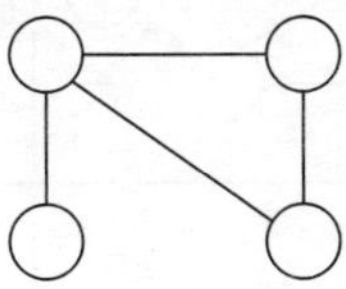	There exists at least one pair of vertices, V_i and V_j, such that an edge does not exist between V_i and V_j.
Cyclic graph	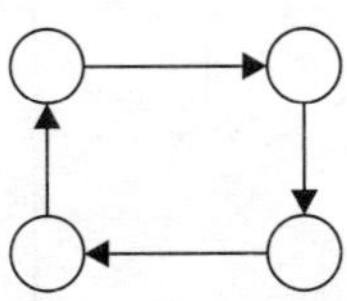	Cycle is a path which starts and ends in the same vertex. A graph which contains a cycle is a cyclic graph.

Contd...

Type of graph	Example	Description
Acyclic graph	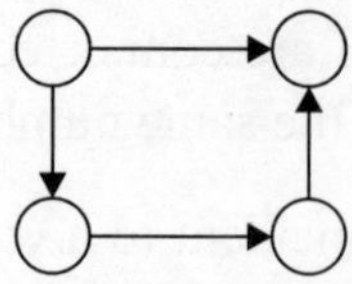	A graph containing no cycles.
Weighted graph	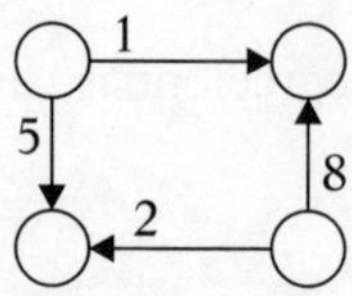	All the defined edges are given certain weights or values.
Unweighted graph	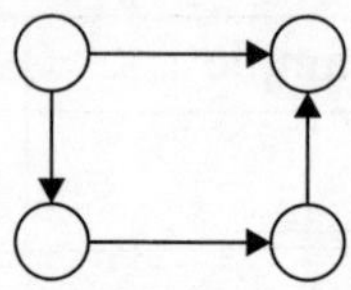	The defined edges are not given certain weights or values.
Null graph	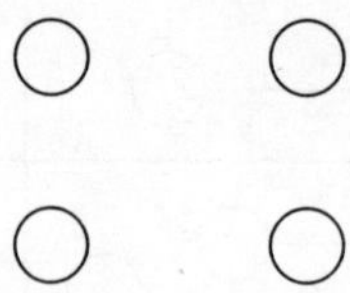	An empty graph with no vertices and edges, or a graph with no edges.
Pendant graph	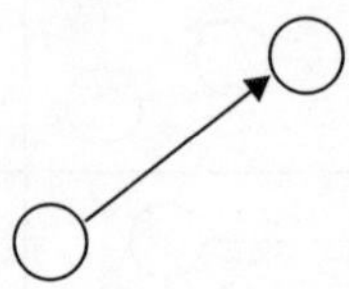	A graph containing a pendant vertex.
Hamilton graph	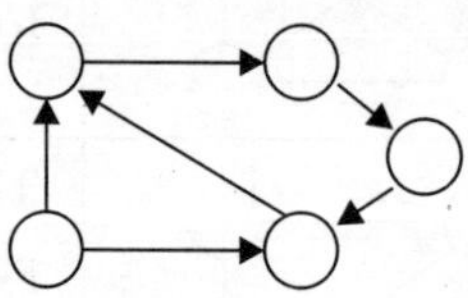	A graph which has a Hamiltonian path. A Hamiltonian path visits each vertex exactly once.
Euler graph	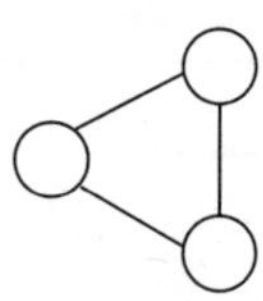	A graph which has a Euler path. A Euler path is one which contains all the edges in a graph exactly once.

Graph theory

Graph theory was pioneered by Euler in the eighteenth century when he solved the Konigsberg bridge problem. This field was later enriched by contributions from GR Kirchhoff, A Cayley, AK Mobius and WR Hamilton.

Konigsberg bridge problem

Konigsberg was a city located on the banks of the Pregel river. It comprised 4 small islands connected by 7 bridges (Fig. 10.1).

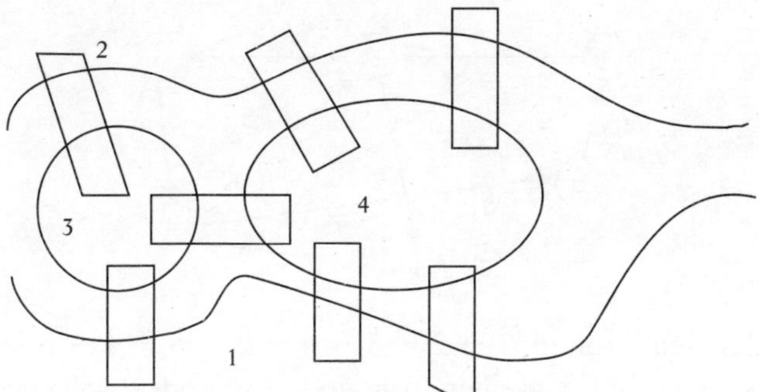

FIGURE 10.1 *Diagrammatic representation of a city with 4 islands and 7 bridges*

The problem is to visit all the islands by crossing all the bridges exactly once and returning to the starting point.

The situation can be represented graphically as follows.

Input: A city map with 4 islands and 7 bridges. The vertices represent the 4 land masses or islands and the arcs represent the 7 bridges.

Output: A city tour, with same starting and end points, visiting all bridges exactly once (Fig. 10.2).

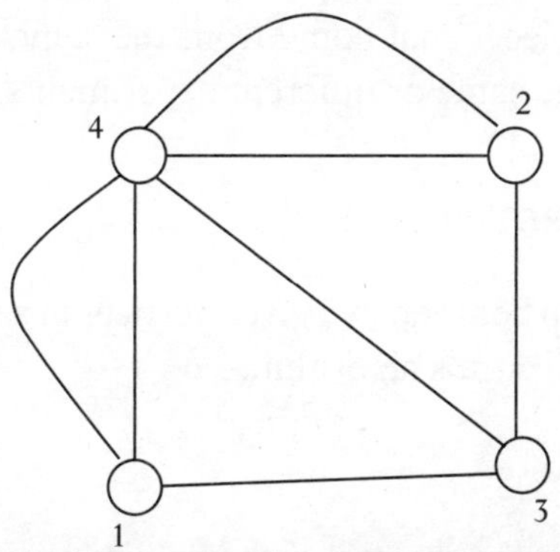

FIGURE 10.2 *Graph representation of a city with 4 islands and 7 bridges*

Now the problem is reduced to that of finding a Eulerian cycle in a graph.

Euler's cycle problem

Find a cycle in a graph that visits every edge exactly once.

Input: G as a graph.

Output: A cycle in a graph visiting all edges exactly once (Euler's path).

For example, consider the following graph.

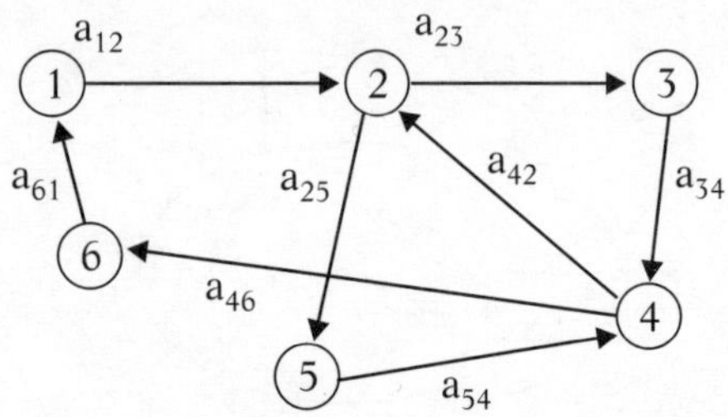

The Euler's path found: 1 → 2 → 3 → 4 → 2 → 5 → 4 → 6 → 1. That is, if we start from node 1, travelling from node 1 to node 2 will cover edge a_{12}, then from node 2 to node 3 will cover edge a_{23}, and so on. It is clear that all nodes have been travelled only once and all nodes are covered.

Euler proved that such a path cannot exist in the Konigsberg bridge problem.

Using graph theory we can solve various bioinformatics problems. We can obtain sequences in pieces from experiments and use these algorithms to finalise the string. Different graph algorithms are used to find out the evolutionary history among different gene or protein sequences, where distance is computed to understand how much and where the sequences are similar. Searching for the smallest path finds the basic sequence string from different sequence pieces that come from the same string with many common portions from the same or different experiments.

Shortest path problem

Searching the shortest path between two given vertices in a weighted directed graph can be solved by Dijkstra's algorithm.

Dijkstra's algorithm

This algorithm searches for the shortest path in a directed graph. The locally optimum solution is checked at each step to produce the globally optimal solution. It starts from a selected vertex and, at each step, it searches for the shortest path to some vertices in the graph and continues till the shortest paths to all vertices are found. The searched vertices at each step can be referred to as final vertices.

Algorithm

Input: A weighted directed graph G.

Output: The shortest path in graph G from the start vertex to the end vertex.

At first, the source vertex is marked with distance zero and all the other vertices are marked as infinity (as the path length is not known).

1. Now we have only one final vertex, which is the source vertex. The vertices that are connected to the source vertex are checked and marked with the distance of the connecting edge.
2. Out of these vertices the one with the minimum weight can be added to the final vertices. The vertices that are connected to the final vertices are considered and the distance is computed.
3. If the new distance is smaller than the marked distance, it is replaced with the smaller one.

This process is continued until all the vertices are added to the final vertices.

Example 10.1

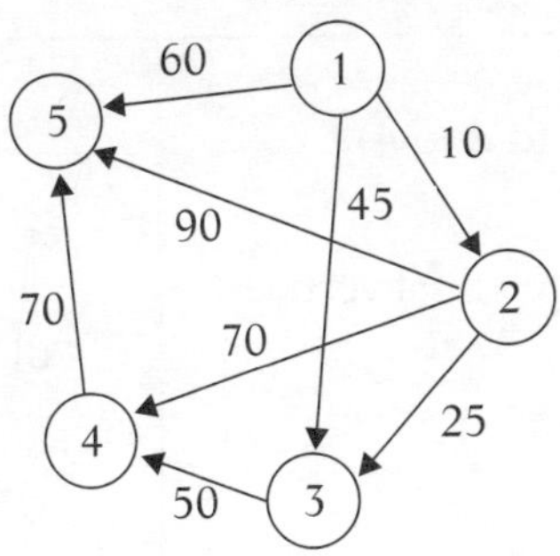

A weighted graph with 5 vertices and 8 edges is given. Compute the single source shortest path for the given graph from any vertex.

A weighted cyclic graph for single source shortest path problem

Step 1: Select any vertex (here 1 is selected) as the source vertex. The distance from the source vertex to all other vertices is computed as follows:

1 → 2 = 10
1 → 3 = 45
1 → 4 = ∞ (as no direct path from one)
1 → 5 = 60
Vertex 2 is added to the final vertices.

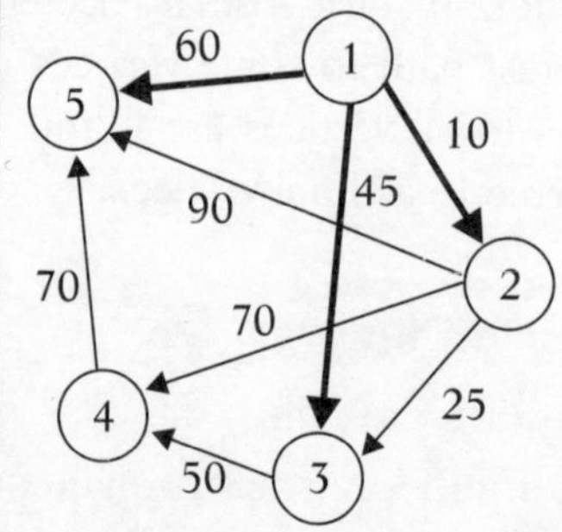

Step 2: Now we have two vertices to search for the shortest path for vertices 3, 4 and 5.

1 → 3 = 35 (path 1 to 2 to 3)
1 → 4 = 80 (path 1 to 2 to 4)
1 → 5 = 60
Vertex 3 is added to the final vertices.

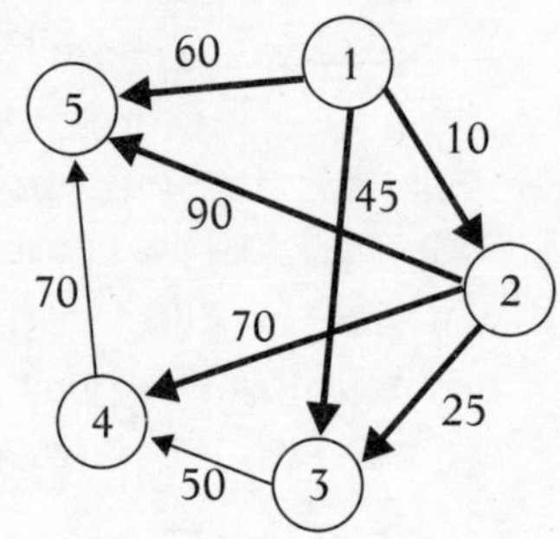

Step 3: Search the least distances for vertices 4 and 5.

1 → 4 = 80 (path 1 to 2 to 4)
1 → 5 = 60
Vertex 5 is added to the final vertices.

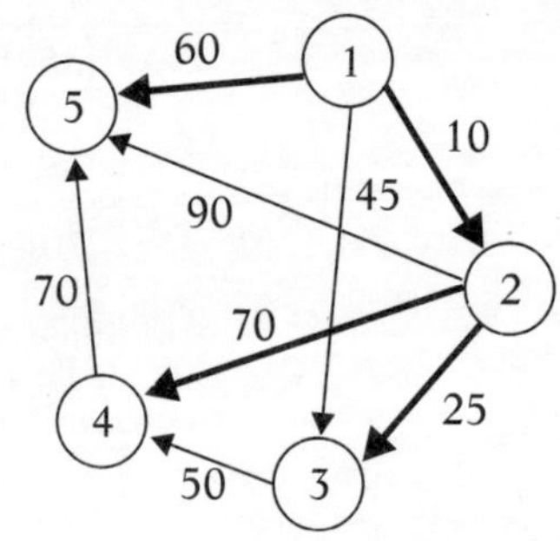

Step 4: The least distance for vertex 4 is searched.

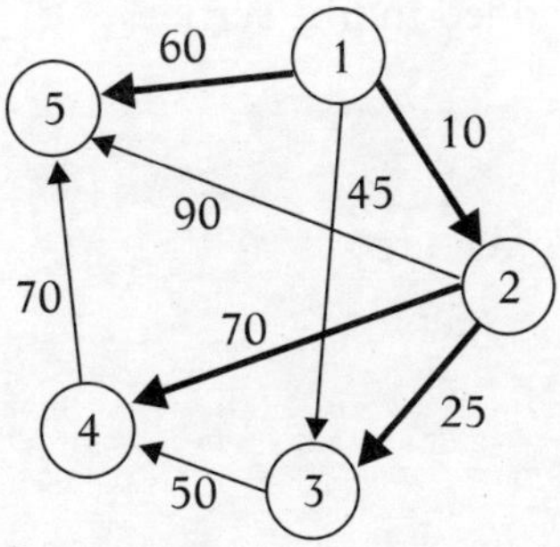

This can be explained with the table below. S. No. 1 gives the starting position, that is, all the distances from node 1. In 2, we start the process, so the distance will be the same as in 1 and we show the minimum in bold. (1,2) shows the minimum is 2, so we move from 1 to 2. Any distance that is not direct in the graph, for example, 1 to 4, is given the value infinity. Similarly the other lines can be explained.

SNo.	Final Vertices	Destination vertex (with least distance in that row)	Distance with 2	Distance with 3	Distance with 4	Distance with 5
1	1	Start	10	45	∞	60
2	(1, 2)	2	**10**	45	∞	60
3	(1, 2, 3)	3	10	**35**	80	60
4	(1, 2, 3, 5)	5	10	35	80	**60**
5	(1, 2, 3, 5, 4)		10	35	**80**	60

Minimum cost spanning tree

A minimum cost spanning tree is a special case of the path-finding problem for a connected, undirected, weighted graph. A spanning tree of a graph G with n vertices is a tree of G with all n vertices. The cost of a spanning tree is the sum of all costs on its edges. A minimum cost spanning tree is a spanning tree with minimum cost (finding a path with minimum distance).

Prim's and Kruskal's algorithms can be used to find a minimum cost spanning tree.

Prim's algorithm

Prim's algorithm follows the greedy method and is very similar to Dijkstra's algorithm. This also starts with a selected vertex and goes on to construct a spanning tree by selecting the minimum weighted edge. At each stage the selected vertices can be added to tree vertices.

Algorithm

Input: A connected, undirected, weighted graph.

Output: Minimum cost spanning the

- Before the first step, the tree vertices consist of the selected vertex only.
- At each step, we consider all the edges originating from the tree vertices which do not form a cycle with the partially constructed spanning tree.
- Out of these edges, the one with the minimum weight is added to the tree and the corresponding vertex is added to the tree vertices.
- This is continued till all the vertices are added to the tree vertices.

Example 10.2

Find the minimum cost spanning for the following graph

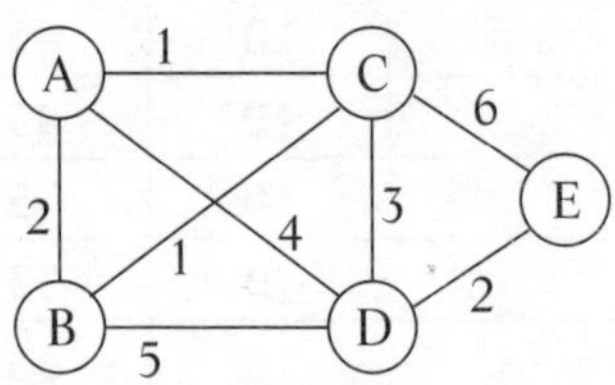

Select A as the starting vertex. The minimum cost spanning tree is constructed as follows:

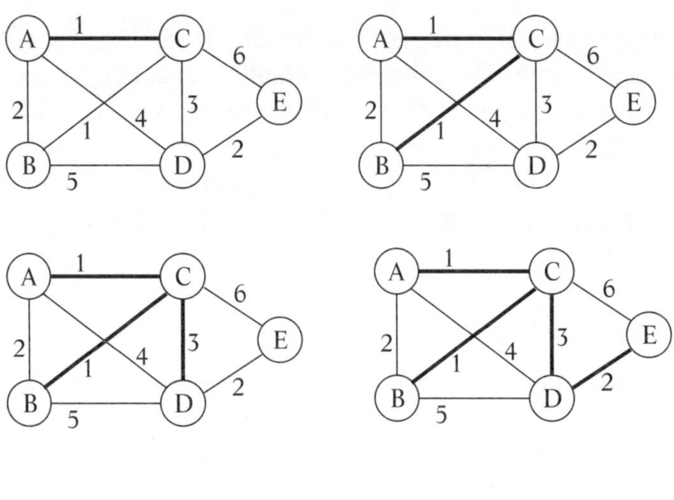

Kruskal's algorithm

Kruskal's algorithm also follows the greedy approach. Here, the edge with the minimum weight is first added to the tree. Then in each consecutive step, the edge with the next smallest weight is added to the minimum cost spanning tree, making sure that the edge being added does not form a cycle.

Algorithm

For example 10.2, the following steps can be written

Step 1: There are two edges with minimum weight 1: AC and BC. Select any one edge arbitrarily. In the given example, AC is selected and added to the minimum cost spanning tree.

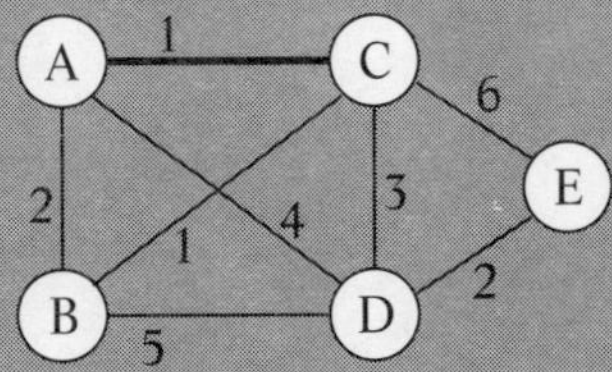

Step 2: Out of the remaining vertices, the one with the minimum weight is BC and it does not form a cycle with the spanning tree. So BC is added to the minimum cost spanning tree.

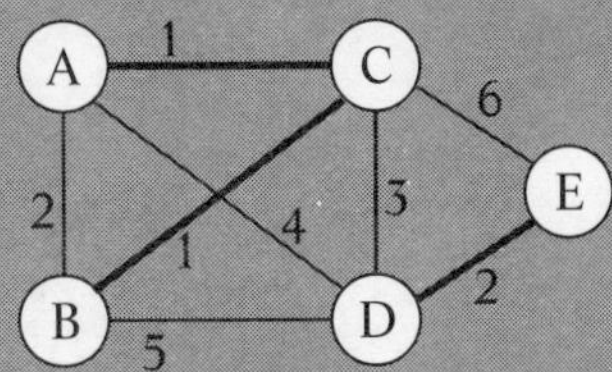

Step 3: The next minimum weighted edges are AB and DE, both with weight 2. Since AB forms a cycle with the spanning tree, it cannot be added. So DE is added.

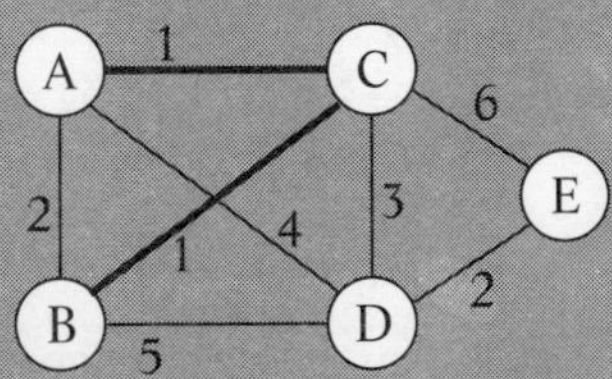

Step 4: The edge with the next minimum weight is CD with weight 3. This edge also does not form a cycle with the already formed spanning tree, so it can be added.

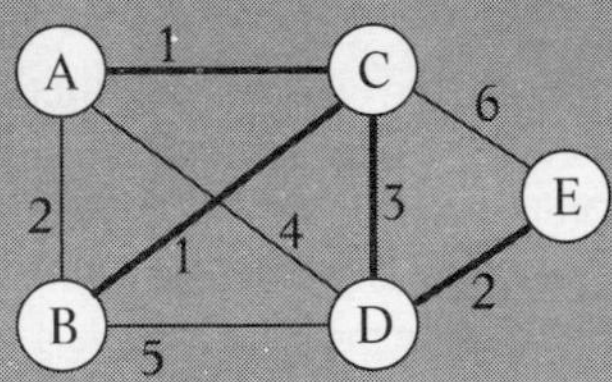

After finding the minimum cost spanning tree, this procedure will stop.

Exercises

1. How can you travel to each square exactly once and return to the first square again in the given checker board?

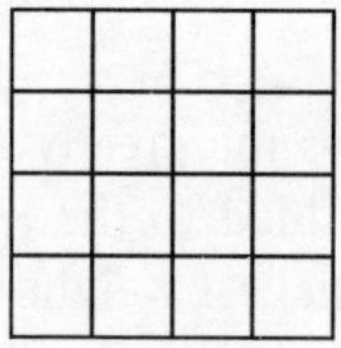

2. What is graph theory? State the importance of graphs in bioinformatics analysis.
3. Explain the given graph and write the 'degree' for vertex B and D.

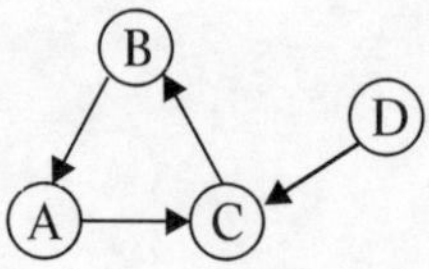

4. Using Dijkstra's algorithm, solve the single source shortest path problem for the given example:

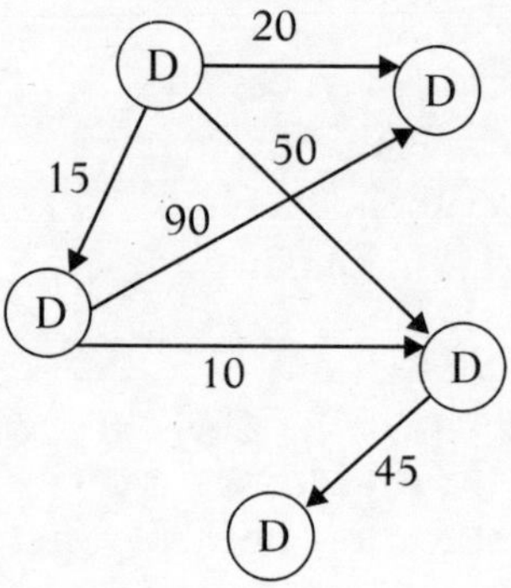

5. Design an efficient algorithm to find the longest string shared by two sequences.
6. For the given four hypothetical branched structures of a gene, construct a graph showing overlaps. (Hint: Gene A has some part of the sequence common with genes B and D. Gene B has some common portions with C and D but C does not have any similarity with gene A. Gene C has some common sequences with D. So the graph will have 4 vertices A, B, C and D, with the edges showing their relationship).

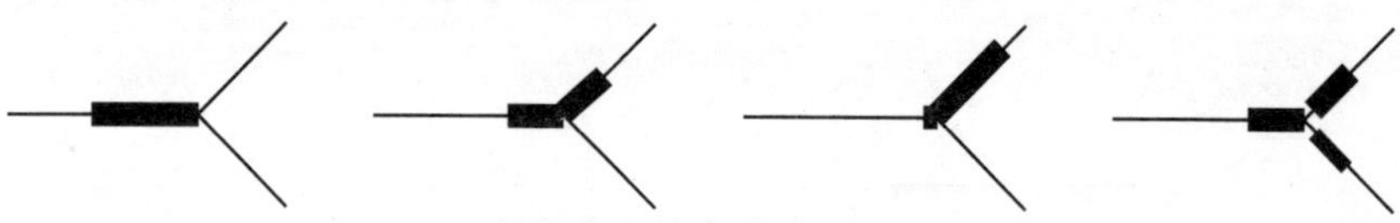

CHAPTER 11

Sequencing Algorithms

LEARNING OUTCOME

- Explain the shortest superstring problem
- Explain sequencing by hybridisation (CBH)
    - Hamiltonian path problem
    - Eulerian path problem

Shotgun sequencing method

In the shotgun sequencing method of genome sequencing, the genomic DNA sample is split into small pieces by the ***sonication technique***. The fragments of almost 500 bp length are cloned into a vector and multiplied in the bacterial host. The cloning process produces multiple copies of the 'insert', and these copies are sequenced using any DNA sequencing method. It produces copies of fragments of DNA overlaps. A major problem is to now arrange them in order and sort the overlapping pieces to obtain the short string from which all the fragments have been obtained. Finding the shortest superstring that represents the sequence is accomplished by applying a graph algorithm to the sequence fragments.

Shortest Superstring Problem

Assembling sequences from various small sequence fragments or concatenating a number of small sequence fragments into one fragment overlap representing the main superstring is solved by using graph algorithms.

Example 11.1

To find the shortest superstring (F) that contains all the fragments f_1, f_2, f_3...f_n.

Input: Sequence fragments f_1, f_2, f_3...f_n.

Output: A string 'F' that contains all the fragments f_1, f_2, and f_3- - - - f_n substrings. Here the length of the string should be as small as possible.

Searching for the strings with maximum overlap till only one string is left solves this problem. This is done initially by the greedy method. The dynamic programming algorithm for sequence alignment finds matches between the suffixes of one fragment with the prefix of another, and finally the shortest sequence with all the fragments is obtained.

```
A = ACGTACG                D = TCCAAC
B =     GCTTC              A =    ACGTACG
C =      CGTAGGC           C =     CGTAGGC
D =          TCCAAC        B =          GCTTC
```

Shortest superstring (F) = TCCAACGTACGTAGGCTTC

SEQUENCING BY HYBRIDISATION

In this method, the DNA sample is hybridised to a certain length composition (ℓ-mers) and sorted by the Hamiltonian path or as a Eulerian path problem. It is very difficult to obtain the final sequence by using these methods because of the repeat sequences present in genomic DNA. These methods do not report repeats as they are considered as multiple copies of the same fragments. For such a problem, ℓ-mer (a sequence string of size ℓ) of larger than the repeat is chosen.

Reconstruction algorithms first find the correct overlapping fragments and the order of reads along the DNA. The DNA sequence is derived from its final ***layout***. Finding the overlaps is the main problem. This is done by finding a match between the suffixes of one fragment with the prefix of another. The dynamic programming algorithm for sequence alignment is used to find matches between the suffix of one fragment with the prefix of another.

Layout construction is a bigger problem than obtaining the overlapping fragments because of the presence of repeats in a genome sequence. As discussed before, this problem can be reduced by using ℓ-mers that are larger than the repeats. The error in obtaining the final layout is reduced by checking each position with many copies of the fragments.

Reconstruction of a sequence by Hamiltonian path problem

A graph is constructed with the sequence fragments considered as vertices. The overlaps are searched by visiting each vertex exactly once to produce the original sequence.

Example 11.2

Construct the shortest string from the given 3-mers: TGC CAA GCA AAT ATG (Fig. 11.1).

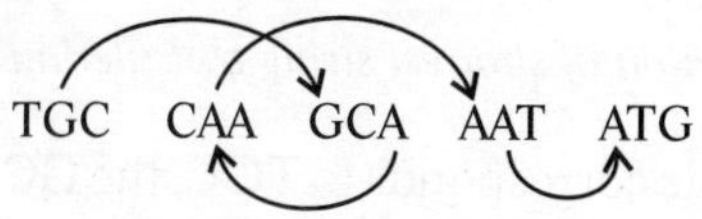

FIGURE 11.1 *Reconstruction of shortest string by Hamiltonian path*

Following the Hamiltonian path will lead to the shortest string, which could be the original string. To make it easy, follow the ladder and pick the first letter from each fragment.

TGC
GCA
CAA
AAT
ATG

Shortest string: TGCAATG

Reconstruction of a sequence by Eulerian path problem

A graph is constructed with the (ℓ – 1)-mer sequence fragments (one character of the vertices will be common so we will choose ℓ, that is, the string size taken, –1 sequence fragment here) considered as vertices. In the Eulerian path problem, the edges corresponding to ℓ-mers form the sequence. Visiting each edge exactly once to produce the original sequence searches the overlaps. The graph is built with all (ℓ – 1)-mer fragments (for the Hamiltonian path, it is ℓ-mer).

Example 11.3

Construct the shortest string from the given 3-mers: TGC CAA GCA AAT ATG.

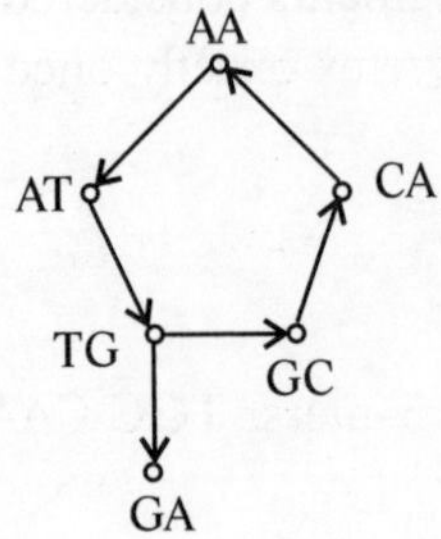

FIGURE 11.2 *Reconstruction of shortest string by Eulerian path*

Here the TG–GC edge corresponds to TGC, the GC–CA edge corresponds to GCA, and so on. The final shortest string representing the fragments from the Eulerian path is: TGCAATGA.

Exercises

1. Reconstruct the shortest common superstring from the given 3-mers: {TGC CAA GCA AAT ATG}.
2. How can you solve the sequence strings given in Exercise 1 using the Hamiltonian and Eulerian paths?
3. Explain how the sequence given in Exercise 1 can be solved by using other graph algorithms.

Assignment

Take ten 3-mer sequences; concatenate them to get the shortest superstring. Write an algorithm for the same using the C programming language. Input the sequences and check the output.

Reconstruct the sequence from the given ten 3-mers by using both Eulerian path problem and Hamiltonian path problem.

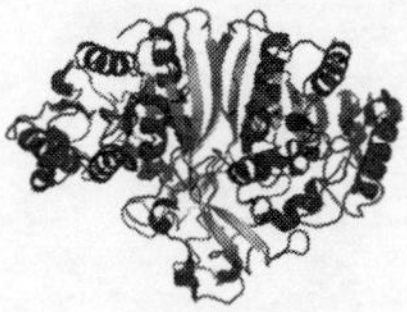

Section V

APPLICATIONS OF BIOINFORMATICS

Chapter 12: Transcriptomics
Chapter 13: Metabolomics
Chapter 14: Pharmacogenomics
Chapter15: Combinatorial Synthesis
Chapter 16: Genomics
Chapter 17: Proteomics

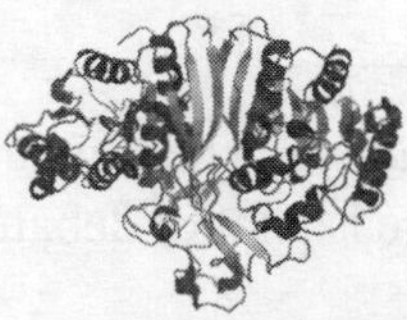

CHAPTER 12

Transcriptomics

LEARNING OUTCOME

- Explain hybridisation
  - o Northern hybridisation
- Define differential display
- Define microarrays
  - o cDNA microarray
  - o Oligomicroarray
  - o Designing microarrays
  - o cDNA microarray experiment
  - o Microarray data variability
  - o Normalisation
  - o Image analysis
  - o Microarray databases

A set of all mRNA molecules, or 'transcripts', from a cell or a population of cells is called '***transcriptome***'. It can refer to all the transcripts present in different cells of an organism, or the transcripts for a certain cell type from different organisms. ***Transcriptomics*** is the study of transcriptomes. It is the study of genes being expressed at a given time and the mRNA expression level in a given cell population.

The ***gene*** is the basic unit of inheritance. Each organism has a set of genes or a set of segments of nucleic acids. These genes are transcribed to produce an expression. The gene is a hereditary unit consisting of a sequence of DNA that occupies a specific location on a chromosome and determines particular characteristics and traits in an organism. The human body contains about 25,000 to 35,000 genes, though there is a lot of debate over this estimate.

Messenger RNA or mRNA is a type of RNA that reflects the exact nucleotide sequence of the genetically active DNA. It carries the 'message' of the nucleus to the cytoplasmic DNA, where proteins are synthesised (Fig. 12.1) based on mRNA specifications.

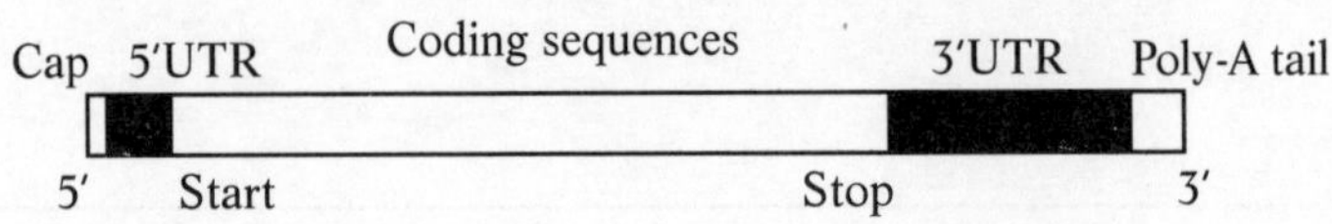

FIGURE 12.1 *Structure of a typical human protein coding mRNA*

Hybridisation

Hybridisation is a technique in which the nucleic acid or protein is immobilised on the membrane and then challenged with a known probe or antibody. It is a widely used technique to confirm the presence or absence of DNA/RNA/protein in an unknown sample.

In the hybridisation technique, the sample (single-stranded DNA/RNA/protein) is first run onto a gel and then blotted onto a membrane. The single-stranded nucleic acid present on the membrane binds to it by the phosphate and thymine molecules (negative charge). Now the membrane is placed in a labelled single-stranded DNA or RNA solution (probe), where the nucleic acid present on the membrane forms hydrogen bonds with the probe, if the complementary sequence is found. Special conditions are required for the probe to hybridise with the nucleic acid present on the membrane. Hybridisation can be detected using the autoradiography method (for radio-labelled probe) or by the biotin streptavidin method (non-radioactive probe). Depending on the sample and probe sequence, hybridisation can be DNA:RNA, DNA:DNA or RNA:RNA.

PROBES

Probes are small nucleotide sequences (15–30 base pairs long) that are used to detect the presence of complementary sequences in nucleic acid samples. They work on the basis of the hybridisation technique. Hybridisation occurs only when complementary base pairs join. Hence the search for a certain stretch of nucleotide sequences can be carried out using its complementary sequence as a probe.

Both DNA and RNA sequences can be used as probes. ssDNA is frequently used as a probe, as mRNA is easily denatured by RNAase in samples. mRNA is changed into ssDNA for the hybridisation experiment. Denatured dsDNA can also be used as a probe. Probes can be:

- Highly purified mRNA (but it is not stable in nature)
- cDNA prepared from mRNA and which limit the copy by reverse transcriptase to only one strand
- Synthetic oligonucleotide (single-stranded)

Labelling of probes: Radioactive labelling is done by ^{32}P; but as its overheads (safety and discharge cost) are high, non-radioactive labelling (biotin, dioxygenin) is more common.

Importance of probes

- Inherited disease can be identified.
- Infectious agents present can be screened.
- Restriction sites in single copy genes can be mapped.

NORTHERN HYBRIDISATION

This is a procedure in which RNA fragments are transferred from an agarose gel to a nitrocellulose membrane and then hybridised to a labelled probe (Fig. 12.2). The blotting procedure was originally developed by Southern in 1975 to detect fragments in an agarose gel that are complementary to a given DNA sequence; this is called the Southern blotting procedure. In this method, nitrocellulose or nylon membranes are used to transfer DNA fragments from agarose gel. RNA does not bind to nitrocellulose membranes. The fragments are transferred from the gel onto chemically reactive paper where they covalently bind to the membrane. This membrane, called diazobenzyloxymethyl paper (DBM paper), is prepared by diazotization of aminobenzyloxymethyl paper. This paper can be prepared from Whatman 540 paper in a series of simple reactions. In 1980, Thomas found that RNA can be blotted onto nitrocellulose membranes under appropriate conditions.

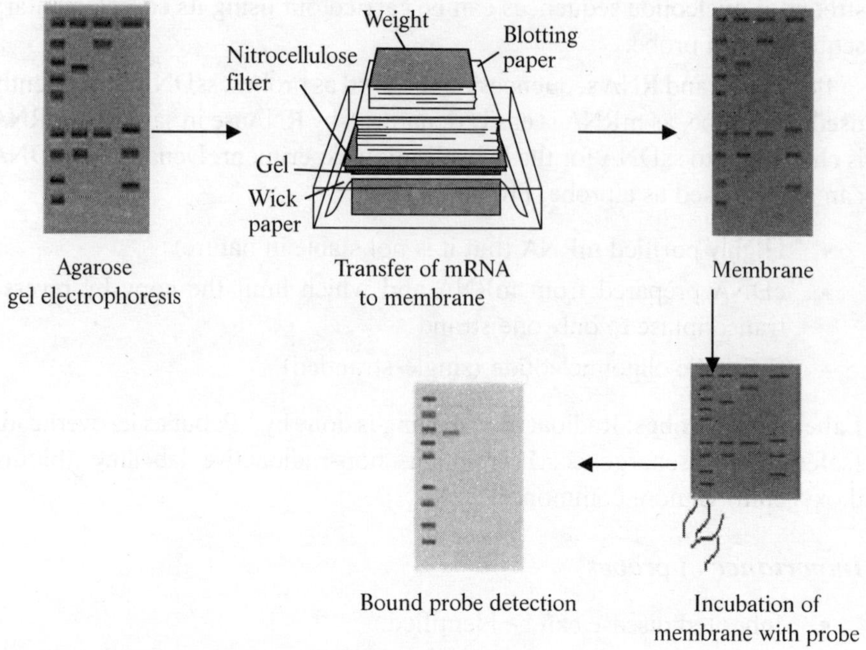

Figure 12.2 *Northern hybridisation procedure*

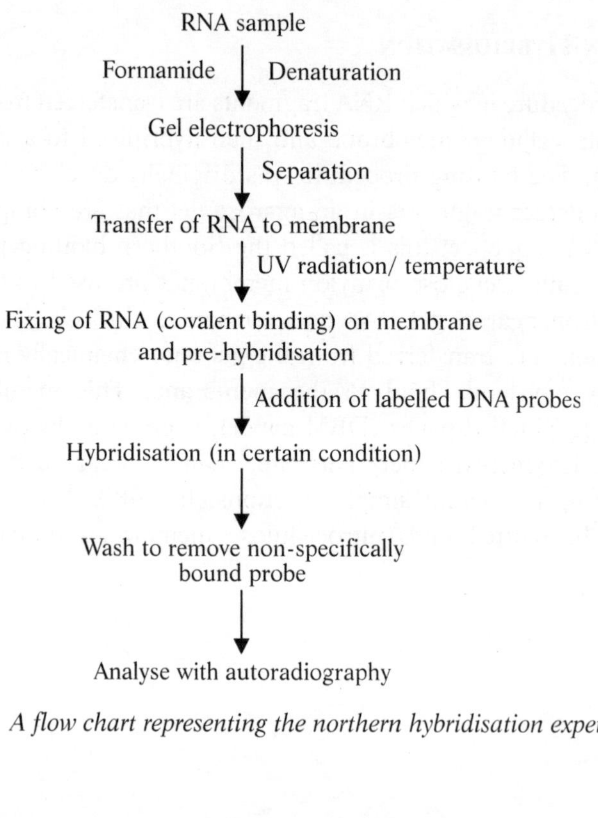

FIGURE 12.3 *A flow chart representing the northern hybridisation experiment*

The northern hybridisation procedure is extensively used to compare the amount of a particular mRNA in a cell under different conditions. This results in the identification and separation of RNA that is complementary to a specific DNA probe (DNA–RNA hybrid is generated here, whereas in Southern hybridisation, it is the DNA–DNA hybrid). RNA is single-stranded but formamide is still used to denature the H-bond between the RNA base pairs (found as pseudoknots or hair-pin loops). This is done to confirm that all the RNA has unfolded linear conformation. A low level of expression of genes produces faint bands, while dark bands are produced by genes with a high expression level (Fig. 12.3).

Differential display

For isolation of genes of unknown function, differential display (DD) and subtractive hybridisation technique is used. Developed by Liang and Pardee, this method quickly identifies and isolates differentially expressed genes in different conditions or from different cells.

In this method, mRNA samples from different cells or different experimental conditions are taken and reverse transcription polymerase chain reaction (RT–PCR) is performed with a random primer to make copies of mRNA of interest. Due to the polymerisation step, this method can be performed with a very small amount of sample. Finally, gel electrophoresis is performed and the results are analysed.

For all the genes present in the sample, we get bands, based on the fragment size or sequence length. The band present in one sample and not found in another is called differentially expressed genes. Depending on the quantity of that fragment, the band appears faint or dark. Now bands induced (band not present in first sample and present in another sample) or repressed (band present in first sample and not present in another) are recovered and cloned for further analysis (Fig. 12.4).

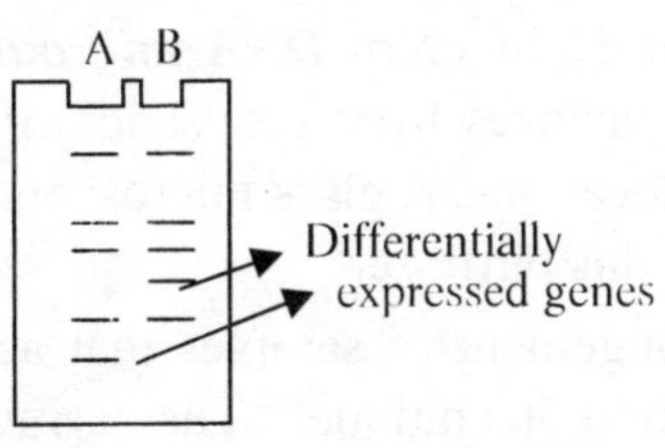

FIGURE 12.4 *An experiment showing differentially expressed genes*

Limitations

- False positives may be generated in the PCR step.
- Generally the amplified fragment corresponds to the tail region (poly-A tail) of mRNA only
- Band contamination; mRNA present in abundance produces a proper band.

Modified differential display method

In this method, for more specific hybridisation, in the PCR step, longer and better designed primers are used. This helps rectify the first two problems with the original DD method:

- PCR is performed first with few initial low stringency cycles followed by several high stringency cycles favouring more specific hybridisation in PCR.
- Additional elements are added into the primer sequence to facilitate reamplification, analysis and cloning of cDNA fragments.

Microarrays

Traditionally, measurement of gene activity was performed as one gene analysed in many samples on blots using the northern hybridisation, differential display and subtractive hybridisation procedures. The most widely used recent technology for genome analysis is the microarray technique, where thousands of genes are analysed at a time in a single experiment. Microarray technology allows us to look at thousands of genes simultaneously to determine which genes are expressed in a particular sample.

First introduced by Pat Brown's lab in 1995 (cDNA microarray), and by Affimatrix in 1996 (oligomicroarray), it is of immense biological importance. These experiments rely on the principle of hybridisation. Thousands of known probes are fabricated onto a small solid slide in a particular order and called DNA microarray or DNA chip. ***DNA microarrays*** are small solid supports on which the sequences from thousands of different genes are attached at certain known locations. A glass microscope slide or silicon or nylon membrane is used for this purpose.

An ***array*** is an orderly arrangement of samples that acts as a blotting membrane in the hybridisation technique. The array searches for complementary DNA strands from DNA sample(s). An array can be a microarray or macroarray on the basis of the size of the sample spot. The size of a microarray sample is usually less then 200 microns and a macroarray sample spot can be more than 300 microns in diameter. One array contains around thousands of spots of that size. A cDNA microarray is fabricated by using a robotic technique while oligomicroarray or gene chip is a collection of gene spots arrayed on a solid surface (chip/slide) by covalent attachment to a chemically suitable matrix.

TYPES OF MICROARRAYS

To detect and measure gene expression, two types of microarrays are synthesised using different technologies: cDNA microarray and oligonucleotide microarray.

cDNA microarray

First introduced by Pat Brown of Stanford University, this is also termed spotted microarray because it is fabricated by spotting a cDNA template on an array. In this technique, DNA fragments (genes) are amplified by polymerase chain reaction and then spotted onto a glass slide in a grid-like pattern. A cDNA microarray can be explained by Fig. 12.5. This is a two-channel microarray that is typically hybridised with cDNA from two samples to be compared on the same slide for visualisation of up-regulated and down-regulated genes. These samples are fluorescently labelled (Cys3 and Cys5) so that when they hybridise with the complementary gene present on the slide they can be detected easily. The intensity and colours provide information about how much and which sample (spot) is expressed in the sample. Data from a cDNA microarray provides information about the relative expression of genes in two different biological samples.

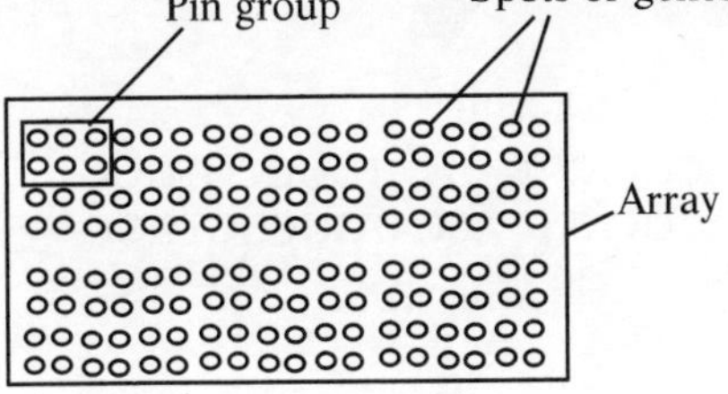

FIGURE 12.5 *Common features of a cDNA microarray*

The common features of a cDNA microarray are subarray, pin groups and spots.

Spots: They are the basic unit containing cDNA clones that are fixed to a glass substrate. Measurements are taken for analysis from these spots, generated by a robotic printing device.

Pin groups: The robotic printing device has multiple printing tips or pins that generate multiple spots at once, called pin groups. The same gene may be present at many spots on a slide for better reading.

Oligonucleotide microarray

In this method, a DNA microarray slide is fabricated by synthesising 11–16 short oligonucleotides (approximately 25 bp in length) at very high density for each expressed gene on a slide. Here oligonucleotides are synthesised at fixed locations by photolithographic technique and chemical synthesis technique. One by one the nucleotides are laid on one another using photolithographic techniques.

In Affimatrix (a company generating oligonucleotide microarrays), 25-mer (25 bp long) oligos are taken and a total of 100 light masks are made for each base at each layer. The resulting gene chip is an array of tens of thousands of distinctive oligonucleotides on a small slide. These arrays are used in genotyping experiments, where sequences of alternate gene forms are synthesised to detect polymorphisms or mutations.

An oligo-MA contains two sets of probe pairs for each gene. One set for 'perfect match' and another that contains 'mismatch nucleotides'. Perfect match sets contain perfectly matched exon sequences at different positions along the sequence of the represented gene. Mismatch nucleotides are identical to perfect match oligonucleotides, except for a mismatch nucleotide in the middle.

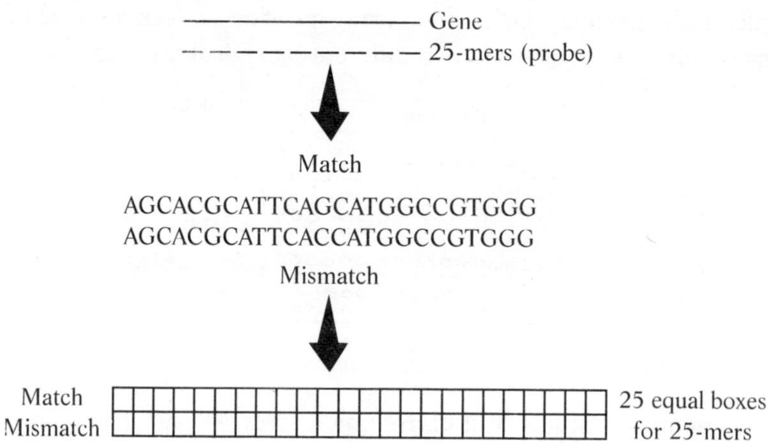

FIGURE 12.6 *A layout of an oligonucleotide microarray*

In oligonucleotide microarray, hybridisation occurs at a critical temperature in a perfect environment. At this time a single mismatch of nucleotides in the middle can prevent hybridisation. Here, two or more samples can be compared at a time but each sample needs different microarray slides. These oligonucleotide microarray slides measure the intensity of the signal from each match probe and less specific binding measurement to the mismatch probe. A white spot is generated for strong hybridisation and no hybridisation produces black spots. In between these two colours is marginal hybridisation.

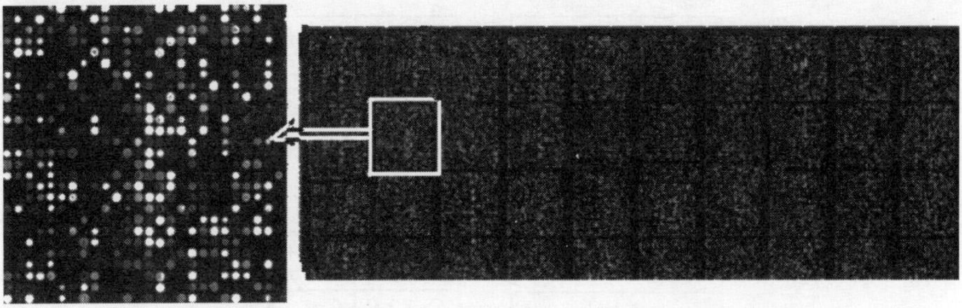

FIGURE 12.7 *An oligonucleotide microarray with enlarged figure for detail*

Oligonucleotide microarrays (Fig. 12.7) avoid the cross-hybridisation that may occur with the cDNA microarray, but are very expensive and also need very accurate gene annotation to fabricate match and mismatch probes. The slides that usually hybridise with only one sample are highly specific and need a smaller quantity of RNA sample for analysis.

DESIGNING A MICROARRAY

Two dyes are used by a cDNA microarray, as two samples are analysed on the same slide. The oligonucleotide microarray uses only one dye, as only one sample is analysed on one slide, for labelling. Due to this difference in array technology, both the arrays use different principles (Fig. 12.8) of design.

External factors to the experiment (like labelling with dye and slide itself) are blocked while designing a cDNA microarray. Dye swap is performed on the sample to analyse the effect of the dye. For dye swap, the sample is divided into two parts. One half is labelled CY3 and the other half is labelled CY5. The other sample is also divided and labelled in this way. This checks the effect of both the dyes on the sample. To analyse the effect of the slide on the result, each slide is given one reference sample and one sample in question, and the results are compared (indirectly) statistically. This type of designing technique requires large quantities of reference sample and half of each slide is used for the reference sample. Hence, if more genes are to be detected, many slides are needed to obtain the results.

To overcome these problems, the loop design technique is used to design a microarray. In this technique, each slide gets a different pair of biological samples and uses all possible combinations of possible samples/treatments. But this method is relatively better for fewer number of samples/treatments as otherwise more slides are needed for the corresponding reference design. An oligonucleotide microarray is a single-dye method, and hence does not need to analyse the dye effect while designing a slide.

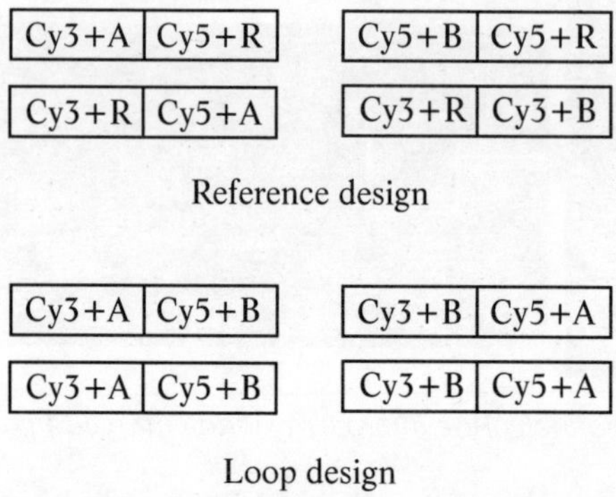

FIGURE 12.8 *Two ways to design a microarray: reference design and loop design*

cDNA MICROARRAY EXPERIMENT

1. Samples are taken under different conditions. They can be from different tissues (tissue-specific genes), cellular responses (temperature, pH, other environmental changes, etc.), cell cycles (mitotic or meiotic stages) or from healthy and diseased cells (regulatory gene defects).
2. RNA is extracted from the sample by any RNA extraction technique. mRNA is just 3% of the total RNA content in a cell. The chromatographic technique is used for mRNA extraction. This is done by using oligo dT column as mRNA has a Poly-A tail that is bound to the 'T' of the column.
3. mRNA is not stable and is susceptible to degradation in an environment that is full of RNA degradable enzymes; so it is now converted into cDNA, a more stable form, using reverse transcriptase. There are some problems in this method as not all the mRNA can be reverse transcribed into cDNA and sometimes only a part of mRNA can be transcribed (starting from the Poly-A tail). To rectify this problem, a random primer is used.
4. cDNA is now labelled to detect the sample by its fluorescence. For each sample, a different dye is used. In microarray experiments, Cy3 (rhodamine) is used for red and Cy5 (fluorescin) for green.

5. The labelled samples are added to the microarray slide, where they get hybridised with the corresponding complementary sequences on the array. Finally, the hybridised array is washed to clear off the unhybridised strands of nucleotide.
6. The array is scanned (scanning) to analyse the spots with hybridised strands using the type and intensity of colours. Fluorescence of different colours has different excitation wavelengths. The detector is sensitive to the emission wavelength from the array and it filters out the excitation wavelength. This way, fluorescent light is separated from the laser light scattered from the array slide.
7. The scanned image is analysed (image analysis) by checking the type and intensity of colour (Fig. 12.9). This is a challenging job, requiring the removal of noise (non-specific hybridisation, dust and others) by normalisation of the data detected to obtain a clear picture. Image analysis and scanning is explained in detail later in this chapter. Many approaches are available for the computational analysis of microarray data, but no general consensus exists as to the standard microarray data analysis protocol (Fig. 12.10).

Various computational methods are available to detect the intensity of colours on a microarray slide and analyse the data to interpret the result.

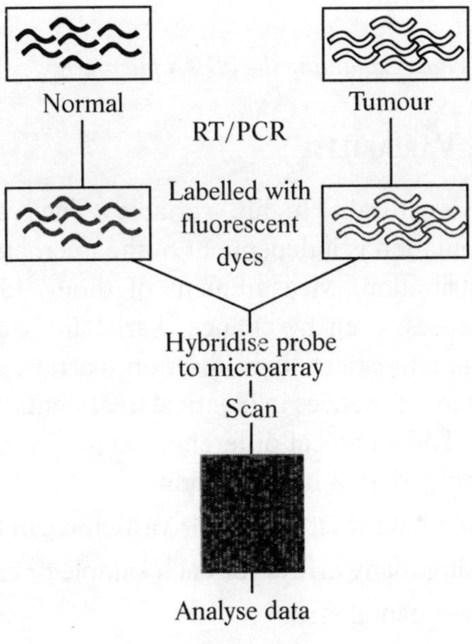

FIGURE 12.9 *Gene expression analysis in tumours and normal cells using a microarray chip*

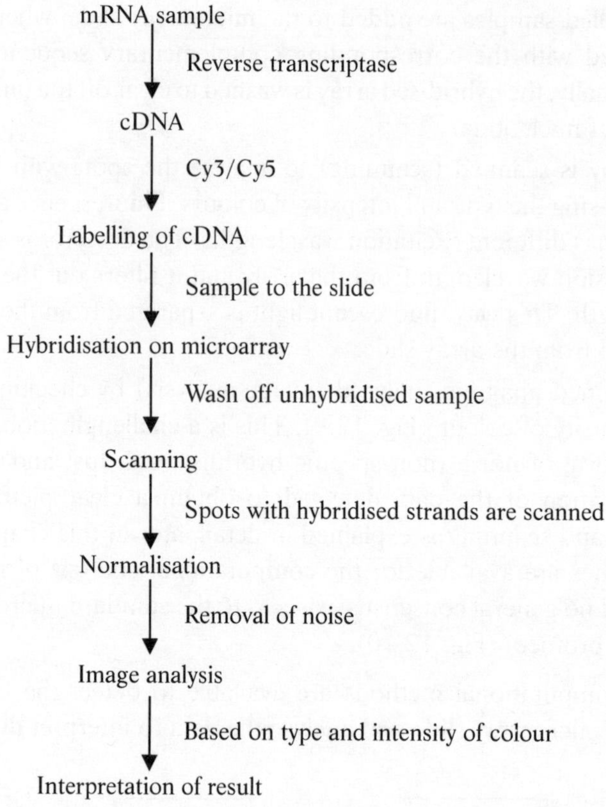

FIGURE 12.10 *A flow chart explaining the cDNA microarray experiment*

MICROARRAY DATA VARIABILITY

Microarray data are naturally highly variable. The variation between individuals in the population is independent of the microarray process. This is called normal distribution. Measurement of thousands of values may produce large differences, even by chance. Variability can be at different levels—between characteristics, hybridisation, array and population. Variability can be due to differences in identical treatment, spot size variation and scanning errors. The technical difference occurs in the extraction and labelling of RNA samples and in hybridisation.

A good result should have least variation. Variation can be controlled by:

- replication (using many arrays for each sample or each treatment)
- correcting experimental error
- increasing accuracy and quality control
- reducing biological variation

Normalisation can control many of the experimental sources of variability and bring each image to similar standard intensity.

NORMALISATION

Normalisation is standardisation of data by removing all the uneven data or non-linear trends in intensity values. It is a crucial procedure in the analysis of DNA microarrays used to compare data from different arrays or colour channels. Normalisation means to adjust microarray data for effects due to technology variation rather than from biological differences between the RNA samples or probes. Usually, adjustment is done to obtain intensity log ratios as a median of zero for each slide. With normalisation, variation in data is removed. It is very important to understand when and how to normalise, as wrong normalisation can remove important data that can affect the final result. It is an indispensable procedure in the analysis of DNA microarrays to compare data from different arrays or colour channels.

The normalisation process has two steps: background correction and transformation, that is, roughly adjusting variance to the same scale for all intensities. Normalisation can be done to reduce variation between dyes or between slides. Even removal of dirt or background variation subtraction is done by normalisation methods. The mean or median of each dye can be used to normalise. First, select a set of non-differentially expressed genes according to experience, and then use these genes to normalise. Invariant genes can be selected computationally and then LOWESS can be applied for normalisation. There are three different methods for normalising a data set: LOWESS, LOESS and Quantile.

Normalisation consists of four steps:

- Background correction
- Image analysis (local background)
- Quantile (global background)
- Transformation

Image analysis

Extraction of meaningful information from microarray images is done using image analysis. This process requires complex computation to extract information from image data. Software for image analysis are inspired by human visual perception models. These software analyse an image by performing three fundamental processes—gridding, segmentation and information extraction.

Gridding: Locates each spot on the slide.

Segmentation: Differentiates the pixels within a spot-containing region into foreground (true signal) and background.

Information extraction: Information is extracted by spot intensity extraction (calculation of fluorescence signal from the foreground from previous step) and background intensity extraction (background signal due to non-specific hybridisation on the slide).

Software tools used for image analysis include Able Image Analyser, ArrayFox, GeneSpotter and Array-Pro Analyser.

Microarray databases

A public microarray database is a public repository of microarray data with some data analysis and visualisation tools.

- Gene Expression Omnibus (GEO) at NCBI
- ArrayExpress: http://www.ebi.ac.uk/arrayexpress
- ExpressDB
- Stanford Microarray Database (SMD)
- Microarray Gene Expression Data (MGED)

Exercises

1. How will you prepare different types of probes for hybridisation?
2. Explain the principle of oligonucleotide microarray with a diagram.
3. Explain the common features in the layout of a cDNA microarray slide.
4. What is hybridisation? Name the different hybridisation techniques and explain the differential display technique.
5. Discuss the advantages, disadvantages and limitations of the microarray approach. Write a detailed account on image analysis and the scanning process. Name any two software tools for image analysis.
6. What does variability and replication explain with respect to microarray normalisation?
7. Among human hemoglobin α and human hemoglobin β, hemoglobin α and rattus hemoglobin β, and human hemoglobin α and human hemoglobin β, which pairs are orthologous, paralogous or none?

CHAPTER 13

Metabolomics

LEARNING OUTCOME

- Define metabolomics
- Explain the reconstruction of the metabolic pathway
- List some metabolic pathway databases
- Explain the importance of metabolomics

A ***metabolome*** is the complete set of small molecules present in living organisms or the metabolites present in a biological sample. These metabolites include metabolic intermediates such as substrates, enzymes and products, hormones and other signalling molecules. Secondary metabolites can also be included in the metabolome.

Metabolomics is "the study of unique chemical fingerprints of all the cellular processes and their small molecule metabolite profile". It is sometimes referred to as 'metabonomics' by some researchers. Knowledge of the metabolomics of a sample gives a complete picture (almost) of its function. "Metabolic pathway is a process where a substrate generates a product through a series of intermediates".

Modelling of metabolic networks can be performed using two approaches: one from the kinetic parameters (mechanisms of absorption and distribution of a ligand) involved in the activity of each component, and another based on the static properties of the system such as Boolean logic (that assumes that reactants and products are isolable, separable and individuated) and stoichiometry (relationships of the reactants and products in a balanced chemical reaction) of the components.

Reconstruction of metabolic pathway from complete genome sequence

Metabolic reconstruction is a process of inferring the metabolism and functional organisation of an organism from its genomic sequence data, supplemented by its known biochemical and phenotypic data. First reported in the phylogeny of unicellular organisms with metabolism and alignment (PUMA) and Kyoto Encyclopedia of Genes and Genomics (KEGG), the reconstruction is based on the available data and known biochemistry.

The complete genome sequence of an organism contains information that has not been fully utilised in the current prediction methods of gene functions, which are based on piece-by-piece similarity searches of individual genes.

Gene prediction methods that are done in parts do not give complete functional information. Reconstruction of the metabolic pathway from the complete genome sequence gives more information by reconstructing the complete functional unit (though 30%–60% of genes are still not identified using reconstruction techniques). The information is stored in metabolic databases. Identification of the function is done by sequence similarity search.

Metabolic pathway reconstruction: The metabolic pathway in a metabolic database is made up of networks of interacting molecules. It is the same as the general pathway, except that it is written as a diagrammatic representation. Traditionally, metabolic pathways have been represented as graphical arrow diagrams. The arrow represents reactions that connect metabolites. The metabolite is written as a label on the node, and over the arrow, the name of the enzyme is written.

Assigning enzyme classification number: In reconstructing the metabolic pathway, the enzyme classification (EC) number plays a key role. The EC numbers are the identifiers of the nodes that tell us about the enzyme in a pathway. It is also a key for linking various genomic information related to that enzyme. Finding enzyme relations is all about modifying the subsystem and checking for correctness along with providing assistance during the creation of a subsystem. GFIT (Gene Function Identification Tool at http://www.genome.ad.jp/kegg/comp/GFIT.html) is a tool used in KEGG that makes use of the orthologous relations of known genes to identify new gene functions. It is used to assign EC numbers. For example: EC: 1.1.1.95 is the enzyme phosphoglycerate dehydrogenase from the amino acid biosynthetic pathway in *Homo sapiens*.

Incomplete reconstruction: After reconstructing a genome, if a specific metabolic pathway is found complete, we can say that the enzyme genes have been correctly assigned. When it is incomplete we say the gene function has not been done extensively because of which it is not possible to assign an EC number. KEGG (also SEED) is used not only to find missing enzyme links, but also to discover exactly which reactions are required to arrive at the missing enzyme. In the KEGG database, the tool PATHCOMP (http://www.genome.ad.jp/kegg-bin/mk_pathcomp.html) is used for this purpose. PATHCOMP searches for alternative reaction paths to fill unidentified reactions.

Steps for reconstructing a metabolic pathway:

1. Start reconstruction with a complete genome sequence.
2. Perform a similarity search and search for orthologs for the sequence.
3. Assign gene function on the basis of top scoring orthologs.
4. Different organisms have different sets of functionally related organisms. Now annotate it by trying to apply the information obtained from Step 3 to the enzymatic reactions and metabolic pathways accumulated from biochemical experiments.
5. After annotation we will know about the genes present in that genome. It will then be easy to find out the reference pathway using all the enzymes based on the existing biochemical pathway.
6. Once the enzyme genes are identified based on sequence similarity and positional correlation of genes, the EC number is assigned correctly for each gene.
7. The organism-specific pathway is constructed using the computational approach by correlating genes in the genome with enzymes from the genes.
8. As intermediary metabolism is well conserved among most organisms (bacteria to humans), reference pathways can be manually drawn and other organism-specific pathways can be generated computationally. Each reconstructed metabolic pathway has one reference pathway and many organism-specific pathways.
9. The regulatory pathways are drawn separately for each organism as they are not similar for all or at least for most of the organisms.

The next step in metabolic pathway reconstruction is quantitative simulation. It requires a lot of data on kinetic parameters and concentration of intermediates. It also requires methods that exploit mathematical simulations to predict missing control mechanisms and parameter values.

Here, the structure and parameters of mathematical models to the known functions of stimulated metabolic systems are optimised.

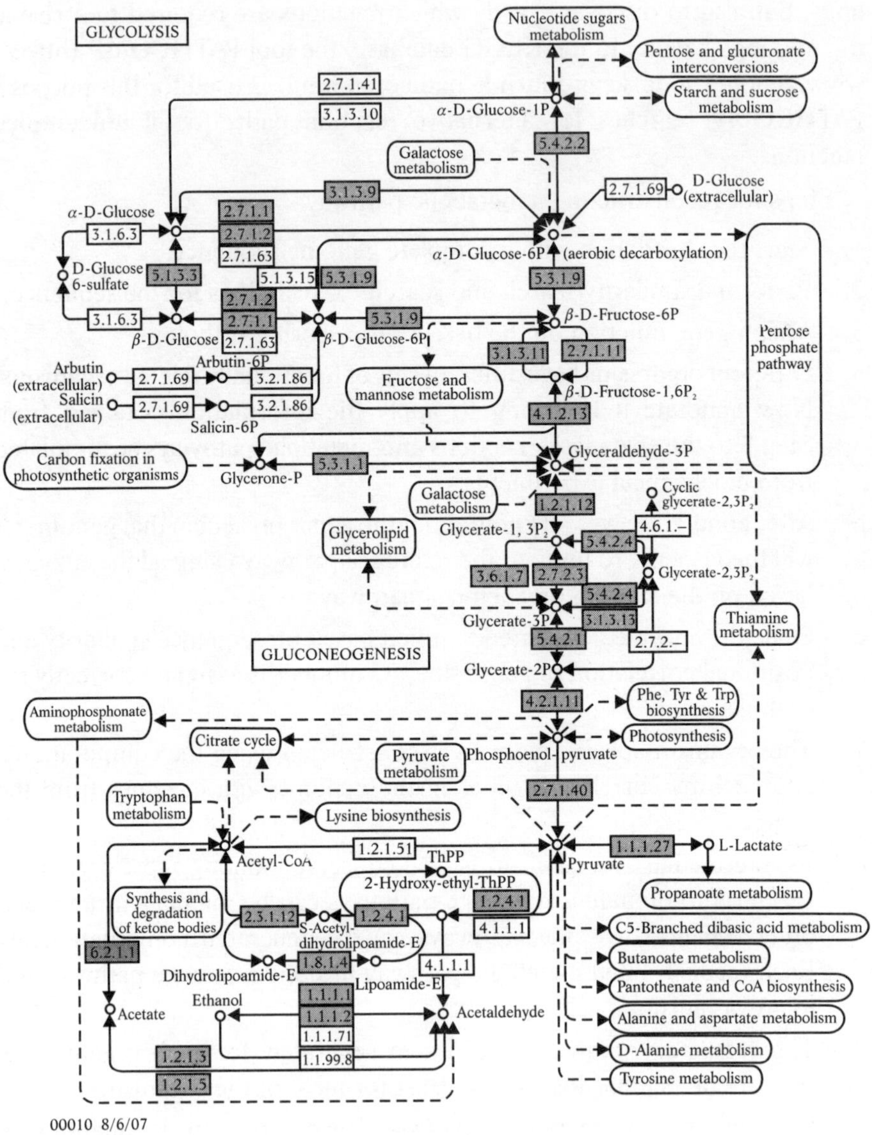

FIGURE 13.1 *A screenshot from the KEGG metabolic pathway database available at genome.jp/kegg/, showing a part of the glycolytic pathway in* Homo sapiens. *The highlighted portion shows the enzymes present in glycolysis in* H. sapiens.

Different objects and arrows represent the ***pathway diagrams***. For example:

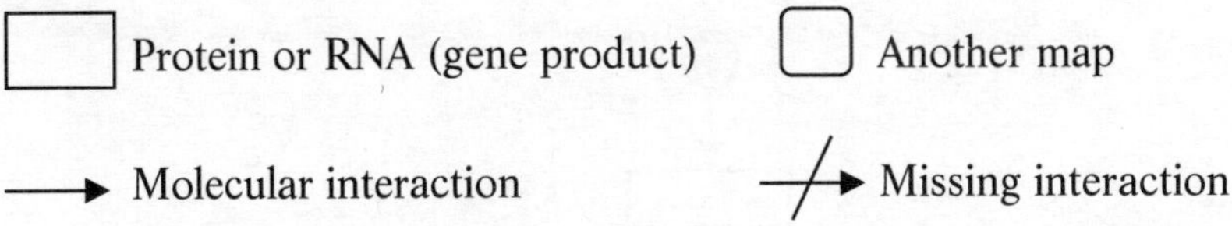

Protein–Protein interaction

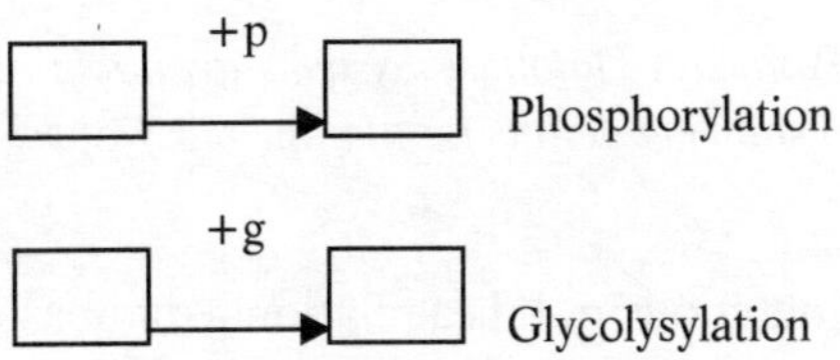

Gene expression reaction

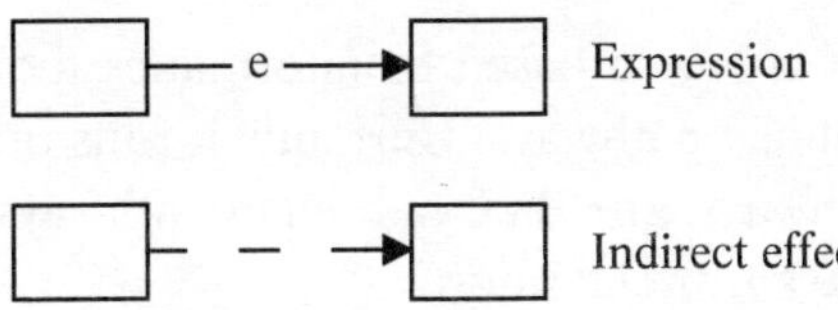

METABOLIC PATHWAY DATABASES

KEGG (Kyoto Encyclopedia of Genes and Genomes): It is a bioinformatics database that contains information on genes, proteins, reactions and pathways. It is the most used database. It consists of four different databases: KEGG BRITE, KEGG GENES, KEGG LIGAND and KEGG PATHWAY. The KEGG PATHWAY database is a collection of graphical diagrams called ***KEGG pathway maps*** that represent molecular interaction networks in various cellular processes.

Gene DataBase (GeneDB): This has a hierarchical organisational structure for metabolism, due to which one can see at what level of the chain one is currently working on.

BioCyc: It is a collection of over 200 pathway/genome databases, containing whole databases dedicated to specific organisms.

WIT2 (What is there?): It is a database for metabolic reconstructions from the sequence data, with genetic sequence and comparative analysis of sequenced genomes. This tool has been replaced with two new systems: SEED and PUMA2.

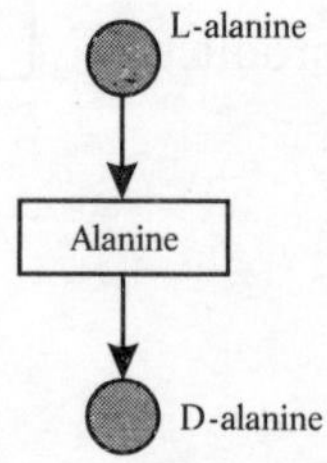

FIGURE 13.2 *A snapshot from PathCase Pathways Database Systems available at nashua.case.edu/pathwaysweb/ and a graph showing details for alanine biosynthesis in humans.*

PathDB: PathDB is a database of plant metabolism. It is a relational database with a non-redundant, hierarchical design. It stores related data like kinetic information, locations ranging from sub-cellular to whole organism level, taxonomic information, compound structures and chemical properties.

PathCase (Path Database System): It is a web-based bioinformatics tool used to store, query and visualise metabolic pathways. Currently it runs on three different datasets: (i) KEGG pathways, (ii) BioCyc human pathways (alpha version) and (iii) sample pathways from literature.

Applications of metabolomics

1. The major diagnostic application is the detection of SNPs and gene prediction.
2. It is used in drug development using metabolic biomarkers of disease.
3. The biochemical pathway associated techniques help in disease target search.
4. The effect of any disease or drug on an animal can be studied by looking for its biochemistry. Example: insecticides, herbicides and growth regulators for agriculture, veterinary and public health.
5. Changes in crops and food to provide health benefits to people are done by modifying their biochemistry.
6. Metabolic changes to fruits or crops (as genetic engineering products) to obtain greater yield.

Exercises

1. Give the KEGG representation of gene expression reaction and **protein–protein** interaction.
2. Define metabolomics. Explain PathDB in detail.
3. What are the different approaches to model metabolic networks?
4. How is EC number assignment done to reconstruct a metabolic pathway?
5. How can you reconstruct a metabolic pathway from sequence and function? Explain in detail.
6. Explain how metabolic studies are important for animal health and breeding.
7. Search enzyme ACE; EC 3.4.15.1. Using any metabolic pathway tool to write its function in humans.
8. For EC 2.7.1.11, using the KEGG Pathway database,
   a. Identify the enzymes and metabolic pathway involved
   b. Display the enzyme for the first pathway
   c. For the same pathway, identify the difference between *Homo sapiens* and *Pseudomonas aeruginosa*

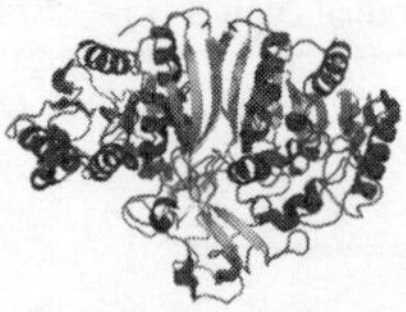

CHAPTER 14

Pharmacogenomics

LEARNING OUTCOME

- Define drugs
- Explain drug receptors
- Describe drug designing
- Explain drug discovery and development
- Define pharmacokinetics
    - Single nucleotide polymorphism
    - Benefits of pharmacogenomics
    - Limits of pharmacogenomics

The word pharmacogenomics is a combination of the words pharmacology and genomics. ***Pharmacology*** is the science of drugs and ***genomics*** is the study of genes, genomes and their expression. The drugs related to genes are studied in pharmacogenomics. It includes both genomics-derived drugs and traditional drugs. Genomics-derived drugs have information about at least one known target. If it is a gene, direct drug targetting can be investigated. If it is a protein, the gene coding differences that change the protein and influence its response towards the drug are explored. Non-target proteins also influence drug targets by affecting drug absorption, distribution, metabolism and excretion.

"An intersection of pharmaceuticals and genetics", pharmacogenomics aims at customising drugs for each individual, that is, drugs created according to each person's genetic makeup.

Drugs

Drugs are small molecules that bind to the receptor to produce the desired effect and to modulate the activity of specific biological receptors. Drugs can also be defined as substances that cure and prevent disease. A drug can be a medicine (with a positive response in the human body) or it can be a poison (if it shows a negative reaction to the body). Drugs produce physiological effects based on receptor occupancy and the propensity of the drugs to activate the receptor.

AGONIST

A molecule that binds to the receptor at its active site to initiate a response is called an agonist. An agonist should have both affinity and intrinsic activity. Affinity is the parameter of tightness of drug and receptor binding, while intrinsic activity is the parameter that measures the effect of the drug, that is, the change in cellular activity after the agonist binds to the receptor. So affinity and intrinsic activity are the factors that govern the action of a drug.

Full agonists produce maximum response once they are bound to the receptor molecule (intrinsic value equal to one), while partial agonists can activate receptors but are unable to produce maximum response (intrinsic activity less then one). Drug activity changes from a full agonist to a reverse agonist (it reverse the receptor activity) in the following way:

Full agonist > partial agonist > neutral agonist > partial inverse agonist > full inverse agonist

Sometimes the affinity of a ligand with the receptor site is so high that it does not dissociate. In this case a ligand is considered as the prosthetic group. Sometimes it is too low to reveal any biological significance. The binding affinity is measured by the dissociation constant for the binding equilibrium.

$$\text{Protein (P)} + \text{Ligand (L)} \underset{K_d}{\overset{K_a}{\rightleftharpoons}} \text{Protein . Ligand (PL)}$$

Affinity constant $K_a = [PL]/[P][L]$

Dissociation constant $K_d = [P][L]/[PL]$

[P], [L] and [PL] are the concentrations of the protein, ligand and complex, respectively. Affinity describes the degree of attractiveness between a drug and a specific receptor. The dissociation constant measures the propensity of a larger object to separate or dissociate reversibly into smaller components. The dissociation constant is usually denoted by K_d and is the opposite of the affinity constant. By comparing K_d values among drugs, we can compare their affinities for a given receptor.

The binding of a protein with a ligand is specific to a particular ligand or group of ligands at a specific binding site and should be reversible. Three forces determine the binding of a drug to a receptor: hydrophobic interactions (main driving force), hydrogen bonds and ionic bonds.

ANTAGONIST

Molecules that have an affinity for the receptors but do not have intrinsic activity (binds but produces no specific reaction) are called antagonists. They partially bind to the receptor site. Though they do not produce any response directly by binding to the receptor, antagonists block the receptor site and hence do not allow an agonist to bind. In this way, they reduce the effect of agonists.

INHIBITORS

Molecules that inhibit the activity of a ligand/substrate are called inhibitors. A reversible inhibitor can be competitive, non-competitive or uncompetitive.

In ***competitive inhibition***, the inhibitor binds to the active site and so the ligand/substrate cannot bind at that site to produce the effect; hence no reaction will occur. Here the inhibitor competes for the active site with the substrate and hence this is called competitive inhibition (Fig. 14.1 (a)).

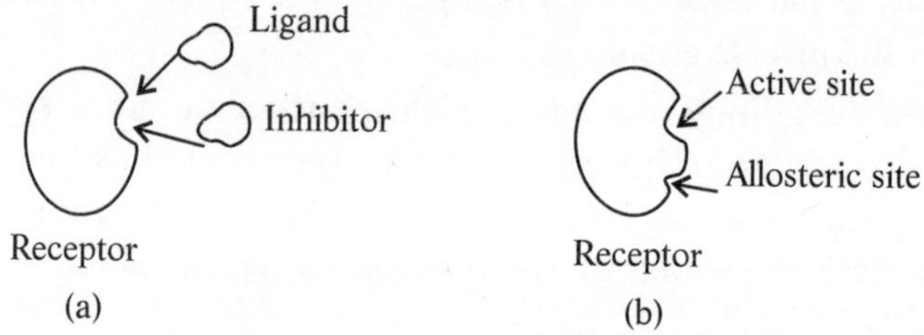

FIGURES 14.1 *(a) Competitive inhibition and (b) Non-competitive inhibition*

In ***non-competitive inhibition***, the inhibitor binds to the allosteric site (a site other than an enzyme active site). Binding of inhibitor to the allosteric site produces some conformational changes in the active site due to which the substrate cannot bind to the active site and thus reduces the activity. Binding of inhibitor to the enzyme reduces its activity but does not affect the binding of the substrate (Fig. 14.1 (b)).

In ***uncompetitive inhibition***, an inhibitor binds only to the complex formed by the enzyme and the substrate (the ES complex) and hence reduces concentration of the ES complex. This increases the enzyme's affinity for the substrate (Le Chatelier's principle) and decreases the maximum enzyme activity (V_{max}).

Irreversible and ***reversible inhibition*** can be both competitive and non-competitive. Reversible inhibitors bind to the receptors with non-covalent interactions such as hydrogen bonds, hydrophobic interactions and ionic bonds. So they can be easily removed and recovered. These receptors generally do not undergo chemical reactions when bound to the receptor site. Irreversible inhibitors bind with covalent bonds, so they block the site permanently. Irreversible inhibitors are usually specific to one class of enzymes and do not inactivate all proteins.

Drug receptors

A drug receptor is a cellular macromolecule (mostly a protein) to which the drug binds and then initiates its effects. Receptors are mostly found on cell surfaces (intracellular receptors), but are also present inside the cell (intracellular receptors).

INTRACELLULAR RECEPTORS

These receptors are located inside the cell, in the cytoplasm or nucleus. These receptors can be nucleus (receptors inside the nucleus) or IP3 receptors (receptors on the endoplasmic reticulum); for example, steroid and thyroid hormone receptors. Receptors located inside the cell function as ligand-dependent transcription factors. Hormones entering the cell form a hormone–receptor complex and enter the nucleus. This binds to the promoter regions of the genes responsible and changes its transcription according to the signal.

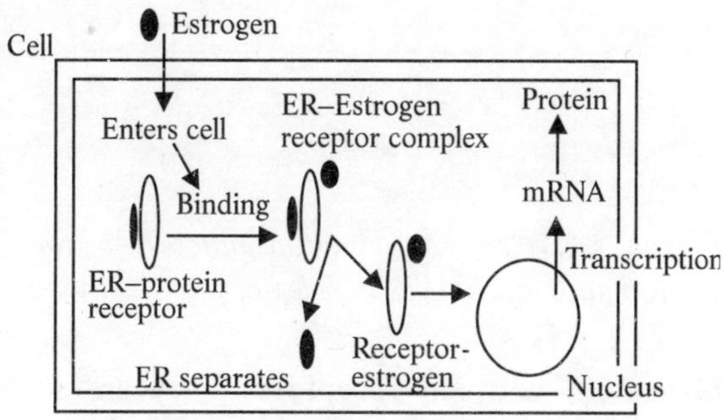

FIGURE 14.2 *The ER complex: Estrogen enters a cell and binds to the intracellular protein receptor. The ER complex separates and the estrogen binds to the receptor that sends a signal to the nucleus to alter transcription to generate various functional and structural proteins.*

The estrogen receptor is an example of an intracellular receptor; steroids and thyroid hormones act as the ligand here. The steroid hormones modulate gene expression in target cells that affect transcription, which in turn changes the phenotype of the cell (Fig. 14.2).

EXTRACELLULAR RECEPTORS

These receptors are of three types:

- Ion channel receptors that can be ligand gated, voltage gated or secondary messenger regulated
- G-protein–coupled receptors that are secondary messenger regulated
- Tyrosine kinase receptors that work by activating cell signalling pathways

Ion channel receptors: They are specific for different ions like Na^+, K^+ and Ca^{2+}. The ion channels are much controlled and open up only when signalled to open the ion channel. Ion channel receptors are ligand gated, voltage gated or secondary messenger regulated. Neurotransmitters are the ligands for ion channel receptors (Fig. 14.3).

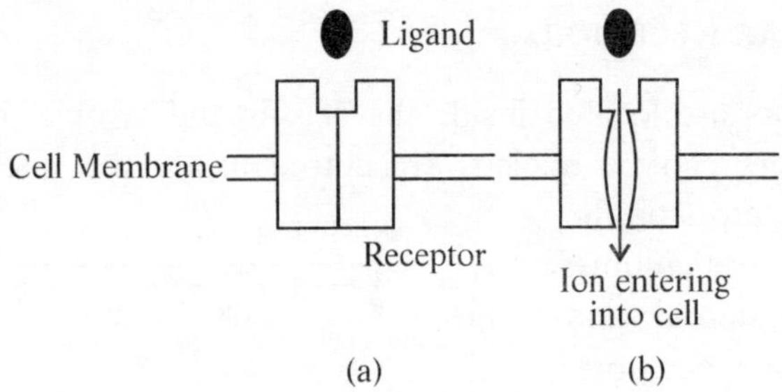

FIGURE 14.3 *(a) A neurotransmitter near the ion channel receptor and (b) Conformational changes in receptor protein structure so that ions enter the cell.*

G-protein–coupled receptors: They are secondary messenger–regulated receptors. This extracellular ligand binding site once bound with the ligand (for example, hormone) produces some changes in the receceptor and opens up the G-protein binding site present in the intracellular region of the receptor. This change in G-protein shape alters the G-protein binding site in such a way that it favours GTP (guanosine triphosphate) over GDP (guanosine diphosphate). So, instead of GDP, GTP now binds at that site. G protein again changes its shape in such a way that the α-subunit splits off with GTP from its β- and γ-subunits. Now, another G protein can bind to this site. This detached α-subunit with GTP (acting as the signalling unit) via the cell membrane reaches inactive adenyl cyclase, which is now activated and signals ATP to get converted into cAMP. cAMP is a secondary messenger that activates the signalling cascade in the cell (Fig. 14.4).

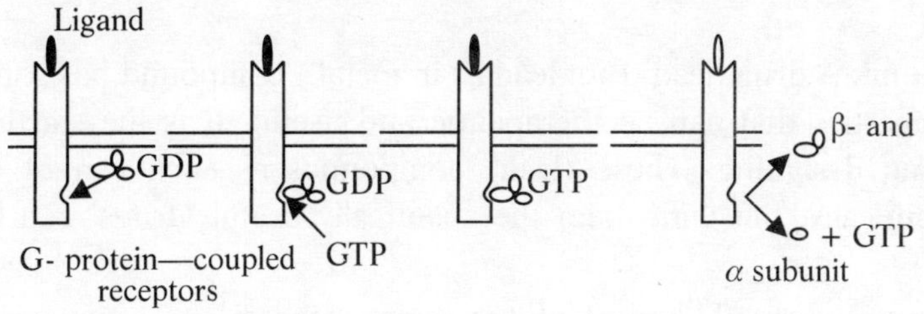

FIGURE 14.4 *Ligand binding interactions in G-protein–coupled receptors*

Tyrosine kinase receptors. These have an extracellular region where the ligand binds and sends the signal to the intracellular region where changes take place due to ligand binding. Tyrosine kinase receptor is a dimer and hence a bivalent ligand is required, that is, one for both the receptors. Once the ligand (for example, insulin, cytokinins and growth factors) binds to the extracellular region of the receptor, the kinase active site present as the intracellular binding region opens up and phosphorylation of tyrosine takes place, which in turn finally activates cell signalling. ***Phosphorylation*** is the addition of a phosphate (PO_4) group to a protein or other organic molecule and it plays a significant role in a wide range of cellular processes (Fig. 14.5).

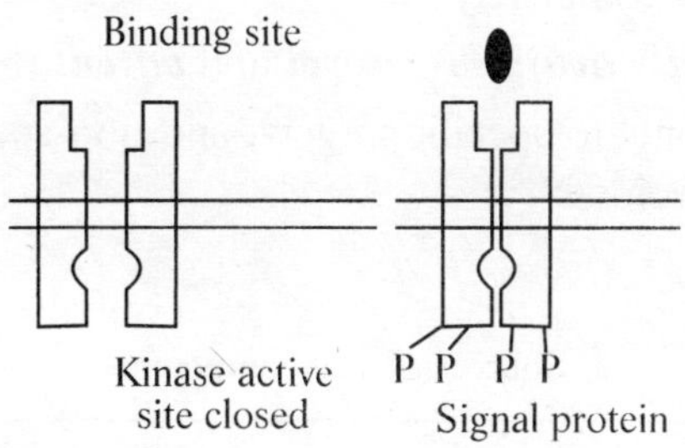

FIGURE 14.5 *Ligand binding interactions in tyrosine kinase receptors*

Drug designing

This is the process of designing a new drug. It is an approach for finding a new drug on the basis of its biological target. A drug is made from substances or compounds obtained from natural plant or animal sources or it is derived from chemical compounds. The starting compounds from which drugs are designed are called ***lead compounds***. A drug attempts to stop the functioning of any malfunctioning metabolic signalling or to enhance the normal pathway affected due to a disease state. Drug designing aims to improve the desired properties of a compound and reduce the undesirable ones.

Lead compound: A drug 'lead' (not lead as in metal!) compound has some desirable properties that can be therapeutic and useful. It is the starting point for drug designing. These (lead) compounds as such cannot be used therapeutically, but with them therapeutically useful 'drugs' can be developed.

A lead compound should have the following properties:

1. It must be ***effective***. This property of a lead compound is called 'potency'.
2. It must be ***safe***, that is, it should not produce any fatal side effect, or should not be poisonous to the host.
3. It must be ***soluble*** in water for quick action.
4. It should not be changed chemically once introduced into the body, that is, it should be ***stable*** chemically and metabolically.
5. It should be mildly lipophilic for ***lipid solubility***, to penetrate the plasma membrane.
6. It should not be toxic or less ***toxic***.
7. It should remain in the body for a specific time (***retention time***) and then be excreted completely.
8. It should be ***easily available***, ***novel*** and ***patentable***.
9. It should bind only to specific targets, and non-specific targets should be completely avoided.

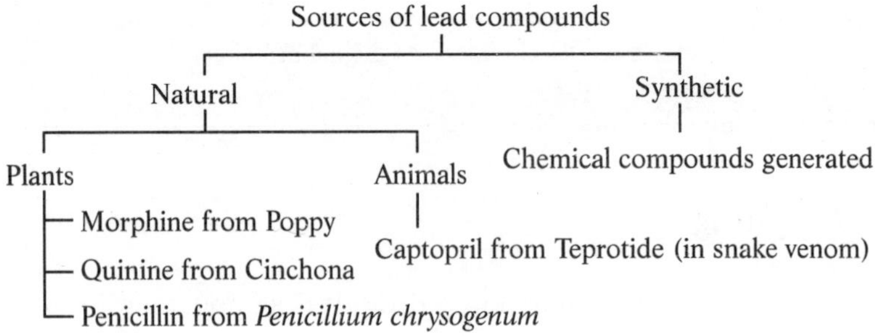

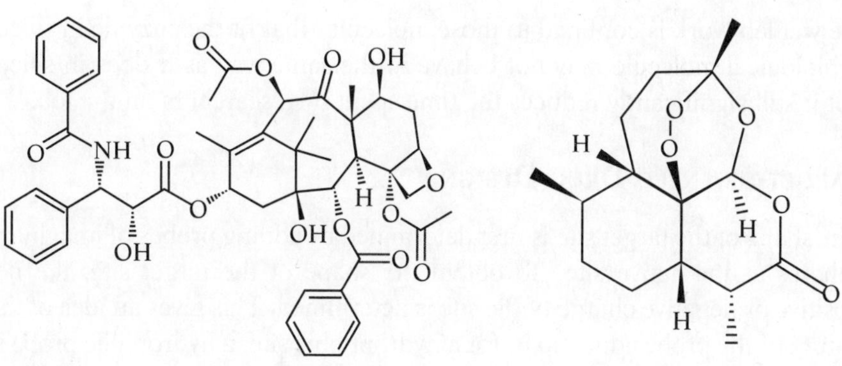

(a) (b)

FIGURE 14.6 *(a) Paclitaxel (taxol), a natural product from the yew tree; (b) Artemisinin from* Artemisia annua, *an antimalarial*

There are various ways of designing drugs:

1. Structure-based or rational drug design
2. Target-oriented drug design
3. Computer-aided drug design

STRUCTURE-BASED DRUG DESIGNING

This approach requires an understanding of interacting molecules and active site groups. This technique uses the 3D structure of proteins and other receptor molecules to assist in the development of new drug compounds. After a number of lead compounds have been found, the structure-based drug designing technique refines their 3D structure to improve their binding to the target active site (***lead optimisation procedure***). This method provides a high level of detail of interaction between the drugs and the protein targets.

Drug molecules have to be designed in such a way that they bind only with the target molecule and not affect any other molecule that may be similar in appearance to the key molecule. Traditionally, new drugs are designed in two ways: by redesigning existing drugs or by testing the interactions of thousands of compounds in the laboratory, which is time consuming and sometimes not effective.

Applying the structure-based strategy, with the help of molecular modelling and chemical sketching software, we can make a mould of the natural molecule (substrate) that can fit into the target enzyme (disease responsible site). Here, the goal is to plug the lock with 'moulded molecules' that fit the enzyme and hence prevent entry of the natural substrate. Thus the wet lab work is confined to those molecules that fit the enzyme in silico. A biological molecule may not behave in the same way as it does in silico, but it still significantly reduces the time spent by researchers on the job.

TARGET-ORIENTED DRUG DESIGN

The shape of the target site is first determined by adding probes of imaginary spheres at the active site. To obtain the shape of the target site, the net positive or negative charge of the site is determined. This gives an idea of the nature of the probe added to it; for a hydrophobic site; a hydrophilic probe is used and vice versa. Layer by layer, from outside to inside, the probe enters the target site till it reaches the centre of the depression called the active site point (ASP). This is done on a trial and error basis. Computationally this procedure is performed using a genetic algorithm and the probe generated binds loosely at the active site. The probe generated can be whole or in several parts for the same receptor. Probes generated in parts for one target site need to be linked by using a link program (for example, Ludi). Finally the biochemical analysis (for checking its strength, purity, identity, quality and potency) of the ligand generated is performed to check and validate its feasibility in a biological environment.

COMPUTER-AIDED DRUG DESIGNING

Computational methods to simulate drug–receptor interactions can be used to design drugs. This discipline is an emerging and very promising field with a lot of potential for growth, though no single drug has been designed solely using computer techniques. It is dependent on bioinformatics tools, applications and databases. Computer-aided drug designing is cost effective and it avoids ***dead end compounds***. It provides deep insight into the new molecular models, their putative drug compounds, their protein targets and how the two bind together.

Drug discovery and development process

The steps to be followed are listed below.

1. Identify the causative agents or type of problem for which the drug is being designed.
2. Identify the target for the disease: X-ray crystallography or NMR can determine target structure experimentally.
3. Search for the drug candidates or lead compounds that can fit the identified target. Check if this target can be fitted with any existing

ligand or if the ligand is to be generated from a lead compound, that is, any biological chemical substrate that can produce the desired effect.

4. Develop the lead compound. In this process, toxicity is reduced and the functional groups or even the main chain are changed to enable specific binding with the desired activity.
5. Check the activity of the lead compound which has been changed into a drug candidate, first in vitro and then with animals. After positive results from these tests, file an application.
6. Start clinical trials once the application is approved. Here the effect of the drug candidate is checked on human volunteers and patients; this finally confirms approval or rejection of the candidate drug into a new permitted drug sent to market.

Clinical trials

A clinical trial is research performed on human volunteers to check the effect of the drug, and to ensure that there are no side effects. This is a very important step (carried out in four phases) that is necessarily carried out on all drug candidates before they come to the market. There are many regulatory bodies that require results from clinical trials.

FDA, Food and Drug Administration in the USA is the main body that finally decides whether a drug can be sent to the market or not. It checks for drug validation results and for any undesirable side effects or toxicity. The FDA also approves drug labelling, dose and directions for use.

EMEA, European Medicines Agency, is a European agency for the evaluation of medicinal products.

NDA, New Drug Application, is the agency that checks the efficiency and safety of a drug in the United States of America. After approval from the NDA and FDA, any modification in drug synthesis or its analytical procedure needs approval from both organisations.

CHMP, the Committee for Medicinal Products for Human Use, carries out evaluation for quality safety and efficacy of medicinal products. This committee begins work when an application for a marketing authorisation comes to the EMEA.

IND, Investigational New Drug, is the means for obtaining exemption from the FDA to transport and use in clinical trials, before getting approval for the market.

Fast tracking is permitted for drugs used for rare and fatal diseases. Such drugs are known as ***orphan drugs***.

Clinical trials are conducted in four phases. There are many guidelines a volunteer has to follow during a clinical trial study:

- They should know the history of previous treatments and any other medical problems.
- They should sign the informed consent form, a document with details about clinical trials. Volunteers should view the details of the trial and discuss them with their doctors before participating in the trial.
- They should not take any other medication, alcohol or smoke cigarettes, to avoid drug–drug reaction complications.
- Volunteers get access to the latest in medical care and can also contribute to medical research by participating in clinical trials. They can however withdraw at any step of the clinical trial.
- Volunteers should be aware that apart from positive aspects there may be some risks involved in clinical trials, as a new drug may have side effects or could even be fatal. Carefully controlled protocols are used for this purpose and results are reported to some government agencies and in scientific and medical journals.

Phase I is carried out on healthy volunteers. It gives information about drug safety, method of administration, dose calibration and pharmacokinetics. It takes about one year and 100–200 healthy volunteers are involved. In case of drugs with high side effects, volunteer patients can be taken instead of healthy volunteers. A trial can be terminated at any stage if any major side effect is seen.

Phase II may start before Phase I is complete, on 200 volunteer patients to check the therapeutic properties of the new drug. In this phase, short-term toxicity and pharmacokinetics of the drug are also studied. It can be divided into two parts: Phase IIa and Phase IIb.

Phase IIa is the initial trial that involves fewer number of patients. After positive results, Phase IIb (late trials) with a large number of patients begins. It is done as double-blind, placebo controlled studies, where volunteers are divided into two groups. One group is given the drug in question and another group is given a placebo. For rare drugs and life-threatening diseases, a placebo is not given but an existing drug is given. This phase takes about two years.

Phase III: The third phase may begin before the end of Phase II and runs for almost three years. This is also divided into early (Phase IIIa) and late (Phase

IIIb) studies. Here also a double-blind placebo controlled study is done. It requires two thousand volunteer patients. Phase IIIa studies suggest the best way for drug administration and its therapeutic value. This phase checks if the new drug is better than the best available treatment. After obtaining a positive result, a new drug application is filed with the NDA in USA (with TGA in Australia and with AMEA in the European Union) with data from all clinical trials. Phase IIIb studies start after filing the application, but before getting an approval. In this phase, the new drug is compared with the best treatment available.

Long-term toxicity and side effects are also checked as volunteer patients responding to the drug can be permitted to continue with it. After approval from the concerned authority, the drug is sent to the market.

Phase IV: Subsequent to the approval for marketing study, the drug is checked for new side effects that may turn up in some patients. These unexpected side effects and interactions may lead to restriction of its use or even removal of the drug from the market. It takes almost 5 to 10 years to conclude a clinical trial.

Pharmacokinetics

Pharmacokinetics is the study of what happens to a drug when it is administered to a patient. While designing a drug, pharmacokinetics should be considered to check whether the compound will be able to reach the target, before perfecting it with expensive and time-consuming procedures. A pharmacokinetics study can be done under four heads: absorption, distribution, metabolism and excretion.

Drug absorption: It is necessary for most drugs to travel across the cell membrane in order to enter the blood supply and reach its target. Drugs must have a balance of both hydrophilic and hydrophobic characteristics and should also be polar for better transportation. For better absorption, a drug should be soluble in both polar and non-polar environments. Modifying the drug polarity or pK_a changes its relative solubility and also improves its pharmacokinetic properties. The polarity of a drug can be reduced by masking polar functional groups and increased by replacing aromatic rings with hetero aromatic rings, or by removing hydrocarbon groups.

Drug distribution: After absorption, drugs first enter the blood, then the tissues and organs. Sufficiently hydrophobic drugs pass through the cell membrane and into the cell. The blood–brain barrier and placental barrier allow only a few drugs to reach the brain and cross the placental barrier, respectively. By increasing the polarity of the drug, it can be prevented from crossing the blood–brain barrier. Some polar drugs require carrier proteins to cross the blood–brain barrier.

Drug metabolism: The reaction that a drug undergoes in the body is called drug metabolism. It can be studied in two phases: Phase I and Phase II. In Phase I metabolism, a polar functional group is introduced or an existing polar group is modified to enhance its polarity. Oxidative reactions are important in Phase I metabolic reactions.

Phase I metabolic reaction

$$\text{RCOOR} \xrightarrow{H_2O} \text{RCOOH} + \text{ROH}$$

Phase II reactions are conjugation reactions where a polar molecule is linked to a suitable functional group. This increase in polarity makes a drug conjugate more easily than the original drug.

Phase II metabolic reaction

$$\boxed{\text{Ar–OH}} \xrightarrow{\text{Enzyme}} \boxed{\text{Ar–O}}\ \text{S–}(O_2)\ \text{OH}$$

3′ phosphoadenosine–5′ phosphosulphate Drug   Sulphate conjugate

Drug excretion: Drugs must be excreted after a specified shelf period. They are excreted via a number of routes. The kidneys are the major excretory route for drugs. Gaseous and volatile drugs are excreted via the lungs, and some are excreted through sweat, saliva and breast milk.

Drug toxicity: Studies are carried out to test the safety of a drug. This can be studied as short-term and long-term toxicity. Short-term toxicity studies are carried out to test exact dose levels that lead to toxic effect. Long-term toxicity tests are used to test the drug for chronic toxicology, carcinogenicity, mutagenicity and reproductive abnormalities.

SINGLE NUCLEOTIDE POLYMORPHISM

A DNA sequence variation that occurrs in an individual DNA sequence when any one of the nucleotides (A, T, G or C) replaces itself with any of the other three nucleotides is called SNP (pronounced 'snip') or single nucleotide polymorphism. For example,

GGTAAGT to GGTTAGT (A changed into T).

SNP is important in medical research, diagnostics and the development of pharmaceutical products; it is mostly found outside the coding exons. If present in the coding region, it may change the function of a protein and hence is of immense biological importance. Even if it is found outside the coding region, it affects gene splicing, transcription factor binding or non-coding RNA sequences. Ninety per cent of human genetic variation is caused by SNPs. They are present throughout the human genome, with an average frequency of 1 per 1000 base pairs.

SNPs that produce the same protein are said to be synonymous, and if they produce different proteins they are said to be non-synonymous. Since most DNA do not make proteins, most of the SNPs have no effect on DNA function or on health and disease. However, some SNP variants can cause major health problems. SNPs do not themselves cause disease but are mostly found near the diseased target sequence. For example, ApoE4 is a common SNP in the apolipoprotein E gene that increases the risk of Alzheimer's disease. It carries information about a disease that a person can develop in the near future or with an environmental change. Each person's genetic material has a unique pattern of SNPs and it is stable evolutionarily and genetically. The frequency, stability and relatively even distribution of SNPs in the genome make them particularly valuable as genetic markers for tracing a disease on the genome map.

Pharm GKB: Pharmacogenetics Knowledge Base (htttp://www.pharmgkb.org/) is a database of information from pharmacogenetic studies and provides tools to browse and work on that information.

BENEFITS OF PHARMACOGENOMICS

- The correct drugs created for specific patients can be administered. It would be better than the standard trial-and-error method and would also be safe. It would increase recovery time and reduce side effects.
- Drugs based on the protein of genes (genomic mapping) ease drug discovery. This enhances the therapeutic effects and also saves surrounding cells from getting damaged due to trial-and-error treatment.
- As it is targeted for an individual, drug doses will be calibrated for that person only; hence doses will be accurate and appropriate.

- Better and safer drugs and vaccines can be made using pharmacogenomics. By finding out an individual's genetic code, certain diseases can be predicted and their effect reduced by changing the environment early and by starting medication at the right time.
- Clinical trials for drug approval would be faster and more successful and hence would decrease the cost of drug development.

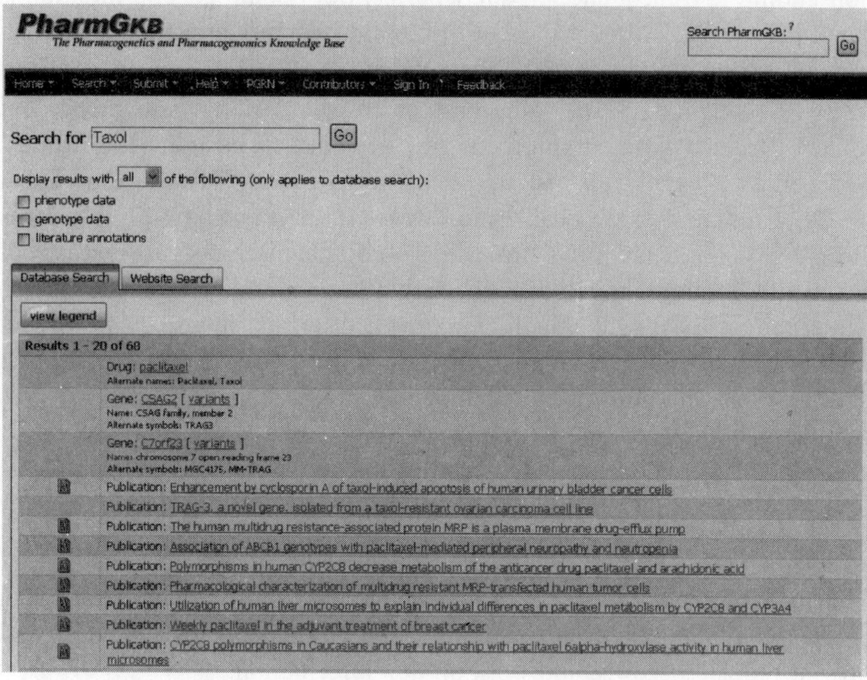

FIGURE 14.7 *A screenshot from the PharmGKB database showing results for Taxol, an antitumour drug*

LIMITS OF PHARMACOGENOMICS

1. The drug alternatives would be limited and if in due course the genetic makeup of an individual changes, that drug would be of no use. It is not necessary for the drug trial to yield positive results. Hence in life-threatening diseases, it may be fatal to wait for the next trial if the first trial fails.
2. It is not easy to obtain a gene target, as SNPs are found near disease targets; SNPs are identified for gene targets.

3. For an individual, it would be useful to have a personalised drug. But it is not practical for pharmaceutical companies to make such individualised drugs.
4. A major problem with personalised drugs is to find knowledgable physicians who would be able to diagnose and determine which drug would suit the patient. So besides their specialisation, all healthcare providers need knowledge of gene target genetics and pharmacogenomics. So, though pharmacogenomics has made personalised drugs that are safe and of lower cost possible, its use is limited because of the above mentioned reasons. It is used only in a few serious diseases like cancer, heart disease and depression. Sometimes personalised medicines are used to treat metabolism problems as well.
5. Many ethical issues may arise. The privacy of an individual might suffer due to access to genome maps. Prior knowledge of a person's problem may affect access to health insurance and even a job.

Exercises

1. What do you mean by agonist and antagonist?
2. Differentiate between non-competitive, competitive and uncompetitive binding.
3. Give a brief account of the characteristics of a lead compound. How is a drug developed from a lead compound?
4. What is a clinical trial? Explain what double-blind, placebo controlled studies are.
5. What is a fair distribution of burdens and benefits in developing the field of pharmacogenomics?
6. Discuss pharmacokinetics and pharmacodynamics.
7. What are drug receptors? Explain receptors for physiological regulatory molecules.
8. Define toxicology. Explain in detail short-term and long-term toxicology. Give some examples of naturally occurring toxins.
9. Mention the pharmacogenomic association of ApoE and LPL genes.
10. Browse and obtain the exact SNP for the ApoE4 gene using the SNP database at NCBI (http://www.ncbi.nlm.nih.gov/SNP/) and report the allele for *Homo sapiens*.

CHAPTER 15

Combinatorial Synthesis

LEARNING OUTCOME

- State the principle of combinatorial chemistry
    - o Solid phase synthesis
    - o Parallel synthesis
- Explain the synthesis of a mixture
    - o Mix and split method
    - o Solution phase synthesis
- Explain solution phase synthesis
- Define the SMILE format

Combinatorial chemistry uses information techniques to generate and analyse the chemical structure of molecules. Born in early 1980, combinatorial chemistry is an innovative method of synthesising various substances. It is faster than traditional methods of chemistry which would involve more time and labour. It is mainly used by the pharmaceutical industry to design new drugs. This method is also applied in semiconductors, superconductors, catalysts and polymers. Combinatorial chemistry has grown rapidly in the last decade; however, there are some areas that need more attention and development.

Combinatorial synthesis involves the small-scale synthesis of large numbers of novel structures using automated solid phase synthetic procedures. Solution phase synthesis also generates chemical structures, but is used in smaller amounts.

A large range of chemical compounds can be created in a very short time by combining molecular building blocks. In this method, one scaffold molecule is present as a base and many other compounds are present as side attachments which react with the 'scaffold' to generate different structures. Combinatorial chemistry generates a large number of different molecules at a time, instead of synthesising compounds one by one using traditional methods. Both preparation and purification happen faster and are less complicated than with traditional methods.

Chemoinformatics (also known as ***cheminformatics*** or ***chemical informatics***) is the use of information technology to solve problems in chemistry. It entails the building of electronic databases with graphic and visual information of the chemical and biological properties and effects of a large numbers of chemical compounds.

Principle of combinatorial chemistry

In combinatorial chemistry, under the same reaction conditions and in the same reaction vessel, huge numbers of analogs are synthesised, which is not possible by simple chemical synthesis techniques.

Example 15.1

Traditional method

$$X + Y \longrightarrow XY$$

Combinatorial synthesis

$$X_1 \text{ to } X_n + Y_1 \text{ to } Y_m \longrightarrow \text{All combinations of } X_{1-n}\, Y_{1-m}$$

These combinations of chemical compounds are made either in parallel, one by one, or in a mixture by using either solid phase or solution phase synthesis.

SOLID PHASE SYNTHESIS

Synthesis of chemical compounds on a solid surface is the most commonly used technique for combinatorial chemistry. Pioneered by Merrifield, a Nobel Prize winner, the combinatorial synthesis technique was developed in 1963 for a biopolymer. It is now used in various other fields. Using this technique it is now easy to create various analogs and store them in a library for use in research. This approach has changed the way in which we now search for a new drug or related discovery.

The solid surface used here is a polymeric support or resin. It must be inert to the reaction conditions of the process. The group that joins the substrate to the resin bead is an essential part of solid phase synthesis and is called the ***linker***. It is a specialised protecting group that must not be affected by the chemical procedure used in combinatorial synthesis. The linker binds with a functional group during chemical synthesis and recurs at the end of the synthesis.

The main requirements for solid phase synthesis are:

1. An insoluble polymeric material that is inert to the reaction conditions. For example, cross-linked polystyrene (polymeric beads), Wang resin (most used solid support).
2. A linker that links the substrate with the solid phase. It should be cleaved rapidly and selectively for good yield and should be inert to the reaction conditions. A linker always has a functional group like the alcoholic (OH) group (Wang resin), carboxylic acid (COOH) or carboxamide.
3. A suitable chemical for selective protection and de-protection of the reactive group.

In this method, for peptide synthesis, the carboxyl terminal of an amino acid is attached to a solid support and the next amino acid is joined or coupled to it. To stop chain growth, the last joined amino group is blocked in the peptide. The block is removed from the primary amino group and the next amino acid is coupled with it. This process is continued until the required peptide or protein is completely formed. Then, the molecule is cut from the solid support and any groups protecting amino acid side chains are removed. Finally, the peptide or protein formed is purified to remove partial products and products with errors (Fig. 15.1).

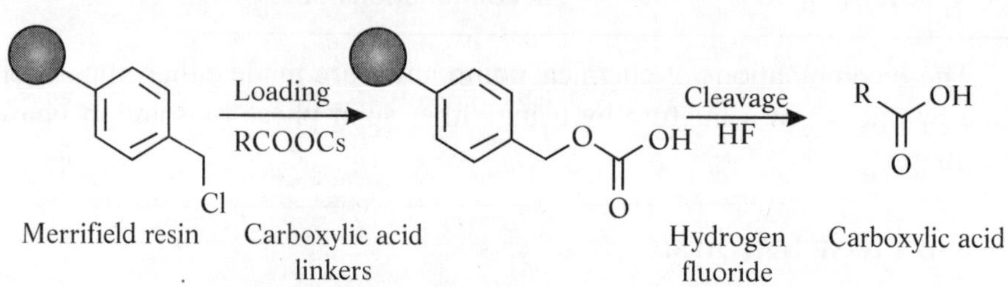

FIGURE 15.1 *Merrifield resin loading and cleavage*

Synthesis of chemical compounds can be done in various ways on a solid support.

SOLUTION PHASE SYNTHESIS

The synthesis of peptides in solution phase has become a well-established science in the field of organic chemistry, with years of research and development by renowned peptide chemists. A few examples have been seen where peptide libraries have been made in solution, though this technique is now replaced by solid phase techniques for the synthesis of combinatorial libraries. However, it is still useful for large-scale production of peptides for industrial purposes.

Normally peptides are synthesised in the carboxyl to amino terminal direction. Protecting groups are selected with great care as they need to be selectively removed. In this process, the carboxylic and lateral functional groups of amino acids are protected. The basicity of the amino group is reduced, while reactivity towards activated carboxylic groups is left unchanged. It can be done using orthodox analogue synthesis, where one compound is made to change form and is then purified. Alternatively, parallel analogue synthesis is used where various compounds are prepared at the same time.

PARALLEL SYNTHESIS

The reaction sequence in all the reaction vials used is the same in this method. But reactants and reagents are different for each vial. Each vial contains the same beads but the structures of the beads are different in different vials. By this method, we can make various analogs with the same skeleton. Each vial will produce a unique chemical structure, based on the reagents and reactants used that vial (Fig. 15.2).

Vial 1: Beads $\xrightarrow{X}$ Bead-X $\xrightarrow{Y}$ Bead- XY $\xrightarrow{Z}$ Bead- XYZ

Vial 2: Beads $\xrightarrow{Y}$ Bead-Y $\xrightarrow{Z}$ Bead- YZ $\xrightarrow{X}$ Bead- YZX

Vial 3: Beads $\xrightarrow{Z}$ Bead-Z $\xrightarrow{X}$ Bead- ZX $\xrightarrow{Y}$ Bead- ZXY

FIGURE 15.2 *Parallel synthesis in three different vials*

SYNTHESIS OF A MIXTURE

Chemical compounds can be synthesised as a mixture of compounds. In this method, in the same vial, beads will have different structures. In each vial, a mixture of structures are synthesized. This can be explained by the mix and split method where each bead has same individual structure but different beads in the same vial have different structures. This way the numerous structures can be synthesized in each vial. [See http://userwww.sfsu.edu/~cberkman/CHEM_640_synth_part_1.pdf]

Mix and split method

In different reaction vials, different starting materials are first attached to beads. So each vial (Vial 1, Vial 2 and Vial 3 in Fig. 15.3 below) will have the corresponding structure and different vials will have different structures. Now all the structures are mixed together in Vial X and again split into different reaction vials (Vial 1', Vial 2' and Vial 3'). Each vial will now have a mixture of structures. The same process is repeated and in each vial different reactants are added so that again each vial has different structures. All the structures are once again mixed and split.

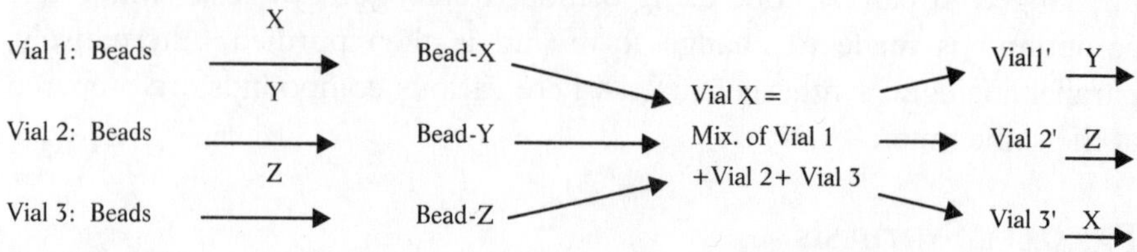

FIGURE 15.3 *Parallel synthesis in three different vials (mix and split method)*

This process is repeated to get various structures with the same skeleton at different levels. This method enables the generation of all possible structures that can be made using the given starting materials. With this method, peptide synthesis and heterocyclic synthesis are performed.

CHEMICAL SKETCHING

Designing chemical structures using conventional drawing software is extremely painstaking and practically unfeasible. Chemical sketching software packages are standalone applications. They serve as the input modules of other database or modelling software.

ISIS/Draw (at ISIS/Base), ChemDraw (incorporated with ChemOffice), ChemSketch (with ChemFolder) and Chemistry 4D Draw (with Chem4D database) are the chemical sketching software packages. ACD/ChemCoder produces and scans 2D barcodes of the structures drawn. 2D structures can be converted into 3D structures. These structures can be written in the SMILE format or can be drawn directly in the 2D form and converted to the 3D form.

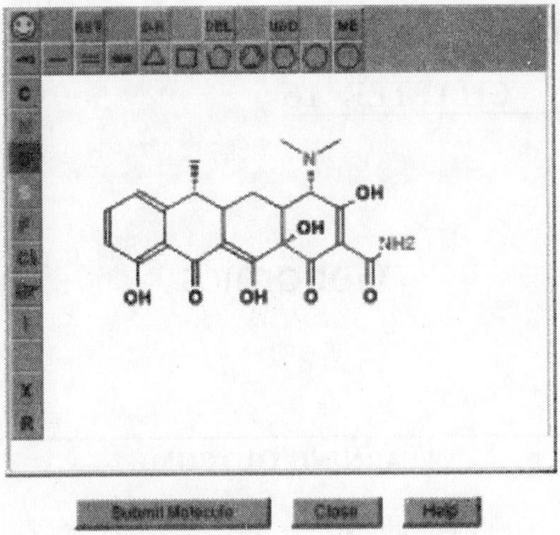

FIGURE 15.4 *A snapshot from a chemical sketching tool*

The SMILE format

Simplified Molecular Input Line Entry Specification or SMILE can be studied in detail using the smile tutorial at http://www.daylight.com/dayhtml/smiles. It is a system for representing chemical formulae as strings, based on a valence model in which all valences are considered to be satisfied by H atoms until otherwise shown. Double bonds are shown as two parallel lines (=) and triple bonds as #. Cyclic molecules are indicated by numbering the atom at which the ring is closed.

Smile format for		
	Methane (CH_4)	-- C
	Water (H_2O)	-- O
	Ethanol ($CH_3CH_2CH_2OH$)	-- CCCO
	Carbon dioxide (CO_2)	-- O = C = O
	Cyclohexane	-- C_1CCCCC_1

Exercises

1. What is combinatorial synthesis? Explain the different methods of combinatorial synthesis.
2. How is a chemical library created? State the importance of a chemical library.
3. Define combinatorial synthesis. Explain the split synthesis and parallel synthesis procedures for random structure generation.
4. What is the SMILE format? Where is it used? Give an example.

CHAPTER 16

Genomics

LEARNING OUTCOME

- Define genomics
- Define genome sequencing
- Describe and list the objectives of the Human Genome Project
- Define gene prediction
- List the tools for gene prediction
- Define comparative genomics
- Define model organisms
- List the tools for comparative genomics

Genomics is the branch of molecular genetics concerned with the study of the genome structure of organisms and its significance to pathology and disease. Genomics identifies and sequences the component genes. It also examines molecular mechanisms and the interplay of genetic and environmental factors in diseases; this has implications for medicine, pharmacy, agriculture, etc. Functional genomics, structural genomics and comparative genomics are sub-disciplines of genomics that can be combined to provide a powerful approach to study adaptive genetic variation.

Eukaryotic and Prokaryotic Cells

Eukaryotic cells contain membrane-bound compartments, like the nucleus and organelles such as mitochondria and chloroplasts in plant cells. Animals, plants, fungi and protozoa are eukaryotes. The basic physical structure of all eukaryotic nuclear genomes is similar; a few organisms have very different structures. The genome size ranges from 10 Mb to 100 000 Mb, with the simplest eukaryotes—fungi—having the smallest genomes, and higher eukaryotes, vertebrates and angiosperms having the largest (Fig. 16.1). The correlation between the complexity of an organism and the size of its genome is still unclear.

FIGURE 16.1 *A eukaryotic gene structure*

Prokaryotic cells lack extensive internal compartments. Based on characteristic genetic and biochemical features, there are two very different groups of prokaryotes: bacteria and archaea. There is some overlap in size between the largest prokaryotic and the smallest eukaryotic genome, but in general, prokaryotic genomes are much smaller. The physical organisation of the genome is also different in eukaryotes and prokaryotes. The traditional view has been that an entire prokaryotic genome is contained in a single circular DNA molecule. However, research has shown that some organisms, for example, *Borrelia burgdorferi* B31, have a linear chromosome of length 911 kb. In many bacteria and archaea, multipartite genomes are also known. Prokaryotes are different from eukaryotes as they do not have introns in their genes and repetitive sequences in the genes are infrequent. However, they do possess certain sequences that might be repeated elsewhere in the genome. Isolation of distinct pieces of a genome and their amplification is carried out by a cloning technique which consecutively enables sequencing of DNA.

Genome sequencing

Detection of the sequences and structures that describe the principal control elements of gene expression, like promoters, specialised sites, etc., has been made possible by analysing genetically well-characterised genes. Once a gene is sequenced, analysed and characterised, it becomes possible to scan new DNA sequences and categorise potential new genes. This procedure, which used to be performed manually, is now facilitated by bioinformatics. The sequence is not easy to work out; the order can only be generated after millions of chemical reactions have taken place.

Human beings are emblematic eukaryotes and an excellent model for eukaryotic genomes in general. The human genome comprises about three billion building blocks. There are two methods to sequence the full genome: shotgun sequencing and clone contig.

Shotgun sequencing

Celera Genomics pioneered an innovative approach. The entire human genome is first fragmented into small random-size pieces (2, 20, 50, 100,150 kb) which are cloned into a vector and multiplied in the bacterial host. The clones are then sequenced by the chain termination method from both ends. Copies of fragments of DNA overlaps are produced and arranged by using the Phred and Phrap assemblers. Computer algorithms assemble the millions of sequenced fragments into a continuous stretch resembling each chromosome. Shotgun sequencing takes maximum advantage of the speed and low cost of automated sequencing.

Clone contig

In this method, a crude physical map of the whole genome is first created. Several copies of the genome are randomly cut into 150 kb-long pieces. They are then cloned and finger-printed based on the physical map. Once again they are fragmented and cloned and finally 500 bp from one end is sequenced. These sequences are then fed into the Phrap program that checks for common overlapping sequences that join two fragments together.

Human Genome Project

The Human Genome Project (HGP) is the most ambitious and challenging quest ever undertaken in research. Its purpose is to completely map and sequence the chemical base pairs that make up DNA, and identify and map all the genetic material of humans. It was started in October 1990 by the National Center for Human Genome Research. Its goal was to identify all the approximately 30 000 genes, determine their sequences, develop faster and more efficient sequencing technologies for data analysis and tackle ethical, legal and social issues (ELSI). Though the objective of the HGP was to understand the genetic makeup of the human species, the project also focussed on several non-human organisms such as *E. coli*, the fruit fly and the laboratory mouse. The draft sequence was completed in June 2000 and analyses of the working draft were published in February 2001. The finished sequence was published in April 2003, two years ahead of schedule. About 95% of the gene-containing part of the human sequence was completed to 99.99% accuracy by April 2003. In May 2006, HGP researchers announced the completion of the DNA sequence for the last of the 24 human chromosomes. It was started with the Public Genome Project using the clone contig method and continued later with Celera Genomics' shotgun technique.

MAIN FINDINGS OF THE HUMAN GENOME PROJECT

- Humans have approximately 24 000 genes; a laboratory mouse also has the same number of genes. How these genes express themselves provides clues to how diseases are caused.
- The human genome's gene-dense areas are predominantly composed of the DNA building blocks G and C. In contrast, the gene-poor areas are rich in the DNA building blocks A and T.
- Chromosome 1 has the most genes (2968), and the Y chromosome has the least (231).
- Less than 2% of the genome codes for proteins.
- Repeated sequences that do not code for proteins ('junk DNA') make up at least 50% of the human genome.
- Racial and ethnic groups show significant genetic differences, regardless of the overall intra-specific consistency of the genome.
- Most genetic mutations occur in the male of the species. They are also more likely to be responsible for genetic disorders.
- Genomics has improved our understanding of how we evolved as humans and also tells us how our body works.
- Scientists have identified about 3 million locations where single-base DNA differences (SNPs) occur in humans. This information is useful in finding chromosomal locations for disease-associated sequences and in tracing human history.

Scientists are faced with the challenge of understanding:

- Gene number, exact locations and functions and regulation;
- DNA sequence and chromosomal structure organisation;
- Non-coding DNA types, amount, distribution, information content and functions;
- Interaction of proteins in complex molecular machines and protein conservation;
- Proteomes (total protein content and function) in organisms;
- Correlation of SNPs with health and disease.

The HGP genome is the foundation for future research in identifying differences among individuals. It has had a profound impact on biomedical research. The project has generated several maps which are useful in finding the genes associated with many genetic conditions. Gene mutations and the effect of environmental agents on health are potential areas for research.

Gene prediction

The sequencing of a gene is productive only when it is analysed and predicted correctly. Gene prediction is carried out to identify the structure of genes in order to differentiate protein-coding genes from non-coding regions, and to identify promoters and other regulatory elements. Gene prediction hence provides

- an understanding of the structure and function of genomes of different organisms;
- information on the evolution of genes, speciation and evolution of species.

Traditionally, there are three different approaches to computational gene prediction:

- ***Extrinsic** or **comparative method*** searches for similarities in protein and nucleic acid sequence databases amid different organisms. In this method, documented genes and proteins are searched for homology.
- ***Intrinsic** or **ab initio method*** uses known properties of coding and non-coding sequences like open reading frame and coding statistics (ORF length, codon usage, GC content, etc.) for gene prediction.
- ***Integrated approach*** combines both intrinsic and extrinsic methods. It combines the calculations of several programs for better prediction.

Gene prediction is easy in prokaryotes. In eukaryotic genes, there are several issues that make finding genes extremely difficult:

- Very long genes with many exons and long introns (the dystrophin gene in humans is composed of 79 exons straddling nearly 2.3 Mb and some introns are >100 kb long)
- Very short exons (3 bp long in *Arabidopsis* genes)
- Introns in non-coding regions
- Overlapping genes (though rarely found in eukaryotic genomes)
- Polycistronic gene arrangement—one gene and one mRNA, but two or more proteins
- Alternative splicing

The current approach to finding genes in newly-sequenced genomic DNA can be roughly classified into the following categories:

- pattern recognition
- protein homology
- use of expressed sequence tags (ESTs)
- domain knowledge

TOOLS FOR GENE PREDICTION

GeneMark is a family of gene prediction programs developed at Georgia Institute of Technology, Atlanta, Georgia, USA. Separate programs are designed here to predict the genes from eukaryotes, bacteria, viruses and ESTs.

Gene Finder is a software tool used to find splice sites and protein coding exons, construct gene models and recognise the promotor and poly-A region, based on which it can predict the gene.

GrailEXP is a software package that predicts exons, genes, promoters, poly-As, CpG islands, EST similarities and repetitive elements within a DNA sequence. It was originally developed by the Biosciences Division, Oak Ridge National Laboratory, to annotate the entire known portion of the human genome.

GeneBee is a molecular biology server for RNA secondary structure prediction.

GENSCAN is a web server at Massachusetts Institute of Technology, Cambridge, Massachusetts, USA, for the identification of complete gene structures in genomic DNA (Fig. 16.2).

GenomeScan is a web server at MIT for predicting the locations and exon–intron structures of genes in genomic sequences from a variety of organisms. It incorporates protein homology information when predicting genes.

ORF Finder (Open Reading Frame Finder) at NCBI is a graphical analysis tool which finds all open reading frames of a selectable minimum size in a user's sequence or in a sequence already in the database.

Promoter 2.0 Prediction Server predicts the transcription start sites of vertebrate Pol II promoters in DNA sequences.

Sequence.fasta : 2767 bp : 51.03% C+G : Isochore 3 (51–57 C+G%)

Predicted genes/exons:

Gn.Ex	Type	S	.Begin	...End	.Len	Fr	Ph	I/Ac	Do/T	CodRg	P....	Tscr..
1.01	Sngl	+	353	2320	1968	1	0	54	47	1816	0.991	166.79
1.02	PlyA	+	2703	2708	6							1.05

FIGURE 16.2 A GENSCAN output for *Mus musculus* epidermal growth factor receptor (Egfr), transcript variant 2; mRNA shows 2767 base pairs with 51%–57% of C + G content. Here Gn.Ex is the gene number and exon number, Type specifies the type of exon, that is, single-exon gene (Sngl) for the first exon and poly-A signal (PlyA) for the second exon. Begin shows the beginning of the exon or signal (numbered on input strand) and End specifies the end point of the exon or signal (numbered on input strand) while Len is the length of the exon or signal (bp). Fr stands for reading frame and Ph for the net phase of exon. The initiation signal or 3' splice site score (I/Ac) and 5' splice site or termination signal score (Do/T) are 54 and 47, respectively, for the first exon and are not present in the second exon. CodRg provides the coding region score (1816 in the first exon), P the probability of the exon (0.991 in the first exon) and Tscr the exon score depending on length (116.79 in the first exon and 1.05 in the second exon). A predicted 5' splice site with a score above100 is considered as strong; 50–100 as moderate; 0–50 as weak; and below 0 as poor. The first exon, with a score of 47, is therefore considered weak.

Comparative genomics

Comparative genomics is the analysis and comparison of genomes from different species. It takes advantage of the information about sequences provided by different techniques to understand the function and evolutionary processes of genomes and the relationships between genomes of different species or strains. This method exploits both similarities and differences in the sequences to infer how selection has acted upon these elements. By using information from well-characterised model systems, comparative genomics hopes to provide candidates for genes implicated in human diseases. Comparative genomics involves the use of computer programs that can compare multiple genomes and search regions of similarity among them. Some of these sequence-similarity tools are publically available over the internet; for example, the BLAST program at NCBI.

The mouse genome is comparable in size to that of humans. It is important to note that almost every human gene appears to have a counterpart in the mouse. Researchers expect to find that almost 90% of gene sequences are similar in mice and humans, with similarities ranging from 60% to 90%. Analyses have shown that highly conserved versions of virtually all single-copy human genes are found in mouse DNA, and mouse and human genes are organised in very similar ways. Hence the laboratory mouse offers great promise in the study of the genetic base of disease susceptibility, development and progress.

MODEL ORGANISMS

A model organism is a species that has been widely studied, usually because it is easy to maintain and breed in a laboratory setting and has particular experimental advantages. It can be classified into three main types:

Genetic model organisms are species that are amenable to genetic analysis, that is, they breed in large numbers and have a short generation time so that large-scale crosses can be set up and followed over several generations. For example, *Saccharomyces cerevisiae* (baker's yeast), *Drosophila melanogaster* (fruit fly) and *Caenorhabditis elegans* (nematode worm).

Experimental model organisms include species that may not necessarily be genetically amenable (they may have long generation intervals and poor genetic maps), but have other experimental advantages. For example, the chicken and the African clawed frog (*Xenopus laevis*) have many disadvantages in terms of genetics, but they produce robust embryos that can be studied and manipulated with ease.

Genomic model organisms include those organisms, which, regardless of their genetic or experimental advantages and disadvantages, are chosen as model organisms because they occupy a key position in the evolutionary tree, or because some quality in their genome makes them ideal to study. For example, *E. coli*, *Drosophila* and *Fugu rubripes* (puffer fish) have a similar gene range to humans but a much smaller genome.

To understand gene function and interaction it is necessary to learn the patterns of gene expression. *C. elegans* is particularly well suited to studying gene expression patterns; it develops rapidly and the fates of all its cells have been mapped. Mice have also been extensively used to establish disease models. The gene defects seen in humans are mimicked in them and hence used to test the efficacy of new drugs.

IMPORTANT TOOLS FOR COMPARATIVE GENOMICS

VISTA is a comprehensive suite of programs and databases for the comparative analysis of genomic sequences. It can be used in two ways. Sequences can be submitted and aligned for analysis (VISTA servers) or pre-computed whole-genome alignments of different species can be examined.

Genomic BLAST at NCBI finds regions of similarity between biological sequences of different genomes.

Graphical Codon Usage Analyser (GCUA) tool displays the codon quality, and different organisms can be compared based on its codon usage.

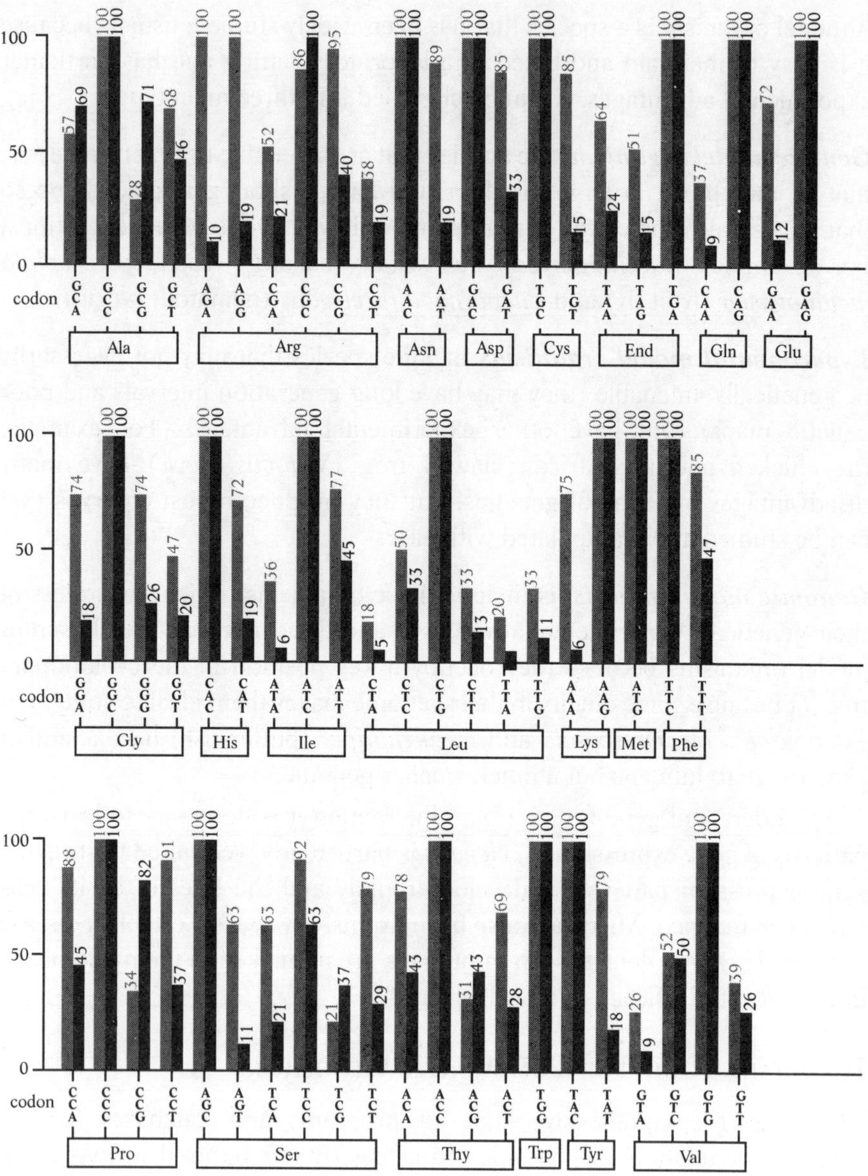

FIGURE 16.3 *A GCUA output showing the codon usage of* Homo sapiens *(in grey) and* Chlorella vulgaris (in black)

Figure 16.3 shows, with relative adaptiveness at the y-axis, that the amino acid arginine (Arg) is coded mostly by codons AGA and AGG in humans and CGC in Chlorella, while other amino acids are mostly coded by the same codons.

Exercises

1. Define genomics and differentiate a prokaryotic gene from a eukaryotic one.
2. The chain termination method can sequence only 500–1000 bp. How can you sequence the whole genome of an organism?
3. Discuss the steps in sequencing the human genome by (a) Shotgun method by Celera and (b) Hierarchical shotgun method used by the public project.
4. List the objectives and major findings of the HGP. What are the future challenges for researchers?
5. What are the different strategies for predicting genes in detail?
6. Name different software tools used for gene prediction and for comparing different genomes.
7. Retrieve any sequence from NCBI GenBank, perform gene prediction analysis and report G+C content and corresponding isochore number, exon type and length, exon score and probability of exon. Similarly, try gene prediction for gi no. 46560583.
8. The genome of corn is not sequenced completely. How can you use information from any other completely sequenced genome to study genetic disease in corn.

   [Hint: Synteny between corn and other genomes; find the region of the genome that corresponds to the gene responsible for the disease.]
9. From the sequence of a chromosome, how can you identify which segments might contain a gene?
10. From the sample of DNA of an unknown organism, how can you determine the origin of the DNA sample? (Hint: Compare the sequence from the unknown organism with sequences deposited in public sequence databases, based on the degree of sequence identity.)
11. Briefly discuss the model organisms for HGP with examples for each.

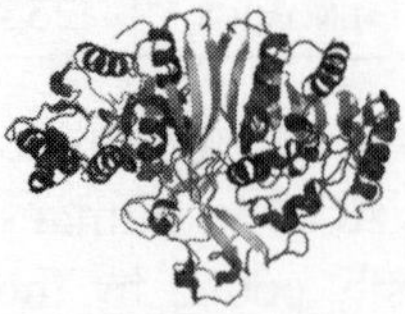

CHAPTER 17

Proteomics

LEARNING OUTCOME

- Define a proteome and proteomics
- Describe the common proteomics methods
  - 2D gel electrophoresis
  - Mass spectrometry
  - NMR
  - X-ray crystallography
- Describe protein structures
  - Primary structure
  - Secondary structure
  - Tertiary structure
- Explain the prediction of protein structures
- List the applications of proteomics

A ***proteome*** is the entire complement of proteins expressed in a cell at a given time, and ***proteomics*** is the study of the proteome. The terms 'proteomics' and 'proteome' were coined by Marc Wilkins and colleagues in the early 1990s. Proteomics is an interdisciplinary science that includes biology, bioinformatics and protein chemistry. It arose as a by-product of several genome sequencing projects and the sequencing of human coding regions. Sequence analysis has revealed many novel genes for which no function can be assigned. The challenge of understanding the function of each gene in the genome led to the development of a new aspect of biology, namely, functional genomics. Proteomics is a branch of functional genomics. In the post-genomic era, the focus of basic research has moved from genes and genomes to proteins and proteomes and their functional analyses.

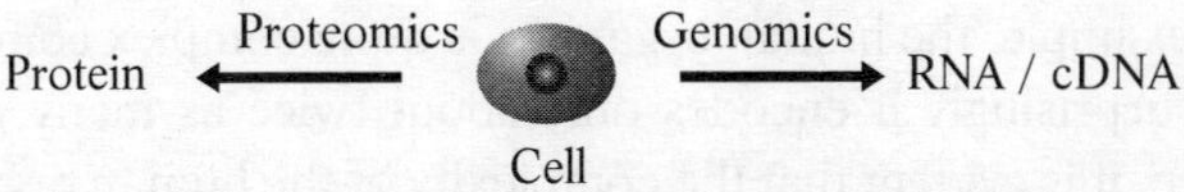

Proteins carry out the majority of the reactions in the cell. Hence proteomics is a complementary approach to genomics and mRNA expression mapping. In proteomics, we study mass spectrometry data analysis and interpretation, analysis and storage of gel images to databases, gel comparison, advanced methods to study protein co-expression, protein–protein interactions, as well as metabolic and cellular pathways to study protein expression, function, activity, regulation and post-translational modifications. Protein structure prediction and molecular modelling can also be considered as a part of proteomics.

In proteomics, the focus is on the relationship of multiple, distinct proteins in their roles as part of a larger system or network. The growth of expressed sequence tags (ESTs) and protein-sequence databases, the introduction of user-friendly bioinformatics computational tools to extract information from these databases and the introduction of the oligonucleotide microarray laid the foundation for this new era of modern biology.

The proteome

All cells contain all the information necessary for making a complete organism. Though all genes are not expressed in all cells, the genes coding for enzymes essential for basic cellular functions like DNA synthesis, glycolysis, etc., are expressed in almost all cells, whereas those with highly specialised functions, for example, rhodopsin in retinal pigment epithelium, are expressed only in specific cell types. Hence, every organism has one genome, but many proteomes.

The protein, a product of a single gene, can exist in multiple forms that vary within a particular cell or between different cells. The proteome in any cell therefore corresponds to some subset of all possible gene products. Proteins are synthesised by the translation of mRNAs into polypeptides on ribosomes. These changes are broadly termed 'post-translational modifications', the chemical modification of a protein after its translation. Post-translational modifications extend over the entire range of functions of the protein. They include attaching to other biochemical functional groups, changing the chemical nature of an amino acid and making structural changes.

As biological complexity is not just due to more numbers of genes, the core proteomes of different organisms exemplify that the relationship between the complexity of an organism and the number of genes in its genome is not simple. For example, the human organism is quite complex compared to the worm, but surprisingly it encodes only about twice as many genes as the worm. Hence, it is evident that the complexity of the human organism lies in the diversity of human proteomes, rather than in the size of the genome.

Proteomics methods

Proteomics methods are mainly used to determine the complement of proteins that are expressed in a cell and how this complement changes under different conditions. New protein characterisation technologies have enabled the identification of several proteins from organisms. The primary goal of proteomics is to provide tools to determine gene function by direct experimentation on proteins.

Proteomics is an incorporation of the following techniques:

- databases, like Protein Data Bank (PDB)
- mass spectrometry (MS), NMR spectroscopy and x-ray crystallography for protein identification and characterisation
- an emerging collection of software that can match MS data with specific protein sequences in the databases
- analytical protein separation technology, such as 2D gel electrophoresis, which resolves complex protein mixtures into individual proteins or small groups of proteins to allow researchers to target specific proteins for analysis.

TWO-DIMENSIONAL GEL ELECTROPHORESIS

A cell contains thousands of proteins. Two-dimensional gel electrophoresis (2D electrophoresis or 2DE) is a powerful and extensively used method for the analysis of complex proteins extracted from different biological samples. It separates and identifies proteins in a sample by displacement in two dimensions oriented at right angles to one another.

Isoelectric focussing (IEF) is used in the first dimension to separate proteins by their isoelectric point (pI). In the second step, it separates the molecules by using a second property in a direction 90° from the first. The second dimension is SDS-polyacrylamide gel electrophoresis (SDS-PAGE), which separates proteins according to their molecular weight (MW).

2D gel electrophoresis is generally used as a component of proteomics for the isolation of proteins for further characterisation by mass spectrometry. Complex mixtures consisting of thousands of diverse proteins can be resolved and the relative amount of each protein can be determined. Although up to

11 000 spots can be separated on one gel, a typical number is approximately 2000. The separation patterns obtained from a test and control sample are shown in Fig. 17.1.

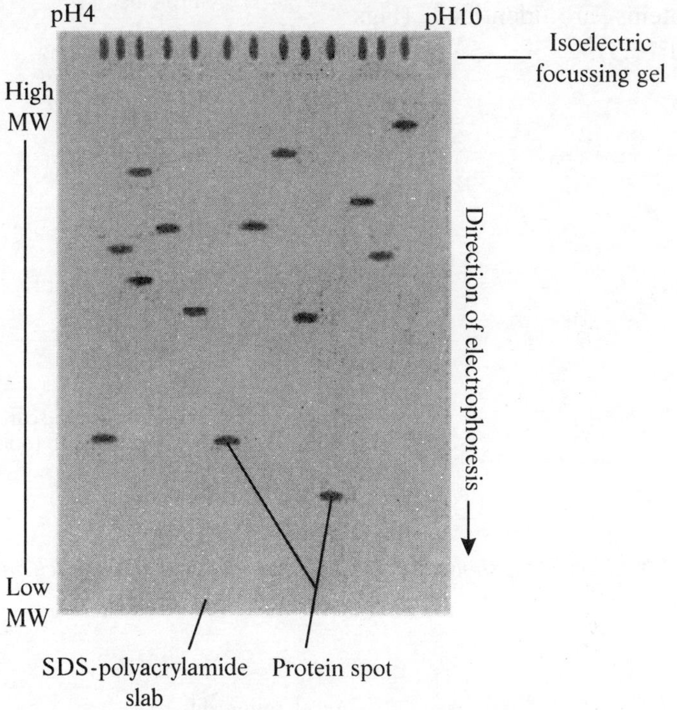

FIGURE 17.1 *Two-dimensional electrophoresis separation*

Mass spectrometry

Mass spectrometry (MS) is an analytical technique used to determine the elemental composition and chemical structure of a biological sample. Fragments are generated and accelerated in a curved path through a magnetic field and the charge-to-mass ratio of the fragments is determined. A single dot on the filter paper, separated by SDS-PAGE, is removed and digested, when it breaks down into several peptides. The peptide solution is loaded into the mass spectrometer where it is vaporised and ionised into positively charged ions that can be moved and manipulated by external electric and magnetic fields. The positive ions are accelerated by a magnetic field and the charge-to-mass ratio of the particles is computed based on the details of motion of the ions as they transit through electromagnetic fields. Each peptide has a specific charge-to-mass ratio and each protein has specific peptides. Hence the protein fingerprint is unique. The detected charge-to-mass ratios are fed into a genome database and the peptides and proteins are identified (Figs 17.2 and 17.3).

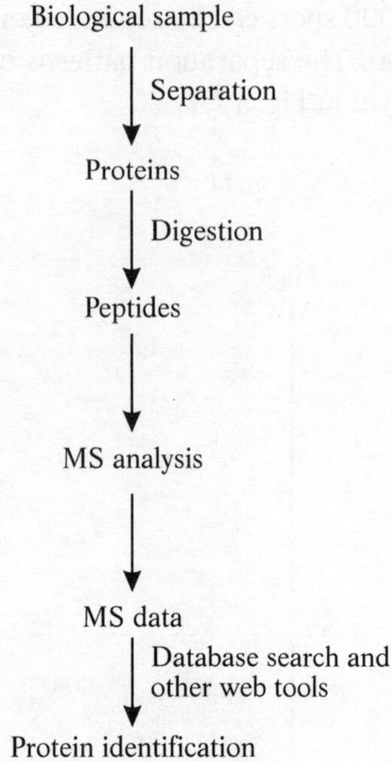

FIGURE 17.2 *Flow chart showing a generalised proteomic analysis scheme*

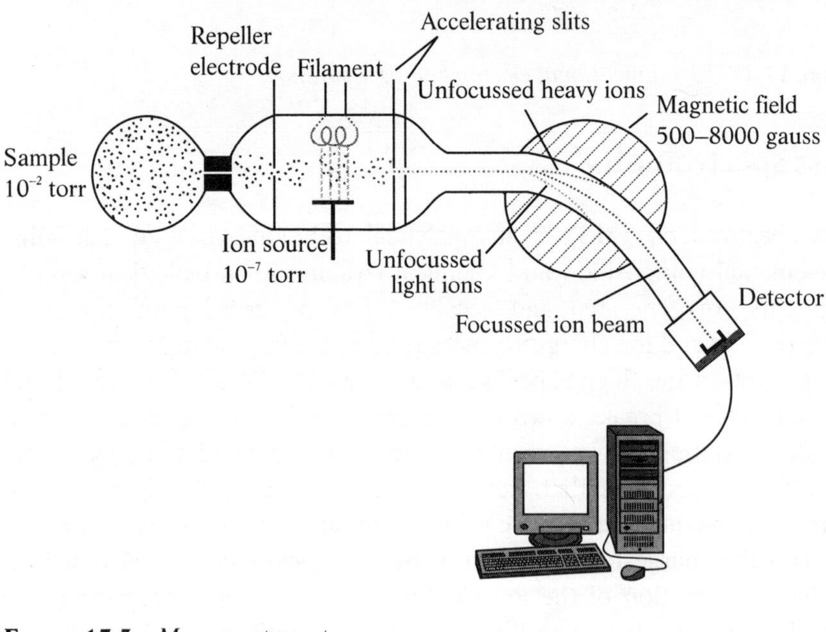

FIGURE 17.3 *Mass spectrometer*

NUCLEAR MAGNETIC RESONANCE SPECTROSCOPY

Nuclear magnetic resonance spectroscopy (NMR spectroscopy) is another powerful analytical tool. Currently it is the most important technique for determining the structure of organic compounds. It is the only spectroscopic method for the complete analysis and interpretation of the entire range of organic compounds.

NMR spectroscopy is one of the main procedures used to obtain physical, chemical, electronic and structural information about molecules. It can provide detailed information on the topology, dynamics and three-dimensional structure of molecules in a solution as well as in the solid state. It is used in quality control and research to determine the content and purity of a biological sample and its molecular structure.

Sub-atomic particles such as electrons, protons and neutrons have spin and hence an associated magnetic moment. In a magnetic field, these particles absorb energy from the electromagnetic field and become excited to a higher energy state. The energy absorbed in excitation is then emitted as rf energy and monitored. For proteins, the NMR spectrum of protons (H) is recorded. The NMR resonance signals are unique for protons in different environments, that is, it is different for H in –NH, –OH, –CH, hydrogen bonds, etc. Using the data gathered from 1D NMR, which depends on the electronic environment, and from 2D NMR, which depends on interactions such as hydrogen bonding, the structure can be found.

X-RAY CRYSTALLOGRAPHY

Crystals are orderly three-dimensional arrangements of atoms that can be described as a repetition of identical unit cells. A unit cell is made up of the smallest possible volume. Multiple repetitions of the unit cells in three dimensions lead to the formation of a crystal. The 3D location of atoms within a unit cell can be listed in terms of their x, y and z Cartesian coordinates.

X-rays were discovered by Wilhelm Conrad Röntgen in 1895. They are electromagnetic radiations with wavelengths ranging between 0.02 Å and 100 Å. X-rays have higher energy as they are of lower wavelength than visible light and can thus penetrate matter more easily. As they have wavelengths similar to the size of atoms, they are used to explore the lattice of crystals.

The method of determining the arrangement of atoms within a crystal is known as x-ray crystallography. Almost 85% of Protein Data Bank entries were determined by x-ray crystallography.

X-rays are produced using a device called an x-ray tube, which consists of an evacuated chamber with a tungsten filament at one end (cathode) and a metal target at the other end (anode). The tungsten filament glows and emits electrons or x-rays when an electrical current is passed. When a protein crystal is bombarded with x-rays, the x-rays are diffracted (or reflected) on striking the atoms within the crystal. The pattern of the reflected x-rays on detection gives a 2D picture of the internal arrangement of atoms. The crystal is rotated in different directions and similar patterns are obtained. By combining the various 2D patterns, a 3D image of the internal structure can be obtained. X-ray crystallography can also be used to measure bond distances and atomic size (Fig. 17.4).

The ExPASy service of the Swiss Institute of Bioinformatics provides the largest selection of internet tools along with the annotated SwissProt sequence database. Other navigation starting points for MS on the web include PeptideSearch and PeptideMass for protein molecular weight calculation and protein sequence tags. MassSearch, MS-Fit, PeptideSearch, Profound and PeptIdent are used to predict peptide mass fingerprinting. AACompIdent, PropSearch and MS-Comp are used to calculate amino acid composition.

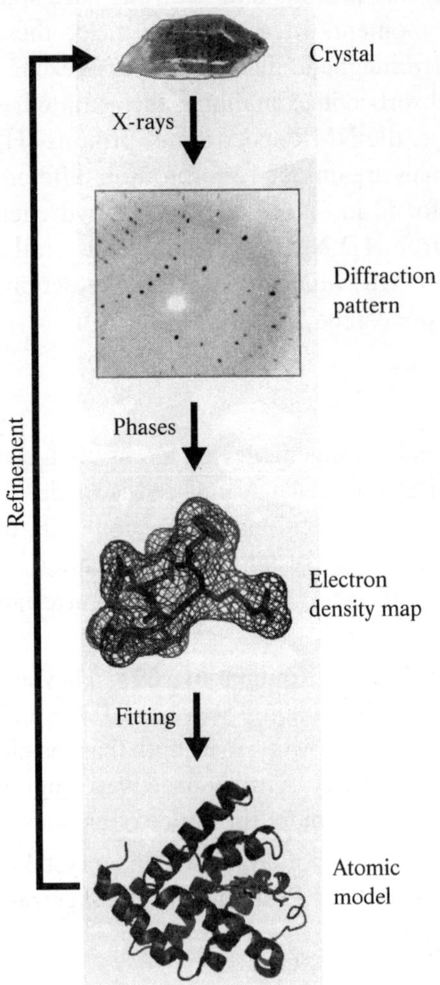

FIGURE 17.4 *Flow chart showing the major steps in single-crystal x-ray crystallography*

[*Source:* Thomas Splettstoesser (Author); http://en.wikipedia.org/wiki/File:X_ray_diffraction.png#file]

Proteomics and disease research

2D-PAGE is a powerful tool for comparing healthy and diseased tissue. Proteins that are more abundant in disease tissue can be identified and new drugs that target these proteins can be developed. The proteins specific to a disease are called ***biomarkers***. Tests for these biomarkers can help in the diagnoses of diseases such as Alzheimer's and cardiovascular (heart) disease.

Structure of proteins

Proteins are made up of amino acid molecules. All amino acids contain the elements carbon, hydrogen, oxygen and nitrogen. Some amino acids also have sulphur and phosphorous, and trace elements such as iron or copper. There are 20 different amino acids (Table 1, *Getting Started*) and they can be linked together in different combinations or sequences to form different proteins. Amino acids are covalently linked through peptide bonds (Fig. 17.5) to form linear polymers called proteins or peptides. A protein can contain several thousand amino acids. The average length is about 300 amino acids.

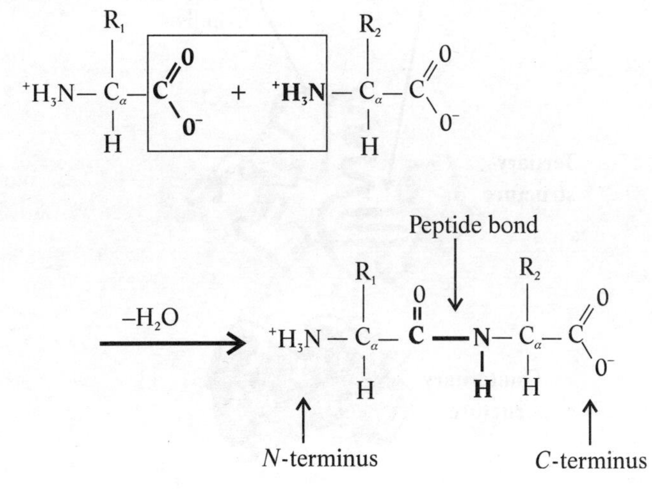

FIGURE 17.5 *Formation of a peptide bond*

The sequence of amino acids in each protein is unique, and each protein has a specific purpose. PDB, a free resource, contains information about thousands of proteins. On synthesis, proteins spontaneously fold into three-dimensional structures, the shape of which determines their biological function.

The structure of proteins (and peptides) can be analysed on four different levels: primary, secondary, tertiary and quaternary (Fig. 17.6).

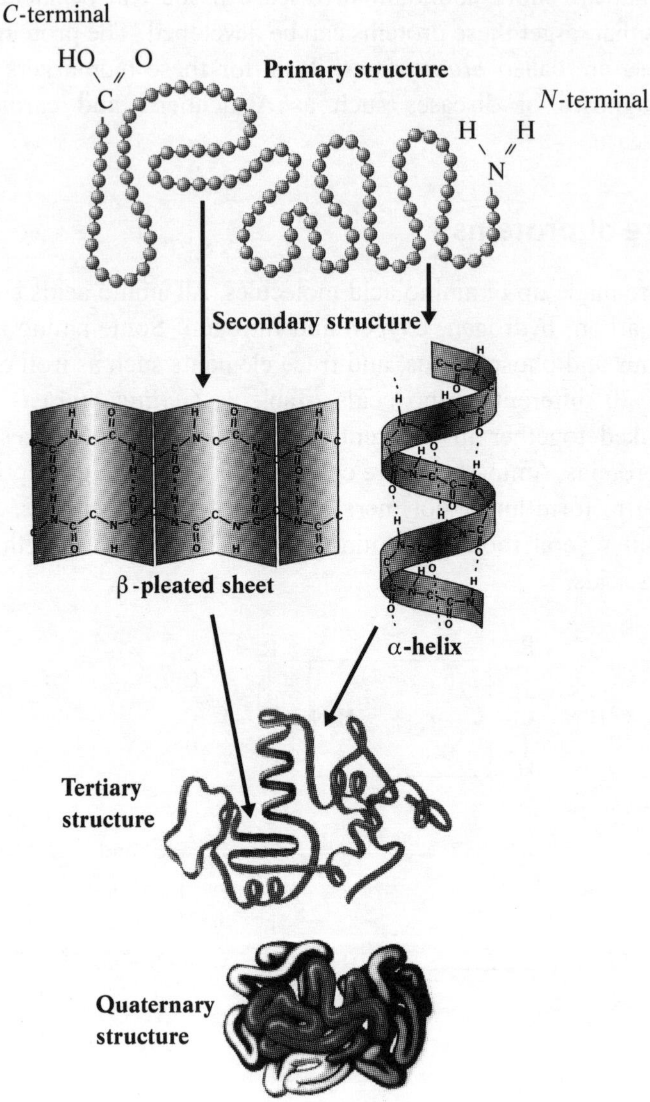

FIGURE 17.6 *The four levels of protein structure*

PRIMARY STRUCTURE

The primary structure of a biological molecule is the sequence of the amino acids or exact specification of its atomic composition and the chemical bonds connecting those atoms. It starts from the amino-terminal (N) end and terminates at the carboxyl-terminal (C) end. The number of amino acids in a protein may range from 2 to several thousand. We mainly study 20 amino acids but there are about six more found in the body. Many others are also known from a variety of sources.

SECONDARY STRUCTURE

The secondary protein structure is the way in which the linear chain orients itself stabilised by hydrogen bonds. The most common secondary structures are α-helices and β-sheets. The random coil is not a true secondary structure, but indicates the absence of a regular secondary structure. Different sequences of amino acids form different secondary structure elements. For example, a sequence comprising methionine, alanine, leucine, glutamate and lysine may prefer to adopt α-helical conformations in proteins; proline and glycine are commonly found in turns; isoleucine, valine and threonine prefer to adopt β-sheet conformations. However, the secondary structure cannot be predicted from the sequence alone.

Specific amino acid sequences and secondary structures derived from these sequences confer unique properties and functions. They are referred to as 'motifs' and 'domains', respectively. In some cases, amino acid sequences within motifs and domains are highly conserved and do not vary from protein to protein. In other cases, some key amino acids occur in a reproducible relationship to each other in a sequence, even though various substitutions in other amino acids occur.

The Dictionary of Protein Secondary Structure (DSSP) is commonly used to describe the protein secondary structure with single-letter codes (G for 3-turn helix, H for 4-turn or α-helix, I for 5-turn or π–helix, E for extended strand or β-sheet, etc.). DSSP defines eight types of secondary structures of which the three dominant states are helix, sheet and coil.

TERTIARY STRUCTURE

The tertiary protein structure is the three-dimensional structure of the protein which it assumes by a folding process. It is stabilised by disulphide bonds and non-covalent interactions like hydrogen bonding, hydrophobic forces, van der Waals forces, ionic interactions, etc.

QUATERNARY STRUCTURE

Several individual peptide or protein chains cluster into a final definite shape—the quaternary protein structure. Hydrogen bonding, salt bridges and disulphide bonds hold the various chains in a particular geometry. There are two main categories of proteins with quaternary structure: fibrous (silk proteins and keratins) and globular (insulin, haemoglobin and most enzymes).

Protein structure prediction

The environment in which a protein is synthesised and allowed to fold is a significant determinant of its final shape. Current prediction methods do not take this into account directly. Using computational methods, various physico-chemical properties and folding patterns can be deduced from a protein sequence. Protein structure prediction is one of the most important goals pursued in bioinformatics as massive amounts of protein sequence data are now being produced by large-scale sequencing efforts.

Primary structure analysis allows the computation of various physical and chemical parameters for a given protein sequence. It computes the molecular weight, amino acid composition, atomic composition, extinction coefficient, estimated half-life, instability index, aliphatic index and grand average of hydropathicity.

Various online software tools such as ProtParam, ProtScale, RandSeq, etc., are available for predicting the primary structure of proteins.

Secondary structure prediction methods were initially based on the helix- or sheet-forming tendency of individual amino acids. It is essentially the prediction of where the helixes, sheets and coils would occur. This was sometimes coupled with rules for estimating the free energy of forming secondary structure elements. Later, multiple sequence alignment was used to increase the accuracy of structure prediction as evolution provides a much better picture of the structural tendencies. For example, a predicted pattern of six secondary structure elements βαββαβ is the signature of a ferredoxin fold.

The Chou–Fasman algorithm, GOR (Garnier–Osguthorpe–Robson) method and neural network components are the main computational methods for secondary protein structure prediction. Online software tools for secondary structure prediction are SOPMA, PHD, etc. Different tools use different methods to predict the structure and, based on the methods adopted, these tools are associated with different levels of accuracy in prediction.

Tertiary structure prediction of a protein is the prediction of the three-dimensional structure of a protein from its amino acid sequence. Predicting protein tertiary structure from its amino acid sequence is a challenging problem. Accurate secondary-structure prediction is a key element in the prediction of the tertiary structure. The different strategies involved in 3D protein structure prediction are:

- *Comparative modelling* or *homology modelling*: It is the best method for tertiary structure prediction.
- *Ab initio method*: It seeks to predict the structure from the amino acid sequence.
- *Swiss PDB viewer* and *MODELLER*: These are the main tools used for homology modelling among those available on the internet either online or downloadable (Fig. 17.7).

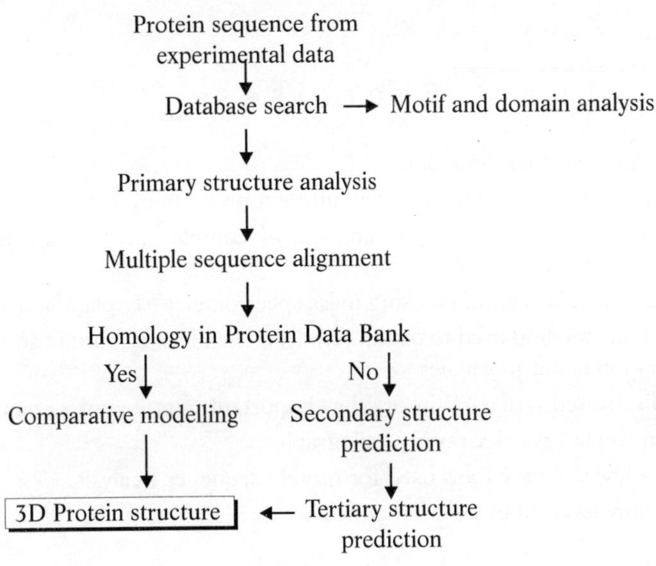

FIGURE 17.7 *A flow chart showing different methods for 3D protein structure prediction*

The predicted structure can be validated using PROCHECK, WHATCHECK, etc. The Ramachandran plot for the 3D structure is used to finally confirm stability based on the free energy of the protein structure. A discussion of these topics is beyond the scope of this book.

Applications

Proteome analysis can be applied to the identification of the function and functional environment of proteins. Identification of proteins is necessary for diagnosis and other disease characterisation, pathogen analysis, search for drug targets and for drug design. The methods used to efficiently analyse the protein complement of cells usually contribute directly to drug development as well, as most drug targets are proteins. Several organisations are involved in researching toxicology, drug development, drug target identification and validation.

Proteomics techniques have helped identify the protein signatures of various diseases, especially at their onset, to aid in diagnosis and treatment. Proteins play the most important part in creating cells and tissues and in directing their functions. In drug design and clinical trials also, protein signatures are extremely valuable.

Exercises

1. Define and explain a proteome.
2. Describe proteomics and name the different proteomics methods.
3. Explain any procedure for the analysis of complex proteins extracted from different biological samples.
4. How are proteins identified using mass spectrometry? Explain in detail.
5. Explain any method used to obtain physical, chemical, electronic and structural information about molecules.
6. Who discovered x-rays? Why are they important in proteomics analysis?
7. Explain single-crystal x-ray crystallography.
8. Name a few software tools used for protein sequence analysis.
9. How many levels of protein structures are there? How do they differ from each other?
10. Name the different methods used to analyse the secondary structure of proteins.
11. What are the tools used to predict the primary and secondary structures of proteins?
12. How can a three-dimensional protein structure be identified from a protein sequence? Write the algorithm for predicting the tertiary structure of a protein.
13. The study of proteomics can be applied to the identification of the function and functional environment of proteins. Explain in brief.

Assignment: Select a protein from *Oryza sativa* responsible for causing an allergy in humans. Using BLAST, find other related sequences. Select proteins from diverse species, varying from grasses to higher plants. Predict the primary and secondary structures using the tools discussed in the chapter. Draw a table listing the details obtained. [Hint: Ory S protein, AAA86533.1 from the NCBI server.]

Bibliography

Allen FH, Bellard S, Brice MD, Cartwright BA; Doubleday A, Higgs H, Hummelink T, Hummelink-Peters BG, Kennard O, Motherwell DS, Rodgers JR and Watson D, 1979 *Acta Crystallogr.*, Sect. B: 1979, 35:2331–39.

Attwood T and Parry-Smith D, 2001, *Introduction to Bioinformatics*, Pearson Education Limited.

Baldi P and Brunak S, 2001, *Bioinformatics: The Machine Learning Approach*, Second edition (Adaptive Computation and Machine Learning), MIT Press, Harvard.

Baxevanis AD and Francis Ouellette B, (eds), 2001, *Bioinformatics: A Practical Guide to the Analysis of Genes and Proteins*, Second edition, John Wiley & Sons.

Bourne PE and Weissig H, (eds), 2003, *Structural Bioinformatics*, John Wiley & Sons.

Brown TA, 1999, *Genomes*, John Wiley & Sons.

Carter CW, Jr and Sweet RM, (eds), 1997, *Methods in Enzymology*, Academic Press.

Durbin R, Eddy S, Krogh A and Mitchison G, 1998, *Biological Sequence Analysis. Probabilistic Models of Proteins and Nucleic Acids*, Cambridge University Press, Cambridge.

Eddy SR, 1996, Hidden Markov Models, *Current Opinion in Structural Biology*, 6: 361–65.

Eddy SR, 1998, Profile hidden Markov models, *Bioinformatics*, 14: 755–63.

Gibas C and Jambeck P, 2001, *Developing Bioinformatics Computer Skills*, Cambridge: O'Reilly.

Gibson G and Muse SV, 2004, *A Primer of Genome Science*, Second edition, Sinnauer Associates, Inc.

Gusfield D, 1997, *Algorithms on Strings, Trees, and Sequences: Computer Science and Computational Biology*, Cambridge University Press, Cambridge.

Higgins D and Taylor W, (eds), 2000, *Bioinformatics: Sequence, Structure and Databanks: A Practical Approach*, Oxford University Press, Oxford.

Jones NC and Pevzner PA, 2004, *An Introduction to Bioinformatics Algorithms* (Computational Molecular Biology), MIT Press, Harvard.

Leibler DC, 2002, *Introduction to Proteomics: Tools for the New Biology*, Humana Press, Inc., NJ, USA.

Lesk AM, 2007, *Introduction to Genomics*, Oxford University Press, Oxford.

Lesk AM, 2002, *Introduction to Bioinformatics*, Oxford University Press, Oxford.

Mount DW, 2004, *Bioinformatics: Sequence and Genome Analysis*, Second edition, Cold Spring Harbor Laboratory Press, Cold Spring Harbor, New York.

Palzkill T, 2002, *Proteomics*, Kluwer Academic Publisher, USA.

Primrose SB, 1998, *Principles of Genome Analysis*, Second edition, Blackwell Science, Inc.

Rhodes G, 1993, *Crystallography Made Crystal Clear*, Academic Press, San Diego.

Rothstein MA, (ed.), 2003, *Pharmacogenomics: Social, Ethical, and Clinical Dimensions*, John Wiley & Sons.

Schena, M, (ed.), 1999, *DNA Microarrays: A Practical Approach*, Oxford University Press, Oxford.

Schumacher, A, *Progressive Alignment Methods*, schumach@rbg.informatik.tu-darmstadt.de

Sharma R, Singh AK and Umashankar V, 2009, Characterization of Allergemic Epitopes of Ory S1 Protein from Oryza sativa and its homolegs, *Bioinformatics*, 4(1):12–18.

Sharma R and Singh AK, 2009, target Identification in Ory S1 Pollen Protein Allergen from Oryza sativa in the Course of Construction of Hypoallergenic Vaccines, *American Journal of Infectious Diseases*, 5(2):147–154.

Twyman RM, 2004, *Principles of Proteomics*, BIOS Scientific Publishing.

INTERNET REFERENCES

http://www.ncbi.nlm.nih.gov/

http://www.ebi.ac.uk/

http://www.rcsb.org/pdb/

http://www.ddbj.nig.ac.jp/

http://wikipedia.org/

http://www.expasy.org/

http://www.biw.kuleuven.be/vakken/i287/bioinformatica.htm

http://myhits.isb-sib.ch/cgi-bin/dotlet

http://www.genome.jp/kegg/

http://www.expasy.ch/prosite/

http://www.medscape.com/home

http://www.geneontology.org/GO.tools.microarray.shtml

http://www.ccp14.ac.uk/solution/2d_3d_model_builders/index.html

http://www.ch.embnet.org/CoursEMBnet/CHIP02/ppt/Liechti02_images.ppt#260,5,Images from scanner

http://www.genome.jp/kegg/

http://wit.mcs.anl.gov/WIT2/

http://www.cem.msu.edu/~reusch/VirtualText/Spectrpy/MassSpec/mspec.htm

http://cmgm.stanford.edu/WWW/www_predict.html

http://www.tulane.edu/~sanelson/eens211/x-ray.htm

http://dl.clackamas.edu/ch106-08/

http://www.cem.msu.edu/~reusch/VirtualText/Spectrpy/MassSpec/masspec1.htm

Index